Communication, Intimacy, and Close Relationships

Communication, Intimacy, and Close Relationships

Edited by

VALERIAN J. DERLEGA

Department of Psychology
Old Dominion University
Norfolk, Virginia

1984

ACADEMIC PRESS, INC.

(Harcourt Brace Jovanovich, Publishers)

Orlando   San Diego   New York   London
Toronto   Montreal   Sydney   Tokyo

ACADEMIC PRESS, INC.
Orlando, Florida 32887

United Kingdom Edition published by
ACADEMIC PRESS, INC. (LONDON) LTD.
24/28 Oval Road, London NW1 7DX

Library of Congress Cataloging in Publication Data

Main entry under title:

Communication, intimacy, and close relationships.

Includes bibliographical references and index.
1. Interpersonal communication. 2. Intimacy
(Psychology) 3. Interpersonal relations. I. Derlega,
Valerian J.
BF637.C45C647 1984   158'.2   83-21559
ISBN 0-12-210840-X (alk. paper)

PRINTED IN THE UNITED STATES OF AMERICA

84 85 86 87   9 8 7 6 5 4 3 2 1

In loving honor of my father, Wally Derlega;
and in affection for my friends and colleagues,
including Janusz Grzelak, at the Institute of Psychology,
University of Warsaw, Warsaw, Poland

Contents

4. Identities, Identifications, and Relationships

BARRY R. SCHLENKER

5. Intimacy, Social Control, and Nonverbal Involvement: A Functional Approach

MILES L. PATTERSON

6. Implications of Social Psychological Concepts for a Theory of Loneliness

STEPHEN T. MARGULIS, VALERIAN J. DERLEGA, and
BARBARA A. WINSTEAD

7. Selectivity and Urgency in Interpersonal
   Exchange

LYNN C. MILLER and JOHN H. BERG

Epilogue   The Dangers of Intimacy

ELAINE HATFIELD

Contributors

Numbers in parentheses indicate the pages on which the authors' contributions begin.

JOHN H. BERG (161), Department of Psychology, University of Mississippi, University, Mississippi 38677

GORDON J. CHELUNE[1] (11), Department of Behavioral Medicine and Psychiatry, West Virginia University Medical Center—Charleston Division, Charleston, West Virginia 25330

VALERIAN J. DERLEGA (1, 133), Department of Psychology, Old Dominion University, Norfolk, Virginia 23508

ELAINE HATFIELD (207), Department of Psychology, University of Hawaii at Manoa, Honolulu, Hawaii 96822

MARTIN J. KOMMOR (11), Department of Behavioral Medicine and Psychiatry, West Virginia University Medical Center—Charleston Division, Charleston, West Virginia 25330

STEPHEN T. MARGULIS (133), Buffalo Organization for Social and Technological Innovation, Buffalo, New York 14216

DAN P. McADAMS (41), Department of Psychology, Loyola University of Chicago, Chicago, Illinois 60626

LYNN C. MILLER (161), Department of Psychology, Northern Illinois University, DeKalb, Illinois 60115

MILES L. PATTERSON (105), Department of Psychology, University of Missouri—St. Louis, St. Louis, Missouri, 63121

JOAN T. ROBISON (11), Department of Behavioral Medicine and Psychiatry, West Virginia University Medical Center—Charleston Division, Charleston, West Virginia 25330

BARRY R. SCHLENKER (71), Department of Psychology, University of Florida, Gainesville, Florida 32611

BARBARA A. WINSTEAD (133), Department of Psychology, Old Dominion University, Norfolk, Virginia 23508

[1]Present address: Department of Psychiatry (M—003), University of California, San Diego, La Jolla, California 92093.

Preface

Most people will be involved one or more times in an intimate relationship, such as a friendship or love relationship. These relationships can provide important sources of social support, including a sense of belonging, aid in coping with life's stresses, and a feeling of closeness with someone as we get along with life's routine and not-so-routine events. On the other hand, people who do not have access to intimate relationships may feel isolated and lonely.

Understanding how intimate relationships occur and how they can be maintained successfully is important for individuals as well as for social scientists. Our book is based on the assumption that intimate relationships can be understood only in the light of theories and research on how these relationships develop and operate. This book presents chapters by various authorities on intimate relationships in the hope that they will contribute to theory development and integration of ideas about the nature of intimate relationships. The book also addresses the development and maintenance of intimate relationships, people's motives and goals in pursuing intimacy, the effects of intimate relationships on people's self-concepts, the nature of social exchanges in intimate relationships, and the consequences for individuals who find themselves socially isolated. A major emphasis in most chapters is the critical role of communication in intimate relationships. Interpersonal communication affects the types of relationships that people have and the success individuals achieve in developing and sustaining intimate relationships.

The first chapter, by Valerian J. Derlega, based on theory and research about self-disclosure processes, discusses the meaning of an intimate relationship. The second chapter, by Gordon J. Chelune, Joan T. Robison, and Martin J. Kommor, presents a cognitive interaction model of the nature of intimacy and intimate relationships. Their approach relies heavily on cognitive–social learning theory and a systems theory approach to communication. Following chapters by Dan P. McAdams, Barry Schlenker, and Miles L. Patterson examine how people's motives affect relationships. McAdams's chapter emphasizes the role of two fundamental human motives—power and intimacy—on love and friendship. Schlenker discusses the importance of the identification process—that is, how people fix their own and others' identities in social interaction—in developing relationships. Patterson's chapter introduces a functional model of nonverbal behavior, showing how a contrast between intimacy and social control motives helps us understand patterns of nonverbal exchange in close relationships. Stephen T. Margulis, Valerian J. Derlega, and Barbara A. Winstead then focus on individuals who do not have intimate relationships and are lonely. Based on social psychological concepts derived from social exchange and cognitive consistency theories, these authors present a model of how and why loneliness occurs. Next, Lynn C. Miller and John H. Berg examine the nature of social exchange processes in intimate relationships, showing how a person selects resources (including communications) to exchange with another person and with what urgency this is done. Finally, the epilogue by Elaine Hatfield provides a perspective, derived from research and her experience as a family therapist, on why people may find it difficult or easy to form intimate relationships. Hatfield's chapter provides a useful bridge between theory, research, and application.

The editor owes a debt of gratitude to many individuals who contributed to the successful completion of this book. Special thanks go to the authors for their interest in the project and for their thought-provoking chapters. Thanks are also due to the editors and staff at Academic Press for their encouragement and patience in the development of this book over a 3-year period. I acknowledge with appreciation the advice and support provided by Barbara A. Winstead, Barbara Paige, and Stephen T. Margulis at various stages of the book's evolution. The idea for this volume emerged partly from conversations with my friend, Janusz Grzelak. It pleases me to dedicate this book to Janusz and his colleagues in Warsaw, Poland. Finally, I am grateful to have a 10-year-old son, John Derlega; John did not edit or write any chapters, but he enriched my life in many ways during this period.

Communication, Intimacy,
and Close Relationships

Self-Disclosure and Intimate Relationships*

VALERIAN J. DERLEGA _____

INTRODUCTION

Consider the following situations:

John is 41 years old and a professor at a state university. He has been dating Susan, a 35-year-old junior faculty member, for 3 months. He has felt depressed in the past year. His father died recently after a chronic illness. John has also felt unhappy about his teaching and research efforts. One evening he and Susan talked for several hours about a wide range of topics. They talked most about John's uncertainties and pessimism about taking control over his life. Susan listened patiently as John talked in an open way about himself. She wished to understand him and to be supportive. Susan said she cared about John regardless of the personal problems he was having. John felt grateful and perceived that she understood him. He was much closer to her after their talk.

Peter is 47 years old. He has spent most of his adult life after finishing graduate school working as an engineer at a shipbuilding yard. He is painfully shy and avoids talking with anyone about his personal life. He is afraid of becoming dependent on others and of others hurting him. He has never had any close friends, though he sings with the church choir every Sunday.

A major feature of interpersonal interactions, as illustrated in the situation between John and Susan, is how we develop intimate relationships. This process may occur one or more times for individuals,

*I gratefully acknowledge the valuable comments of Barbara A. Winstead on an earlier draft of this chapter.

over the life span (in developing friendships and love relationships), or it may never occur, as in Peter's case.

This book presents theories about the development and maintenance of intimate relationships. The how's and why's of relationship development are examined. Topics to be considered include the definition of an intimate relationship, goals individuals pursue in intimate relationships, communication in intimate relationships, the effects of intimate relationships on self-concept, and the consequences of not having intimate relationships. In this introductory chapter, I examine briefly the meaning of an intimate relationship from the perspective of theory and research on self-disclosure processes (see Altman, 1973; Altman & Taylor, 1973; Archer & Earle, 1983; Chelune, 1979; Derlega & Chaikin, 1977; Derlega & Margulis, 1982; Jourard, 1971a, 1971b; Kelvin, 1977; Phillips & Metzger, 1976).

ROLE OF SELF-DISCLOSURE IN INTIMATE RELATIONSHIPS

Self-disclosure has been used to refer to the process by which one person lets herself or himself be known by another person. According to Derlega and Grzelak (1979),

Self-disclosure includes any information exchange that refers to the self, including personal states, dispositions, events in the past, and plans for the future. It can be objectively defined as any verbal message that formally begins with the word "I" (for instance, "I think," "I feel") or any other verbal message about the self. (p. 152)

Self-disclosure involves decisions about whether to reveal one's thoughts, feelings, or past experiences to another person, at what level of intimacy to reveal personal information, and the appropriate time, place, and target person for disclosure.

Self-disclosure plays a major factor in intimate relationships (see Chelune, Robison, & Kommor, Chapter 2; Hatfield, Epilogue, both in this volume). For example:

For most people, one of the nicest things about companionate love is the realization that we know almost all there is to know about another human—and that the other human knows all there is to know about *us,* warts and all. (Berscheid & Walster, 1978, pp. 179–180)

Generally, in intimate relationships, people feel free to reveal far more facets of themselves. As a consequence, intimates share profound information about one another's histories, values, strengths and weaknesses, idyosyncrasies, hopes and fears. (Hatfield, 1982, p. 273)

As relationships develop interpersonal exchange gradually progresses from superficial, non-intimate areas to more intimate, deeper layers of the selves of the social actors. (Altman & Taylor, 1973, p. 6)

These statements by Berscheid and Walster, by Hatfield, and by Altman and Taylor indicate that individuals in intimate relationships are willing to exchange intimate information with one another. As a relationship progresses to more intimate levels, individuals generally disclose more information about themselves and at a more personal level. (See Altman & Taylor's, 1973, social penetration theory for a thorough review of how self-disclosure changes in a developing relationship.)

The reasons people disclose in an intimate relationship are shown in the following:

Self-disclosure leading to shared knowledge between equals is likely to be a reciprocal process; thus it makes possible the development of joint views, joint goals, and joint decisions. Given that, the partners will gradually develop "we-feeling." (Levinger & Snoek, 1972, pp. 8–9)

If a man is reluctant to make himself known to another person, even to his spouse— because it is not manly thus to be psychologically naked then it follows that *men will be difficult to love.* That is, it will be difficult for a woman or another man to know the immediate present state of the man's self, and his needs will thereby go unmet. (Jourard, 1971a, p. 39)

Love as a *relationship* . . . entails the mutual opening of "private" selves. This may lead to exploitation and to hurt: but it is also the basis of the ability to meet one another's needs, and the source of the power to protect. (Kelvin, 1977, p. 373)

As friendship grows into love, and is reciprocated, there is an increasing, mutual, opening of areas of privacy: the lovers come to know, to understand, and to accept more and more about each other; as they do so they validate one another's concept of self, even if only in a *folie a deux.* (Kelvin, 1977, p. 372)

Self-disclosure may act as a vehicle for developing close relationships. In disclosure reciprocity, for instance, one person's disclosure tends to elicit self-disclosure from another. Self-disclosure may also contribute to relationship maintenance. One partner may listen to and help meet the other partner's emotional needs, and this process provides positive outcomes in the relationship. (Derlega & Grzelak, 1979, p. 154)

Loneliness is partly a consequence of not having an appropriate social partner or confidant with whom to communicate. (Derlega & Margulis, 1982, p. 155)

Self-and-other disclosure functions to *acknowledge the interdependence between the participants in an interaction.* (Archer & Earle, 1983, p. 304) [It] provides a medium for couples to inform one another directly about their conceptions of and wishes for individual and joint outcomes rather than being forced to rely solely upon inferences based on behavior. In this way mutual disclosure may serve as a "hot line" to explain motives and so prevent unnecessary escalation of conflict. (Archer & Earle, 1983, p. 305)

These statements deal with the subjective reasons for self-disclosure, emphasizing a *functional* approach (see Derlega & Grzelak, 1979; Phillips & Metzger, 1976). The focus here is on the goals that people can accomplish through their self-disclosing behavior. According to this functional orientation, self-disclosure helps individuals to gain knowledge about themselves and about other persons. It enables the relationship partners to coordinate necessary actions and to reduce ambiguity about one another's intentions and the meaning of their behavior.

A consistent theme in self-disclosure research is the value of verbal openness in gaining feedback about oneself. Obtaining support and confirmation for an individual's self-worth is a major goal of an intimate relationship (Altman, 1973; Jourard, 1971a; Kelvin, 1977; Rogers, 1961). Self-disclosure contributes to this process. The way we understand and see ourselves is influenced by the opinions of others. To the extent that significant others are excluded from having knowledge about us, they cannot provide feedback. Self-disclosure enables others to know us and, in turn, to provide feedback about our self-concept. Ultimately, individuals seek and, if fortunate, gain *acceptance* of their self-concept in a successful intimate relationship.

Many years ago, sociologist William Chambliss (1965) wrote an important essay on how social interactions affect people's selection of friends. His ideas may help us to understand the importance of self-disclosure in intimate relationships. According to Chambliss, people are always attempting to convey some image of themselves in social situations (also see Schlenker, Chapter 4 in this volume). The image being expressed may vary according to the context and the type of interactants. Chambliss argued that "when the actor perceives that his intended expression and the audience's impression do correspond, we want to say that the actor has been *effective* in his or her presentation of self" (p. 371). The image transmitted by persons may or may not agree with how they see themselves. When people perceive that the self they present is reacted to positively by the other, then the interaction is perceived as *successful.* If people perceive that they are seen by others as they see themselves, then the interaction is said to be *validating.* That is, one's self-image corresponds with others' impressions.

As people seek acceptance for their self-concept, social relationships are sought that are perceived, in Chambliss's terms, as effective, successful, and validating. Validation necessarily requires that people be willing to divulge personal information about themselves to others. If others are to see individuals as they see themselves, as in social interactions that are experienced as validating, self-disclosure is critical. Of course, situations may occur in which people do not want their self-image to be perceived accurately. The actor may be skilled in conveying a particular image (the interaction is effective), or others may react favorably to the self-image being expressed (the interaction is successful) without the person's ever being truthful or honest. For instance, a salesperson may simulate interest in a customer's needs in order to sell a product. However, a favorable evaluation for one's self-concept and being understood as a person (i.e., the interaction is successful and validating) are unlikely unless true personal information is revealed.

A problem with this analysis should be noted. Chambliss assumes that individuals seek out relationships that are "validating," meaning that others' beliefs about one's psychological state should correspond with how people actually see themselves. However, some individuals may not have a clear sense of what their personal opinions and feelings are like internally (Buss, 1980; Scheier & Carver, 1981; Schlenker, Chapter 4 of this volume). It is difficult to know what a validating interaction would mean for these individuals and just what they would "disclose." Also, some persons may possess undesirable information, for instance, concerning some supposed defect or negative characteristic about themselves that they prefer to keep hidden (Goffman, 1963). In such cases they may avoid interactions in which it is necessary to divulge negative information about themselves.

The distinction between "self-disclosure" and "self-presentation" has been minimized in some theoretical statements (cf. Derlega & Grzelak, 1979; Schlencker, Chapter 4 of this volume). Derlega and Grzelak (1979) noted that "Self-presentation . . . may represent a particular type of self-disclosure, emphsizing selective use of personal information to control outcomes in social relationships" (p. 160). According to Schlenker (this volume, p. 79), "The label 'self-presentation' is often applied when the goal of creating a desired impression on an *immediate* audience is especially prominent and important; the label 'self-disclosure' is often applied when such a goal is nonprominent and unimportant." These distinctions primarily reflect differences in the importance of controlling the image one seeks to convey to an audience. In contrast to these views, it is important to emphasize what distinguishes "intimate" from other types of relationships—partners' perceptions of one another's honesty and truthfulness. A major developmental task for intimate relationships is for the partners to gain acceptance from one another for their "true selves." This goal cannot be undertaken unless individuals are willing to divulge personal information about themselves. The perceived truthfulness of one's disclosures symbolizes and demonstrates a commitment to pursuing and maintaining a close relationship.

A useful distinction can be made between honest self-disclosure (which almost always includes negative self-information) and selective self-disclosure (which emphasizes positive self-information). People may disclose selectively to establish a positive image of themselves in the minds of others. However, disclosure of negative information (including feelings of inadequacy) contributes to an intimate relationship because it may allow the discloser to feel known and accepted by the other. Theories about intimate relationships must make clear what is the role of negative self-information in a relationship and the effects on a person who feels constrained to hide such information. Genuine intimacy requires spontaneity and the willingness to speak freely.

SELF-DISCLOSURE AND VULNERABILITY

Intimate relationships contribute to one's self-worth by obtaining the support, understanding, and the positive regard of others. This acceptance, since it deals with intimate areas of the self, depends on disclosing personal information and making oneself vulnerable to hurt. The disclosure helps create an intimate relationship, but it can also lead to rejection and exploitation, as the following statements indicate:

On the one hand, the desire to escape loneliness, to find support, reassurance, appreciating, perhaps absolution—all generate the need to share feelings and thoughts with others. Pitted against these advantages are the risks of sharing, e.g., possible criticism, ridicule, loss of power, and the like. (Komarovsky, 1976, p. 163)

The growth of friendship depends on, and progresses with, disclosures of areas of privacy. The disclosure of areas of privacy reveals the underlying causes and motives of the individual's behavior: this potentially gives those to whom they are disclosed power over him; and in doing so, disclosures make him vulnerable to exploitation. (Kelvin, 1977, p. 15)

The central paradox is that the urgency to disclose is matched by the fear of secondhand disclosure. Hurt and betrayal were largely viewed by respondents [in a questionnaire study of friendships] as misuse of disclosed information. Even when there was an urgency to disclose, most subjects felt that they would hold something back (although it was not clear what that something was) rather than give complete possession of their lives to another. There was always the lurking fear of what the other person would do with this information. (Phillips & Metzger, 1976, p. 351)

It is not surprising then that individuals experience ambivalence in their search for an intimate relationship. As persons seek acceptance, they must make themselves known and understood. However, as previously unrevealed information is made known to others, the reasons underlying one's behavior are made available (Kelvin, 1977). This information gives the disclosure recipient the opportunity to predict and possibly control the discloser in an unprincipled way.

The fear of being rejected or exploited may partly explain why men disclose less than women about sensitive issues (Cozby, 1973; Derlega, Durham, Gockel, & Sholis, 1981; Jourard, 1971a; Morgan, 1976). Men may reduce their vulnerability to being hurt or controlled or becoming less powerful by hiding thoughts and feelings. However, an unwillingness to self-disclose contributes to a condition of social isolation (Kelvin, 1977). A preoccupation with being hurt may block men from having intimate relationships even if they choose to have them. If, as Jourard (1971a, p. 38) argues, "Loving, including self-love, entails knowledge of the unique needs and characteristics of the loved person," men as well as women must be willing to incur the potential risk of being hurt. The risk is justified as long as self-disclosure serves to gain understanding and acceptance for one's self-concept and to bring people together.

What risks do individuals incur when they self-disclose? There are many problems that might occur:

Self-Concept Is Rejected People might discover that others don't like them after they make complete disclosure about certain matters. To illustrate, a woman in her late twenties might tell her boyfriend that she is an alcoholic and he subsequently might stop calling her, because the disclosed information makes the relationship unacceptable to him.

Finding Out That the Other Person Is Not Interested in Having an Intimate Relationship An individual may disclose personal information with the idea of developing a close relationship. However, the recipient of the disclosure may not be interested in developing a relationship and may be indifferent to the bid for intimacy.

Information Is Used by Others to Gain Control or Power in the Relationship The disclosure recipient might use the information to gain some advantage over the other. For instance, a male teenager may tell a friend some little-known but potentially embarrassing information about his fear of women. In an angry moment, the friend may remind the young man about his weaknesses in order to establish dominance in the relationship.

Betrayal of Information to Others   A woman might tell her best friend about problems in her marriage, including the infidelities of her husband. The woman finds out at some future date that her friend has told the neighbors about her husband's extracurricular sexual activity.

Breaking Relationship Boundaries by Divulging Information to Others
A sense of "weness" in an intimate relationship may derive partly from keeping certain secrets. The leakage of information to uninvited third parties breaks down the boundary that a couple maintains around itself. For instance, a person divulges personal information to a close friend who happens to be married, while assuming that the disclosure will not be passed along to the friend's spouse. If the information is transmitted by the friend to the spouse, the initial discloser may believe that the friendship bond has been broken (see Derlega & Chaikin, 1977; Phillips & Metzger, 1976).

Inequity Derived from Lack of Equivalent Input into the Relationship
If persons feel that they are on the giving end of an inequitable relationship, they may become resentful and hurt. If one individual always reveals something personal and the second person never does, the high discloser may see this arrangement as unfair. The benefited party may also perceive that this arrangement is unfair, because the discloser has invested more in the relationship in the form of high self-disclosure than has the listener (see Chaikin & Derlega, 1974; Hatfield, 1982; Walster, Walster, & Berscheid, 1978).

Self-disclosure is a risky business. Individuals who divulge personal information risk rejection, betrayal, and maybe even indifference from their confidants. It is doubtful, though, whether individuals can have intimate relationships unless they are willing to undertake such risks.

REFERENCES

Altman, I. (1973). Reciprocity of interpersonal exchange. *Journal for the Theory of Social Behavior, 3,* 249–261.
Altman, I., & Taylor, D. A. (1973). *Social penetration: The development of interpersonal relationships.* New York: Holt.
Archer, R. L., & Earle, W. B. (1983). The interpersonal orientations of disclosure. In P. B. Paulus (Ed.), *Basic groups processes.* New York: Springer-Verlag.
Berscheid, E., & Walster, E. H. (1978). *Interpersonal attraction* (2nd ed.). Reading, MA: Addison-Wesley.
Buss, A. H. (1980). *Self-consciousness and social anxiety.* San Francisco, CA: Freeman.

Chambliss, W. J. (1965). The selection of friends. *Social Forces, 43,* 370–380.

Chaikin, A. L., & Derlega, V. J. (1974). Liking for the norm-breaker in self-disclosure. *Journal of Personality, 42,* 117–129.

Chelune, G. J. (Ed.) (1979). *Self-disclosure: Origins, patterns, and implications of openness in interpersonal relationships.* San Francisco, CA: Jossey-Bass.

Cozby, P. C. (1973). Self-disclosure: A literature review. *Psychological Bulletin, 79,* 73–91.

Deaux, K. (1977). Sex differences. In T. Blass (Ed.), *Personality variables in social behavior.* Hillsdale, NJ: Erlbaum.

Derlega, V. J., & Chaikin, A. L. (1977). Privacy and self-disclosure in social relationships. *Journal of Social Issues, 33,* 102–115.

Derlega, V. J., Durham, B., Gockel, B., & Sholis, D. (1981). Sex differences in self-disclosure: Effects of topic content, friendship, and partern's sex. *Sex Roles, 7,* 433–447.

Derlega, V. J., & Grzelak, J. (1979). Appropriateness of self-disclosure. In G. J. Chelune (Ed.), *Self-disclosure: Origins, patterns, and implications of openness in interpersonal relationships.* San Francisco: Jossey-Bass.

Derlega, V. J., & Margulis, S. T. (1982). Why loneliness occurs: The interrelationship of social psychological and privacy concepts. In L. A. Peplau & D. Perlman (Eds.), *Loneliness: A sourcebook of current theory, research and therapy.* New York: Wiley (Interscience).

Goffman, E. (1963). *Stigma.* Englewood Cliffs, NJ: Prentice-Hall.

Hatfield, E. (1982). Passionate love, compassionate love, and intimacy. In M. Fisher & G. Stricker (Eds.), *Intimacy.* New York: Plenum.

Jourard, S. M. (1971a). *The transparent self.* New York: Van Nostrand-Reinhold.

Jourard, S. M. (1971b). *Self-disclosure: An experimental analysis of the transparent self.* New York: Wiley (Interscience).

Kelvin, P. (1977). Predictability, power and vulnerability in interpersonal attraction. In S. Duck (Ed.), *Theory and practice in interpersonal attraction.* New York: Academic Press.

Komarovsky, M. (1976). *Dilemmas of masculinity: A study of college youth.* New York: Norton.

Levinger, G., & Snoek, J. D. (1972). *Attraction in relationship: A new look at interpersonal attraction.* Morristown, NJ: General Learning.

Morgan, B. S. (1976). Intimacy of disclosure topics and sex differences in self-disclosure. *Sex Roles, 2,* 161–166.

Phillips, G. M., & Metzger, N. J. (1976). *Intimate communication.* Boston: Allyn & Bacon.

Rogers, C. R. (1961). *On becoming a person.* New York: Houghton, Mifflin.

Scheier, M. F., & Carver, C. S. (1981). Private and public aspects of self. In L. Wheeler (Ed.), *Review of personality and social psychology.* Beverly Hills, CA: Sage.

Walster, E., Walster, G. W., & Berscheid, E. (1978). *Equity: Theory and research.* Boston: Allyn & Bacon.

A Cognitive Interactional Model of Intimate Relationships

GORDON J. CHELUNE
JOAN T. ROBISON
MARTIN J. KOMMOR _____

INTRODUCTION

The focus of interest in human relationships appears to be in a state of flux. As Morton and Douglas (1981) observe, from the social wake of the "me decade" a zeitgeist seems to be emerging that is characterized by an increased interest in intimacy and close relationships. As such, there is beginning to be a conceptual shift away from the study of *individuals* within relationships, away from the study of the impact of *situations* upon the individuals within a relationship, and away from the process of interaction during *initial* encounters. While our study of these areas has been productive and enlightening in terms of both the components of interactions as well as the basic processes involved, it has left us short of understanding the meanings of our most important and enduring types of relationships. To study the dimensions of such relationships, we must develop an interactive science of interpersonal relationships that allows us to account for the fact that "relationships influence the nature of individuals, and individuals influence the nature of the relationships they enter" (Hinde, 1981, p. 5). Furthermore, we must also take into consideration that relationships occur across a kaleidoscope of social–situational contexts, which also influence and are influenced by

COMMUNICATION, INTIMACY,
AND CLOSE RELATIONSHIPS
11

the relationships occurring in them. In short, aspects of enduring, close relationships are always emergent entities: that is, more than the sum of their respective parts.

In our chapter, we focus on one qualitative dimension of human relationships—namely, intimacy. The clinical and counseling literatures clearly document the importance of intimacy in adult psychological development, marital adjustment, and family functioning. For example, Horowitz (1979) found that the failure to develop an intimate relationship was the single most common factor identified by patients as to why they sought out-patient psychotherapy. Furthermore, intimacy represents a useful intermediate construct for describing relationships in general (Hinde, 1981). As we shall discuss, we see intimacy as a cognitive appraisal of behavioral interactions that affects the future course and level of commitment in a relationship.

To examine intimate relationships from a cognitive–interactive approach, we found that two levels of study were necessary. The first is a view from a molecular level, and examines the moment-to-moment experience of intimacy in a relationship, taking into account the interactive effects of the individuals involved and the social–situational context in which they find themselves. We then step back and take a more molar cognitive interactional view that incorporates the meanings of these molecular experiences of intimacy within the broader context of close relationships over the course of time. Thus, our approach is analogous to combining a number of still frames into an ongoing and dynamic movie of human relationships.

TOWARD A WORKING DEFINITION OF INTIMATE RELATIONSHIPS

Relationships

Before delineating a model of intimate relationships, it is first necessary to establish a working definition of the phenomenon we wish to examine. First, we begin with Hinde's (1981, p. 2) definition of a *relationship* as "a series of interactions between two individuals known to each other . . . where the interaction is affected by past interactions or is likely to influence future ones." The crucial aspect that is implicit in this definition is the notion that individuals generate relational expectations based upon their cognitive appraisals of their interactions with others. Thus, the term "relationship" implies an expectational association between two or more interactions. The initial encounter between two strangers has no previous relational expectations, yet if these two strangers were to meet again, their interaction would be influenced by the outcomes of their first encounter, and a relationship would be said to exist.

Relationships often arise from situations in which individuals are brought together on the basis of some shared, ongoing activity (e.g., co-workers, church members, doctor–patient contacts). The relational expectations are frequently limited to a specific context or range of contexts, and may or may not include expectations of increasing intimacy. As Delia (1980) describes it, relational development necessitates the consideration of alternative trajectories that vary in the nature and extent of intimate involvement. If we examine our own lives, the majority of our relationships are of limited intimacy, that is, relationships with many co-workers, neighbors, merchants, even relatives do not involve intimacy. However, most of our central relationships do have relational expectations of intimacy. The most frequently studied are marital relationships and their precursor, courtship relationships (see reviews by Burgess, 1981; Cunningham & Antill, 1981; Huston, Surra, Fitzgerald, & Cate, 1981). But there is also active interest in parent–child relationships (see reviews by Pawlby, 1981; Shields, 1981) and friendships (see reviews by Chown, 1981; Kon, 1981; La Gaipa, 1981b; Reisman, 1981).

Intimacy

Arriving at a workable definition of those aspects of relationships that characterize some as highly intimate and others as essentially nonintimate is quite difficult. Almost everyone *knows* what intimacy is, but as soon as one must point to specifics, the concept becomes either elusive or bogged down in idiosyncratic trivialities. The rub appears to lie in the attempt to define intimacy as something specific—a particular class of behavior—rather than as a quality—a cognitive appraisal of certain behaviors. Our basic premise throughout this chapter will be that *intimacy is a subjective appraisal, based upon interactive behaviors, that leads to certain relational expectations.* That is, we see intimacy as an intermediate cognitive construct that derives data from specific interactive behaviors and influences expectations regarding the future trajectory of a relationship and the emergence of higher-order relational qualities (see section entitled "A Molar View of the Model, Qualities").

Let us now look closer at the subjective nature of intimacy. In a rare study that attempted to examine the nature of intimacy without a priori notions, Waring and his associates (Waring, Tillman, Frelick, Russell, & Weisz, 1980) conducted unstructured interviews among the general population, asking subjects "What does intimacy mean to you" (p. 472). A descriptive content analysis yielded five general concepts. Respondents indicated that intimacy involved sharing their private thoughts, beliefs, and fantasies, as well as their interests, goals, and backgrounds. Sexuality, while often a part of intimacy, was not a primary determinant, nor was the expression of anger or resentment. Finally, the subjects reported that their early experiences and observations of intimate relationships and the growth of their own personal identities were important determinants of intimacy.

In reviewing the results of the Waring *et al.* (1980) study, several important points can de deduced about the cognitive appraisal of intimacy: (1) intimacy is based upon the exchange of private, subjective experiences, and therefore involves the "innermost" aspects of oneself, (2) intimacy is viewed as "transactional" in that importance is given to the process of "sharing" as well as to what is shared, (3) intimacy is valued as a positive relational process that entails both mutuality and self-differentiation, and (4) our prior experiences influence our current perceptions of intimacy. If we expand upon these points, intimacy can be seen as a qualitative feature of a relationship that involves the mutual exchange of the meanings of our experiences in such a way as to result in our further understanding of both ourselves and our partners. Stated another way, *an intimate relationship is a relational process in which we come to know the innermost, subjective aspects of another, and are known in a like manner.*

Topographically, intimacy as a relational process bears a striking resemblance to dyadic self-disclosure (Jourard, 1971). Self-disclosure, the revelation of personal information by one person to another, has long been associated with the development of interpersonal intimacy (Altman & Taylor, 1973; Derlega & Chaikin, 1975; Grinker, 1967; Hatfield & Walster, 1981; Jourard, 1971) and is thought to be a major vehicle for self-clarification, social validation, and relationship development (Derlega & Grzelak, 1979). But, as Chelune (1979, p. 247) has questioned, "Is self-disclosure the same as verbal intimacy?" Evidence suggests not. In a recent study examining the relationship between marital intimacy and self-disclosure, Waring and Chelune (1983) found that while self-disclosure was a major covariate of intimacy, the two were not synonymous.

While self-disclosures (both verbal and nonverbal) may be the major interactive behaviors upon which subjective appraisals and relational expectations for intimacy are based, they do not, in themselves, constitute intimacy. Because of the nature of human communication, the same self-disclosure in one social–situational context may have entirely different intended and perceived meanings in another. To understand the process by which individuals come to know and have known the innermost, subjective aspects of self, we must shift our attention away from merely *what* is shared to those factors that influence the *meanings* of what is shared.

THE MODEL: A MOLECULAR VIEW

In the following sections, we delineate a person–situation interactional model of communication that influences our moment-to-moment cognitive appraisals of intimacy. Those aspects of the model's basic components that contribute to these cognitive appraisals are considered individually and then in interaction. We first start with a consideration of the communicational process itself because it represents the primary medium through which the innermost aspects of self are represented and shared with another.

Communication: The Medium

In characterizing intimacy as a sense of knowing the innermost, subjective aspects of another *and* being known in a like manner, we implicitly take a systems theory approach to communication. From a systems theory perspective, interactants are concurrently senders and receivers simultaneously engaged in complex behaviors at a number of levels within a social context (Satir, 1967). As Jackson and Weakland (1961) state,

In actual human communication a single and simple message never occurs, but that communication always and necessarily involves a multiplicity of messages, on different levels, at once. These may be conveyed via various channels such as words, tone, and facial expression, or by the variety of meanings and references of any verbal message in relation to its possible contexts. (p. 32)

For the subjective, innermost aspects of self to be communicated, we imply that interactants can encode and decode both the literal, denotative aspects of a message (what is said) *and* the simultaneous subjective, connotative meanings (the why) of the message. It is this latter aspect that is of central importance to our model of intimacy, and it is synonymous to the systems theorists' notion of *metacommunication* (Bateson, 1972).

Metacommunication is a comment on the literal content of a message as well as on the relationship between the interactants. As Satir (1967, p. 76) remarks, "metacommunication is a message *about* a message." These metamessages accompany every literal, denotative message, and are typically conveyed unconsciously through nonverbal channels (e.g., tone of voice, tempo, and facial expressions). When the literal messages and metamessages are consistent, communication is fairly clear and unambiguous. However, not infrequently the literal messages and metamessages may be at variance, qualifying and/or denying each other, giving rise to possible misunderstandings and conflicts (Bandler, Grindler, & Satir, 1976). In such instances, it is not uncommon for receivers to give more saliency to the nonverbal metacommunication and to the context than to the literal content (Satir, 1967). More than one child (or adult) has been reprimanded not for *what* they said, but for *how, when,* or *where* they said it.

It becomes evident within a systems theory perspective that as long as metacommunications remain at an unconscious or inferred level between interactants, the development of a sense of truly knowing and being known on a subjective level is tenuous at best. If the receiver only attends to the denotative aspects of the sender's statements, he or she is likely to miss the "command aspect" of the metacommunication, which in its highest level of abstraction is a request for validation (Satir, 1967). Thus, in responding to the sender's message, the receiver (now the sender) may communicate that "I understand *what* you said (literal message), but do not know what you *mean* (metacommunication)." In such cases, the interactants are communicating information on a denotative level, but "missing the point," thereby maintaining subjective distance and nonintimacy. Conversely, if the interactants respond on only the metalevel, disregarding the literal aspects of what is said, they enter the realm of mind-reading without reality-based referents. It is only when the interactants transcend the ordinary communication process and can bring their metamessages to a literal level that the innermost, subjective aspects of self can become truly known. Perlmutter and Hatfield (1980) describe this process as *intentional metacommunication,* and consider it the *"sine qua non* of intimate relations" (p. 19). Therefore, we believe that communication is the basic medium through which intimacy is developed, but that the disclosure of personal information is only a necessary, but not sufficient, condition. To develop a sense that we are known and know another, we must communicate and acknowledge the subjective meanings of our messages. Thus, intimacy can be described as "a process in which a dyad—via ideation, sensation, affect, and behavior—attempts to move toward more complete communication, on all levels of the communication transaction" (Perlmutter & Hatfield, 1980, p. 18).

Intentional metacommunication is a risky endeavor, however. When we share the meanings of messages or explicitly acknowledge the meanings of another's messages, we transcend the ordinary rules of social communication. We cannot predict its impact on the other. Yet, Perlmutter and Hatfield (1980) suggest that it is only in the context of such uncertainty that intimacy occurs.

As a relationship begins to unfold, interactants typically disclose personal information on a reciprocal basis, that is, they "return self-disclosure to others in proportion to the amount of self-disclosure they receive" (Kleinke, 1979, p. 69). This mutual exchange of self-relevant information, called the *reciprocity* or *dyadic effect* in the self-disclosure literature, is quite robust. Altman and Taylor (1973) have built upon this notion, and have developed a theory of social penetration, which shows that reciprocal disclosures between interactants follow a systematic and orderly process, moving from nonpersonal to personal areas of exchange. This orderly exchange of information follows implicit social rules, and allows interactants to build a data base from which to infer the subjective meanings of the information exchanged regarding their relationship.

From a systems theory standpoint (Watzlawick, Weakland, & Fisch, 1974), reciprocity at this level involves the use of strategies and tactics designed to effect "first-order change" and maintain the social status quo. That is, the interactants exchange personal information on a denotative level according to implicit social rules, and leave the subjective meanings of this information to be inferred by the other. Of necessity, one steps back from the immediacy of the relationship at this level of interaction to evaluate (infer) the connotative aspects of the messages. From this distance it is not possible to develop a true sense of knowing and being known since the metamessages cannot be consensually validated. As such, these interaction rituals fall just short of intimacy. However, when the interactants begin to metacommunicate intentionally, they enter the immediacy of their relationship and share on a literal level their subjective meanings, unbound by implicit social rules. This is a ruleless domain where the interactants employ novel and spontaneous strategies and tactics in which the outcomes cannot be known until after the change has occurred. It is this context of impending or realized second-order change that Perlmutter and Hatfield (1980) argue is essential for the subjective perception of intimacy. Thus, it is in the face of second-order change that we truly "disclose" ourselves in the phenomenological sense. By suspending the ordinary rules of social communication, the interactants transcend what Buber (1958) describes as the *I–It* nature of relationships and enter the immediacy of an *I–Thou* relationship.

The Person

In order to appreciate how the members of an intimate relationship come to understand and share their internal realities, we must first begin with the relevant person variables that affect the encoding and decoding of communication. Each person brings to a potential relationship his or her own particular skills, competencies, weaknesses, and perceptual biases. These are the product of each person's unique history of learning and experience, and the inherent qualities with which the individuals started life. These individual qualities influence, and are influenced by, new experiences and current relationships (Newman, 1981).

Mischel (1973, 1977) has described five cognitive and social-learning person variables that mediate the impact of stimuli on an individual and form the basis of individual differences. These variables seem especially relevant for understanding the contribution that the individual brings to intimate relationships.

Cognitive and Behavioral Construction Competencies

The first variable involves a person's cognitive and behavioral construction competencies. On an encoding level, this variable deals with the individual's ability to process and organize a wide range of psychological and physical information cognitively, constructing his or her own form of internal reality. Depending on parental role models (Doster & Strickland, 1969) and early experiences, every individual comes to deal with the complexities of human communication in his or her own unique way, transforming linguistic (i.e., words), paralinguistic (i.e., tone of voice, body posture, and facial expressions), and contextual cues into cognitive constructs that have self-relevant meaning. The pervasiveness of social norms and conventions (e.g., Aronfreed, 1968; Derlega & Grzelak, 1979: Gouldner, 1960; Kohlberg, 1969) provides limits to the range of cognitive transformations that are acceptable, thereby giving communication some degree of universality. In terms of decoding, cognitive and behavioral construction competencies refer to the person's ability to generate diverse forms of behavior under appropriate conditions. People differ in their ability to modulate their communicational patterns in response to social–situational demands (cf. disclosure flexibility, Chelune, 1975) much the same as they do in other behavioral domains (Bem & Allen, 1974; Mischel, 1979; Snyder, 1978). "These competencies presumably reflect the degree to which the person can generate adaptive, skillful behaviors that will have beneficial consequences for him" (Mischel, 1973, p. 267).

Encoding Strategies and Personal Constructs

A second individual difference variable identified by Mischel (1973) is encoding strategies and personal constructs. Not only do people differ in how effectively they take in and process an array of information, but they do so in idiosyncratic ways that create very personalized perceptions. Selective attention, interpretation, categorization and adaptation to existing personal constructs are the modes of cognitive transformation through which reality is filtered. These encoding strategies and personal constructs form the nexus of an individual's "innermost self," the very basis of intimacy. Human communication systems, themselves complex representational systems, mirror the person's idiosyncratic encoding strategies and personal constructs (Grindler & Bandler, 1976). For example, consider the following sentence from Hemingway's (1952) *The Old Man and the Sea* describing Santiago, the fisherman: "Everything about him was old except his eyes and they were the same color as the sea and were cheerful and undefeated" (p. 10). In this sentence, Hemingway not only gives us a description of the old man, but also a glimpse of his own reverence and feeling about the sea (i.e., cheerful and undefeated). Communication is, therefore, both the medium and the message when it comes to sharing the innermost aspects of self in an intimate relationship.

Behavior- and Stimulus-Outcome Expectancies

The next cognitive and social-learning variable that has bearing on the development of intimate relationships is the individual's behavior- and stimulus-outcome expectancies (Mischel, 1973, 1977). Behavior-outcome expectancies are essentially hypotheses regarding the expected outcomes for the range of behaviors possible in a given situation, with the individual presumably choosing behaviors that will elicit the most positively valued outcome. These behavior-outcome expectancies hinge upon a recognition of stimulus-outcome expectancies, that is, recognition of the cues or signs in a situation that seem to be associated with particular outcomes. As Mischel (1973) states: "To cope with the environment effectively, the individual must recognize new contingencies as quickly as possible and reorganize his behavior in the light of the new expectancies" (p. 270). When these concepts are extended to interpersonal relationships, they mirror Altman and Taylor's (1973) social penetration theory in which interactions, especially in the early stages of relationship formation, are constantly subject to forecast assessments of current rewards and costs, new revised forecasts for future interactions (expectations), and finally a decision regarding how to proceed in the relationship (behavior). Depending on the individual's cognitive evaluation of the interactions to date, relational expectations for future interactions are generated that determine whether or not the person will choose to reveal increasing amounts of personal information (alternative trajectories). These expectations are moderated to some degree by the social stimulus cue density in the environment, that is, by those aspects in the environment that are "socially relevant to a person's behavior in relation to other individuals" (Taylor, 1979, p. 118).

Subjective Values

Although expectations about outcomes are important determinants of behavior, people may choose widely differing behaviors depending upon the subjective values of the expected outcomes (Mischel, 1973, 1977). These subjective stimulus values are thought to have "acquired strong emotion-eliciting powers, as in conditioned autonomic reactions seen in intense fears" (Mischel, 1973, p. 273), and are affected by such variables as contextual cues and sequencing (Helson, 1964), the cognitive labels used to describe the individual's emotional state (Schachter & Singer, 1962), and social comparison processes (Festinger, 1945). Within the interpersonal sphere, certain interactive behaviors in a given social-situational context may elicit changes in emotional arousal that the person subjectively labels as positive (e.g., love, excitement, liking) or negative (e.g., anxiety, vulnerability, embarassment), affecting the behavior outcomes the person chooses (Patterson, 1976). For example, if a husband comes home from work, snaps at the children, pushes the dog aside, and curtly asks "When will dinner be ready?", the wife might infer that things have gone badly at work and inquire of her husband "Did you have a bad day?" Having the metameaning of his behavior challenged (facing second-order change), the husband may experience a change in arousal level that can be labeled as invasive (negative) or as supportive (positive). If negative, he might reply "What is it to you?", cutting off further intentional metacommunication (maintaining first-order change). However, if he experiences his arousal to his wife's question as positive, he may choose behaviors that elaborate his perceptions of the day, allowing his wife to enter his phenomenal world while clarifying his own experiences (second-order change).

Self-Regulatory Systems and Plans

The final person variable posited by Mischel (1973, 1977) is that of self-regulatory systems and plans. Although external contingencies play a major role in determining one's behavior in a given situation, "the individual also regulates his own behavior by self-imposed goals (standards) and self-produced consequences" through "self-criticism or self-satisfaction to [his] behavior depending on how well it matches [his] expectations and criteria" (Mischel, 1973, pp. 273–274). Depending on the person's past experiences and relational role models, he or she may have very loose or very exacting self-standards for continuing or stopping interpersonal behaviors within a relationship. Such self-regulatory systems can be thought of as dispositional tendencies that vary in their potency for controlling behavior across situations (Chelune, 1980). When situational contingencies are ambiguous or when a relationship transcends the realm of first-order change (Watzlawick *et al.*, 1974), the individual must rely more and more on his or her internal self-regulatory systems (innermost aspects of self).

To summarize, people differ in terms of what they are capable of doing, how they view and interpret situations, what outcomes they expect from certain behaviors and situations, the values they assign to those possible outcomes, and in their internal, self-regulating standards for behavior. Cutting across all of these person variables is the dimension of "discriminative facility," that is, the ability to discern differences between various stimuli and to modulate one's behavior accordingly (Mischel, 1973). We are all aware of how subtle nuances can alter our assessment of another person, of a situation, and our decisions about how to react. "Because most social behaviors produce positive outcomes in some situations but negative ones in other contexts" (Mischel, 1973, p. 259), discriminative facility has functional value. The greater an individual's social discriminative facility, the more stiuationally specific his or her behavior is apt to be. Conversely, reduced sensitivity to changing consequences or requirements may result in indiscriminate responding and ineffectual coping (Chelune, 1975; Freeman & Giovannoni, 1969; Gibson, 1969; Snyder, 1974). This description of person variables serves as a basis for appreciating the uniqueness that each person brings to and maintains in interpersonal relationships.

The Situational Context

Situations, like individual difference variables, also vary with respect to their impact upon behavior. It has long been recognized that situations differ in terms of their social norms for appropriate behavior (Goffman, 1959, 1963). However, the potency of situational differences for controlling behavior is moderated by a given situation's degree of "situational constraint" (Price, 1974; Price & Bouffard, 1974); the higher the situational constraint the narrower the range of potential behaviors that will be seen as appropriate in that situation.

While the appreciation of the social-situational context is widely accepted as essential for understanding relational processes (e.g., Andreyeva & Gozman, 1981; Goodstein & Reinecker, 1974; Huston & Levinger, 1978), it has remained "one of the most confused, ambiguous and least researched branches of modern psychology" (Argyle, Furnham & Graham, 1981, p. 12). Part of the reason for this is that social situations are highly complex and can be viewed from a number of perspectives (e.g., personality theory, systems theory, ecology, symbolic interactionalism). For our purposes here, we will simply consider the effects of social situations upon intimate communications in terms of three very general relational aspects: *who* is in the situation, *what* is going on in the situation, and *where* the transaction is taking place (Pervin, 1976).

Who

On a very general level, there is considerable evidence to suggest that people behave differently depending on who (the target) is in the situation. Perhaps the most widely researched target characteristics that influence the communicational process vis-à-vis social and cultural norms and expectations are age, sex, attractiveness, and status (see reviews by Archer, 1979; Huston & Levinger, 1978; Kleinke, 1979). For example, social custom dictates that a man should not offer his handshake to a woman as a form of greeting unless the woman has extended hers first. Such social proprieties can exert considerable restraint on the range of interactive behaviors that are potentially appropriate, particularly in situations where there are little or no relational expectations derived from prior interactions. In such social situations, the individual must rely on formal target characteristics to yield information on which social rules should mediate the communicational process.

As a relationship develops over a series of interactions, dispositional attributions about more personalized target characteristics such as perceived similarity (Huston & Levinger, 1978) and warmth (Miller, Berg, & Archer, 1983) are added to those that are socially determined. Communication patterns are still influenced by target characteristics, but they are less stereotyped and situationally constrained. A greater range of meanings can be ascribed to the interactive behaviors, thereby creating a greater potential for intimacy.

Where

Just as the formal and personalized characteristics of the target person influence our patterns of communication, so also do the physical features of the setting condition in which the transaction occurs. As Argyle *et al.* (1981) state, "From a very early age we are socialized into behaving appropriately in different physical settings, which often have strong symbolic meanings" (p. 274). Ittelson, Proshansky, Rivlin, and Winkel (1974) have proposed the ideas of "place" and "space" as means of explaining how the setting condition shapes social interactions. *Place* denotes the physical boundaries within which the interaction occurs. For example, churches, offices, classrooms, kitchens, and bedrooms are places, and are symbolically associated with specific social functions. The presence of props such as chairs, tables, desks, and beds reinforce the social functions of the places, and subsequently the types of interactions considered appropriate within them. *Space* "refers to the distances between people and objects" (Argyle *et al.*, 1981, p. 8). The spatial arrangement of furniture, barriers, and other props (e.g., ashtrays, doors, and liquor bottles) facilitate or inhibit interactions (e.g., Mehrabian & Diamond, 1971). To the concepts of "place" and "space," Argyle *et al.* (1981) add the influence of "environmental modifiers that tax or exceed a person's adaptive resources and affect the emotional tone of behavior being enacted within them" (p. 279). Such modifiers include things as temperature, lighting, noise levels, odors, color, and humidity.

Thus, the environmental setting, symbolically and/or physically, can influence the kinds of communications that occur within them. Some physical setting conditions are simply more conducive for intimate communications than others (Chelune, 1976; Frankel & Powers, 1971; Furnham, 1981). The influence of these situational factors upon communication, however, appears to be subordinate to how well known the target is to the speaker (Rosenfeld, Civikly, & Herron, 1979). If the target is a stranger, formal target characteristics will be the major determinants of the communicational patterns, with setting condition variables playing a minor role. Conversely, if relational expectations have been established, the interactions will be more responsive to the nuances of the physical environment.

What is Happening

What actually happens in an interaction is determined by a number of situational factors that define and limit the types of behaviors that can occur. As noted by Argyle *et al.* (1981), "people enter situations because they anticipate being able to attain certain goals" (p. 6), and they follow implicit rules that allow them to attain these goals. When goals are highly structured with clearly defined social roles and rules, there is a high degree of situational constraint, and the range of communications, the language used, and even the sequence of the communications are limited. For example, in a job interview an interviewer might instruct the job applicant to "Tell me about yourself." Given the situational goal of obtaining the job, the applicant will reveal personal information, but only as it applies to the prospective job. While some self-disclosure of a personal nature may occur, the relational expectations do not ordinarily include those of increasing intimacy. However, in other social situations where the goals are less highly structured and where there are fewer social rules to govern the types of interactions that are appropriate, individuals are more free to interact in ways that are apt to present less stylized pictures of themselves.

The Interaction: Intimacy as an Emergent Property

"Behavior as everyone knows is a function of both the person and the situation" (Bem & Funder, 1978, p. 485). While this truism is certainly appropriate for many aspects of behavior, it is likely to be a bit too simplistic, and perhaps even misleading, with respect to intimate relationships. Implicit in the statement is the assumption that person and situation factors are additive, that is, given a knowledge of each person's competencies and social learning histories and the nature of the given social-situational context, one should be able to determine the probable degree of intimacy. Such a model views both the individuals and the situation as essentially independent and passive elements without relational bonds. While this simple interactive view is certainly superior to either a strictly personological or strictly situational view, it does not account for the dynamic nature and growth aspects of intimate relationships.

Intimacy is a relational property. It does not lie within a person or in a situation, but emerges out of their interaction. It is a characteristic of a system, which influences and is influenced by its components. As La Gaipa (1981a, p. 67) notes, "In a systems approach, the parts of a system cannot be identified except with reference to the whole which functions as a whole by virtue of the interdependence of its parts."

If we compare the communicational patterns of strangers with those of intimates, the emergent nature of intimacy becomes clear. When strangers meet for the first time, they exchange information on essentially a denotative level. Since they have no prior relational experiences, they behave and interpret the other's behavior according to their own personal competencies, expectations, and cognitive appraisals of the social-situational context. Especially in highly structured social situations, cognitive dispositional nuances, however, are apt to be minimized and subordinate to social norms and proprieties. In such circumstances, attributions are apt to be more situational than dispositional in nature, varying in relation with the perceived level of situational constraint exerted by the given social-situational context (cf. correspondent inference theory, Jones & Davis, 1965).

Given additional interactions, the two strangers can be said to have developed an acquaintanceship wherein relational expectations are formed and begin to influence the nature of the present transaction. Current behaviors are not only evaluated against the backdrop of the immediate social situation, but are also compared with those from preceding ones. Similarly, communicational patterns incorporate both the current literal messages as well as information from prior interactions. Thus, messages are sent and evaluated in terms of their meanings within the present situation, and also with respect to the previous interactions. Here, the individuals' behavioral competencies, encoding strategies and personal constructs, and expectancies begin to play a much greater role in shaping the course of the interaction. Since both members of the dyad have expectations of how the other is to be, discrepancies and/or consistencies between current perceived behavior and expectations derived from past behaviors become meaningful and make a statement (metacommunication) about the relationship between the interactants. Because the interactants now have a basis of comparison, differences in behavior from one situation to the next can be attributed to either situational influences or more subtle trait characteristics, which are then organized into modified expectations for future interactions. Depending on the individuals' discriminative facility, their communications may begin to incorporate a metalevel of meaning beyond that conveyed on the literal level. However, the metacommunications are still implicit or inferred, and their impact on the relationship depends on how the interactants perceive and interpret their concomitant emotional states.

Assuming that the interactants' emotional states are perceived as positive, they are likely to increase their interactions, sharing more personal information and widening their relational data base. Furthermore, there is a gradual shift in perspective from one of "me and you" to one of "us"—a new system with its own unique properties. Communications become increasingly interpersonal in nature in that they are designed not only to convey information, but to elicit a response (command aspect) from the other (Satir, 1967). "In this effort, an explanation of why the communication was sent is important, both for purposes of understanding as well as for responding" (Newman, 1981, p. 60). Thus, the metamessage (meaning) begins to have precedence over the literal message. Attributions regarding the intended meanings may be assigned to situational or dispositional influences, or they may now be assigned to a new category—"my partner in relation to me." As Newman (1981) states "The influence of 'interpersonal premises' and expectations, as derived from metacommunication, has been understated in previous discussions of factors which affect attribution assignment" (p. 61). The presence of "interpersonal premises" and "expectations" mark the emergence of this new system, characterized not by its component parts but by their interdependence. Although cognitive person factors and the subjective appraisal of the sum of past interactions are now playing a major role in shaping current communicational patterns in the dyad, situational factors too have their influence. In fact, given the emerging knowledge of "the other in relation to me" and "me in relation to the other," situations can be selectively chosen or created in order to facilitate the communication of specific messages, especially where the metamessage consists of "subtle, emotional, or unpleasant information" (Furnham, 1981, p. 112).

With the emergence of interpersonal attributions and the saliency of metacommunication (meaning) for the dyad, our original strangers can be said to have established a "close" relationship. Still, this relationship may or may not be characterized by the quality of intimacy. Unfortunately, many marriages and friendships can be considered "close," but not necessarily "intimate" relationships. As we have noted previously, to truly feel we know our partners and are known by them, we must at least occasionally communicate and acknowledge (intentionally) the subjective meanings of our messages, that is, we must explicitly address the relational context of our messages. Because one cannot predict the outcome of such intentional metacommunications, they are apt to occur within a state of heightened emotional arousal, directly affecting the "subjective value" (Mischel, 1973) assigned to the relationship at that point in time. It is the subjective value that it is "good to know and be known" that results in the qualitative impression of intimacy, and makes intimate relationships dynamic and emergent entities. Conversely, if metacommunication and interpersonal attributions remain solely at an implicit level or are not periodically updated via intentional metacommunication, "potent sources of attributional conflict and relational disturbance" (Newman, 1981, p. 66) can arise, leading to a breakdown in the intimacy of the relationship. This view might help explain why Waring and his associates have found that clinical interventions aimed at encouraging couples to disclose their ideas, attitudes, beliefs, and interpretations regarding their relationships and behavior (Cognitive Family Therapy) have proven effective in treating marital discord (Waring & Russell, 1981). Such "cognitive" (as opposed to affective) disclosures are thought to increase the couples' sense of intimacy through increased mutual understanding. From the perspective of our model of intimacy, such disclosures appear to be useful at reducing potential sources of attributional conflict through facilitation of intentional metacommunication and a fuller sense of knowing and being known.

While intentional metacommunications may give rise to the mutual sense of intimacy in a close relationship, they are apt to be fleeting moments in the course of an ongoing relationship; they are merely the molecular components. We now step back and take a more molar view of these intimate experiences within the broader context of close relationships over time.

A MOLAR VIEW OF THE MODEL

In the first part of this chapter, we have described the basic components of intimate relationships and the general manner of their interaction. As we take a more molar view of our model, we look more closely at the emergent properties of the intimate relationship themselves. We discuss what we believe to be the characteristic qualities of intimate relationships and the influence of time on relationship development.

Qualities

Several earlier investigators attempted to describe the qualities of intimate relationships in terms of specific behavior patterns (Hinde, 1976;

Levinger & Snoek, 1972). According to these authors, an intimate relationship is one evidencing all or some of the following characteristics:

1. frequent interaction,
2. face-to-face interaction,
3. diverse interactions across several behavioral and situational domains,
4. substantial influence on each other's lives,
5. repeated attempts to restore proximity during absence,
6. alleviation of anxiety upon return of the partner,
7. unique communication systems,
8. synchronized goals and behavior,
9. mutual self-disclosure, and
10. seeing separate interests as being inextricably tied to the well-being of the relationship

Walster, Walster, and Berscheid (1978) described more general qualities that they felt increased as intimacy increased in a relationship:

1. intensity of liking or loving;
2. depth and breadth of information exchanged, so that intimates know much more about one another's idiosyncracies, personal histories, and vulnerabilities;
3. actual and expected length of relationship;
4. value of resources exchanged, with partners increasingly willing to invest more of their resources, but also able to punish more keenly, particularly through termination of the relationship;
5. interchangeability of resources; and
6. "we-ness," the tendency for partners to define themselves as one unit in interaction with the external social world.

Both of these conceptualizations seem to be generally appropriate to the understanding of intimate relationships. However, they rely heavily on descriptions of specific behavior patterns. Within our model, the qualities of an intimate relationship are based upon the subjective, cognitive appraisals of each participant. The following six qualities are relational in nature and characterize the meaning of an intimate relationship at a level beyond its basic components:

1. knowledge of the innermost being of one another,
2. mutuality,
3. interdependence,
4. trust,

5. commitment, and
6. caring.

All of these qualities seem to be necessary to the development and existence of intimate relationships. They are also interdependent qualities, different from one another and yet overlapping. Let us consider each one in greater depth.

Knowledge   We stated earlier that an intimate relationship is a relational process in which the partners come to know the innermost, subjective aspects of one another. Several investigators have equated the growth in knowledge about partners with the growth of an intimate relationship (Crockett & Friedman, 1980; Duck, 1977; Levinger, 1974). This correlation does seem to be important. In the development of intimate relationships, mutual self-disclosure of increasingly personal information coincides with reports of increased appraisals of intimacy (Altman, 1973; Altman & Taylor, 1973; Miller, 1976; Taylor, 1979). It seems to be of central importance to people to be able to share with others all aspects of themselves, and to feel understood and accepted as the people they are. It is also important to know, understand, and accept other people thoroughly at the same time. In an intimate relationship, these processes occur simultaneously and reciprocally. They seem to represent a single process characteristic of the relationship as a whole rather than descriptions of the needs and actions of two separate people.

Along with this "existential" need for mutual knowing, several other reasons for self-disclosure have been postulated. Derlega and Grzelak (1979) describe five functions of self-disclosure: (1) self-expression, for the release of feelings; (2) increased self-clarification, where one's consistency and integration of ideas are assessed in order to be presented clearly to another; (3) obtaining social validation through social comparison processes; (4) acting as a vehicle for relationship development; and (5) social control via impression management. The first three functions are individualistic in nature. They do not relate specifically to intimate relationships. The last two functions are interpersonal in nature, and are concerned with the ways in which relationships are mutually defined and controlled. The recognition of these last two functions lead us to the next basic quality of intimate relationships: namely, mutuality.

Mutuality   Intimate relationships are based upon the assumption that both partners are engaged in a joint venture. Both work, share, interact, and come to know one another in great depth. Intimate relationships have at their center a mutual process like finely choreographed dancers in which a balance of movement, of sharing, occurs. When considering the quality of intimate self- and other-knowledge, it is clear that the mutual process of sharing this knowledge is as important as the knowledge itself (Waring, Tillman, Frelick, Russell, & Weisz, 1980).

Levinger and Snoek (1972) felt that there were three levels of a relationship: (1) awareness, (2) surface contact, and (3) mutuality. At the level of mutuality, "the relationship emerges as personal (vs impersonal), uniquely tailored (vs normative and role-bound), and intimate in the kinds of personal exchange and emotional investment of both parties" (Morton & Douglas, 1981, p. 8). In Levinger and Snoek's conceptualization, mutuality was the most important quality of intimate relationships.

It should be noted that while mutuality implies joint, shared interaction, it does not require highly similar or identical interaction patterns. Intimate relationships seem to involve both *reciprocal* interactions, with the partners showing similar behavior either simultaneously or alternately, and *complementary* interactions, in which the behavior of each partner differs from, but complements, that of the other. Reciprocal interactions revealing similarity between partners seem to be associated with consensual validation, the facilitation of communication, and positively shared belief systems (Azjen, 1977; Byrne, 1971; Clore & Byrne, 1974; Duck, 1976, 1977). Similarity in needs, expectations, skills, and view of the world allow partners to interact as equals and to choose life goals and directions satisfactory to both. Complementary interactions allow the partners to satisfy each other (Winch, 1958) and provide opportunities for them to behave in a manner (nurturant, submissive, dominant, altruistic) that they like to see in themselves (Hinde, 1981). Again using the analogy of a dancing pair, sometimes the partners dance side-by-side using identical actions, and sometimes face-to-face using differing, complementary actions. This interweaving creates a complex and mutually satisfying "dance," or relationship.

Another aspect of mutuality is the concept of "fairness" in rewards and costs resulting from interactions within the relationship. We have chosen to use the term "fair" as opposed to "equal" or "equitable," since the latter two terms have not been used with consistent definitions. Investigators have found that intimate relationships are characterized by a sense of fairness, shared by both partners, relating to their needs, input, and outcome (Hatfield & Traupmann, 1981; Lerner, Miller, & Holmes, 1976; Morton & Douglas, 1981). This sense of fairness is crucial to the mutuality of relationship definition and the mutuality of relationship control that characterize intimate relationships (Morton, Alexander, & Altman, 1976).

Interdependence   Interdependence in relationships refers to "the dependence upon the partner for the occurrence of some action, outcome, or event" (Morton & Douglas, 1981, p. 23). Morton *et al.* (1976) feel that an intimate relationship includes the mutual definition of the nature of the interdependence structure upon which the relationship depends. In other words, partners learn in what ways they can depend upon one another for support, resources, understanding, and action, and they agree upon future dependency. There does not seem to be a direct linear correlation between interdependence and intimacy in relationships. Initially, interdependence and intimacy do seem to increase in unison (Kelley, 1979; Kelley & Thibaut, 1978). Partners share knowledge and goals, increase their interactions with one another while limiting others, pooling resources, and slowly intertwining their lives in a variety of ways. However, as intimate relationships become firmly established, there seems to be increasing room for interdependence with persons outside of the relationship also (Weiss, 1974). Clinical descriptions of pathologically enmeshed marriages (Minuchin, 1974) indicate extreme interdependence of the partners without the other qualities central to the existence of an intimate relationship. Thus, an interdependence structure that allows for the delicate intertwining of two lives for the greater satisfaction of each, but with limits and some flexibility, characterizes intimate relationships. Morton and Douglas (1981, p. 24) describe it as a pattern that involves a "shift from maximizing individual outcomes to maximizing shared, or interdependent outcomes."

Before we consider the fourth quality of intimate relationships, it should be noted that interdependence carries with it considerable mutual power. To the extent that interdependency is characteristic of a relationship, the partners will have mutual power to grant or withhold gratification of needs (Kelley & Thibaut, 1978; Morton & Douglas, 1981). One thing that makes this interdependency possible is the quality of trust.

Trust   "The increased vulnerability which arises with intimacy is tolerable only if accompanied by a belief that the partner will not exploit it" (Hinde, 1981, p. 14). This requires trust, a sense of confidence in the integrity, truthfulness, and fairness of the partner. Basically we are talking about a general sense of trust—a shared, mutual trust—that no undue harm will be associated with the relationship. On a more specific level, partners might say that they trust one another (1) to be accepting, (2) to avoid purposeful hurt of the other, (3) to have the best interests of the partner and of the relationship in mind, (4) to feel warmth and caring for the partner, (5) to need the partner and respond to the needs of the partner, (6) to share, and (7) to continue the relationship.

Commitment   Hinde (1981, p. 14) defines commitment as "the extent to which the partners in a relationship either accept their relationship as continuing indefinitely or direct their behavior towards ensuring its continuance or optimizing its properties." As an intimate relationship develops, partners continually assess their own desires for commitment and also those of the other. The other qualities of intimate relationships seem to be influenced by the level of mutual commitment. For example, investigators focusing on reciprocity of self-disclosure (Altman, 1973; Altman & Taylor, 1973; Taylor, 1979) have found that people will disclose easily and at great depth if the relationship is expected to be short-term, while commitment to the possibility of a long-term relationship instills caution, exemplified by slow, stepwise disclosures dependent upon reciprocal behavior in kind. Partners may be committed to the relationship in varying ways; for example, as friends who realize that eventually circumstances will separate them geographically and in time, but who are committed to the continuation of the relationship in an altered form, along with couples who express their commitment to remain together emotionally and physically through the ceremony of marriage. The variations in the type of commitment are not as crucial as the mutuality of understanding and agreement to the terms of commitment. This need for mutuality is described by Hinde (1981, p. 14) when he states that "the course of a relationship may be affected not only by the degree of commitment of the two partners, but by the extent to which each believes in the other's commitment." Misunderstandings in the expression of commitment and alterations in one partner's faith in the commitment of the other may stifle the growth of an intimate relationship or may initiate its decline (Duck, 1981).

Caring   The sixth and final quality of intimate relationships is caring. Individuals come together in relationships for many different reasons (money, companionship, status, power). Intimate relationships may arise from any or all of these reasons, but at least one reason will always be a strong sense of caring and affection between partners (Driscoll, Davis, & Lipetz, 1972).

Thus, these six qualities characterize intimate relationships and indicate their uniqueness. As noted earlier, they are different yet interdependent and overlapping. They emerge from the relational process and describe the interaction of two individuals within a situational context (or many contexts). Another important consideration in our model of intimate relationships is the influence of time.

Time

One of the most outstanding features of any relationship is its dynamic nature. It is continually growing, changing, developing, recalibrating as it passes through time. Although many times when we discuss relationships or when investigators study various aspects of relationships we appear to believe that their qualities are static, there is always an underlying assumption that we know that relationships are more of a process than an entity. We have just discussed six basic qualities of intimate relationships. The influence of time and the dynamic nature of these qualities were only briefly considered. At this point, we will address these issues more directly.

Knowledge, of necessity, must be gained slowly. There is a great deal to know about another person in order to know that person deeply. Also, much of this information is private and personal. There seem to be rules that guide the process of sharing, determined by general internal needs in each person for psychological defense and by societal norms (Jourard, 1959; Jourard & Landsman, 1960). When there is little expectation for future encounters, individuals frequently self-disclose highly personal information with no need for a response from the person to whom they are disclosing. However, when there is an expectation or a possibility of a relationship continuing in time, individuals self-disclose more slowly, beginning with impersonal and progressing to more personal information, and requiring the same amount and kind of self-disclosures, given in a reciprocal fashion, from the partner (Altman, 1973). Partners seem to "test the waters" with one another, assessing whether further self-disclosure will be safe and accepted. This process of mutual self-disclosure is never really complete. The individuals in a relationship are continually changing. The needs and values professed in their 20s will differ in their 30s and 40s (Levinson, 1978). Even childhood memories and assessments of early life events may differ as the maturing personality of the individual remembers the past.

Mutuality, the shared, joint aspect of an intimate relationship, also has fluctuations in patterns over time. Initially there is a high demand for mutuality. Partners wish to share most activities with one another, to spend as much time together as possible, and to exclude other people from their "inner circle" (Berger & Kellner, 1964). Reciprocity is important in the self-disclosure process just described because it defines a degree of similarity that is important to early stage relationship development (Duck & Craig, 1978). As intimate relationships develop over time, mutuality remains important, but the specific evidence of it may be relatively intermittent. Each bit of self-disclosure by one partner does not have to be followed by the same from the other partner (Taylor, 1979). Greater time may be spent apart, and separate interests and friends may develop. The mutuality of later stage intimate relationships seems to be based upon the belief that over time a balance will be maintained and all events will contribute to the stabilization or enrichment of the shared relationship (Hatfield & Traupmann, 1981; Walster *et al.*, 1978).

The quality of interdependence must develop over time. Two separate individuals come together to initiate a relationship. Interdependence develops as each individual shares resources with the other, receives resources, information, joy, and caring from the other, and believes in the continuity of the relationship. As more time is spent together and more aspects of life are shared, the greater the possibility for the growth of interdependence (Hinde, 1981). There is not a linear relationship between time and interdependence, since many other factors have an influence over the type and degree of interdependence that develops. But time does seem to be necessary for the growth of interdependence, and the greater the amount of time, the greater the possibility for complex interdependence patterns to develop.

The qualities of trust and commitment might well be considered together. Persons learn to trust one another slowly through experience. They come into relationships with differing beliefs about the trustworthiness of other people in general, and therefore develop trust within a particular relationship at different rates and to different degrees. In any case, trust is rarely immediate, but must be gauged slowly from judgments about another's character and intentions. Commitment and trust seem to be closely intertwined. Individuals choose to establish commitments with others whom they trust, and certain aspects of trust within intimate relationships seem to be based upon the extent and type of mutual commitment that exists between partners. Commitment not only requires time in which to develop, but also implies an expectation of the future, a time yet to come.

Caring is the sixth quality of intimate relationships that we discussed. It too grows and changes over time. Initially, in intimate relationships caring may be perceived as romantic love or sexual passion. Over time, this frequently changes into mutual concern and affection, followed by a deeper form of love (Cunningham & Antill, 1981).

Time is required for the development and evolution of all of the qualities. It seems to serve as a path over which they travel. There seems to be the implication of a straight path, leading from little "knowledge/mutuality/interdependence" to great depths of knowing and being known. In actuality there are many paths, each having many forks leading in a variety of directions. Intimate relationships, with all of their qualities, are ever developing, changing, redefining, as they move through time.

SUMMARY AND CONCLUSIONS

All too often reductionistic attempts to dissect process variables result in lists of components that do not sum to their original total. One can reduce the human body to so many liters of water and so many kilograms of basic minerals, but simply mixing these elements together will not produce a living body. The same is true of intimate relationships. If one's goal is to determine the basic components of intimacy, a reductionistic strategy is most applicable. However, if one wishes to study the process of intimacy as a dynamic entity, a different approach is needed.

In the preceding pages we have outlined in broad strokes a cognitive interactional model of intimate relationships that attempts to preserve intimacy's vitality and evolving nature. Specifically, we have defined intimacy as a subjective appraisal that emerges out of a relational process between two individuals in which each comes to know the "innermost" aspects of the other, and each is known in a like manner. Over time, these appraisals in turn give rise to higher-order appraisals of relational qualities that influence the trajectory of the relationship itself. As such, our model of intimate relationships is both dynamic and emergent in perspective.

There are three key premises to our model. The first is the belief that all interactive behaviors have a connotative (meaning) aspect as well as a denotative aspect to them. Recognition of this connotative aspect allows us to explain why behaviors that are considered intimate by one couple may not be intimate for another, or even by the same couple at a different point in time. Furthermore, each individual has his or her own unique ways of taking in and processing behavioral information within a changing environment. The meanings of this information are continually evaluated against the accumulation of past experiences, and they affect future expectations and behaviors.

A second facet of our cognitive interactional model is its systemic view of intimate relationships. A dynamic model of intimate relationships must take into account that "relationships influence the nature of individuals, and individuals influence the nature of the relationships they enter" (Hinde, 1981, p. 5). Neither the relationship nor the individuals can be studied without consideration of the other. Relationships as dynamic entities are constantly redefining themselves as they occur across time and social–situational contexts. Each redefinition changes the relational system and affects how the individuals will encode and decode future interactions.

Finally, our model emphasizes the role of cognitive appraisals over time in the development of higher-order relational qualities that characterize intimate relationships. There must be a means for organizing individuals' appraisals of specific behavioral interactions into more molar qualities that emerge within enduring intimate relationships. A cognitive interactional view is especially useful in this respect because it postulates that the "process" of interacting is as important to the relational system as is its content.

Our cognitive interactional model not only provides a different way of viewing intimate relationships, but it also extends a challenge to researchers to approach the study of intimacy in new ways. Rather than focusing on interactive behaviors per se, our model suggests that there may be something useful to be learned by looking at the meanings of such behaviors, and how these meanings change over the course of time and contribute to relational development.

REFERENCES

Altman, I. (1973). Reciprocity of interpersonal exchange. *Journal of Theory of Social Behavior, 3*, 249–261.

Altman, I., & Taylor, D. A. (1973). *Social penetration: The development of interpersonal relationships.* New York: Holt.

Andreyeva, G. M., & Gozman, L. J. (1981). Interpersonal relationships and social context. In S. Duck & R. Gilmour (Eds.), *Personal relationships* (Vol. 1). New York: Academic Press.

Archer, R. L. (1979). Role of personality and the social situation. In G. J. Chelune (Ed.), *Self-disclosure.* San Francisco: Jossey-Bass.

Argyle, M., Furnham, A., & Graham, J. A. (1981). *Social situations.* London: Cambridge University Press.

Aronfreed, J. (1968). *Conduct and conscience: The socialization of internalized control over behavior.* New York: Academic Press.

Azjen, I. (1977). Information processing approaches to interpersonal attraction. In S. W. Duck (Ed.), *Theory and practice in interpersonal attraction.* New York: Academic Press.

Bandler, R., Grindler, J., & Satir, V. (1976). *Changing with families.* Palo Alto, CA: Science and Behavior Books.

Bateson, G. (1972). *Steps to an ecology of mind.* New York: Ballantine Books.

Bem, D. J., & Allen, A. (1974). On predicting some of the people some of the time: The search for cross-situational consistencies in behavior. *Psychological Review, 81*, 506–520.

Bem, D. J., & Funder, D. C. (1978). Predicting more of the people more of the time: Assessing the personality of situations. *Psychological Review, 85*, 485–501.

Berger, P. L., & Kellner, H. (1964). Marriage and the construction of reality. *Diogenes, 46*, 1–23.

Buber, M. (1958). *I and thou.* New York: Scribner.

Burgess, R. L. (1981). Relationships in marriage and the family. In S. Duck & R. Gilmour (Eds.), *Personal relationships* (Vol. 1). New York: Academic Press.

Byrne, D. (1971). *The attraction paradigm.* New York: Academic Press.

Chelune, G. J. (1975). Self-disclosure: An elaboration of its basic dimensions. Psychological Reports, 36, 79–85.

Chelune, G. J. (1976). The Self-Disclosure Situations Survey: A new approach to measuring self-disclosure. *JSAS Catalog of Selected Documents in Psychology, 6*(1367), 111–112.

Chelune, G. J. (1979). Measuring openness in interpersonal communication. In G. J. Chelune (Ed.), *Self-disclosure.* San Francisco: Jossey-Bass.

Chelune, G. J. (1980). *Person-situation interactionalism in self-disclosure.* Paper presented at the 88th Annual Convention of the American Psychological Association, Montreal, Canada.

Chown, S. M. (1981). Friendship in old age. In S. Duck & R. Gilmour (Eds.), *Personal relationships* (Vol. 2). New York: Academic Press.

Clore, G. L., & Byrne, D. (1974). A reinforcement-affected model of attraction. In T. L. Huston (Ed.), *Foundations of interpersonal attraction.* New York: Academic Press.

Crockett, W., & Friedman, P. (1980). Theoretical explorations of the process of initial interactions. *Western Journal of Speech Communication, 44*, 86–92.

Cunningham, J. D., & Antill, J. K. (1981). Love in developing romantic relationships. In S. Duck & R. Gilmour (Eds.), *Personal relationships* (Vol. 2). New York: Academic Press.

Delia, J. G. (1980). Some tentative thoughts concerning the study of interpersonal relationships and their development. *Western Journal of Speech Communication, 44*, 97–103.

Derlega, V. J., & Chaikin, A. L. (1975). *Sharing intimacy: What we reveal to others and why.* Englewood Cliffs, NJ: Prentice-Hall.

Derlega, V. J., & Grzelak, J. (1979). Appropriateness of self-disclosure. In G. J. Chelune (Ed.), *Self-disclosure.* San Francisco: Jossey-Bass.

Doster, J. A., & Strickland, B. R. (1969). Perceived childrearing practices and self-disclosure patterns. *Journal of Consulting and Clinical Psychology, 33*, 382.

Driscoll, R., Davis, K. E., & Lipetz, M. E. (1972). Parental interference and romantic love: The Romeo and Juliet effect. *Journal of Personality and Social Psychology, 24*, 1–10.

Duck, S. W. (1976). Interpersonal communication in developing acquaintance. In G. R. Miller (Ed.), *Explorations in interpersonal communications.* Beverly Hills, CA: Sage.

Duck, S. W. (1977). *The study of acquaintance.* London: Teakfield-Saxon House.

Duck, S. W. (1981). Toward a research map for the study of relationship breakdown. In S. Duck & R. Gilmour (Eds.), *Personal relationships* (Vol. 3). New York: Academic Press.

Duck, S. W., & Craig, G. (1978). Personality similarity and the development of friendship. *British Journal of Social and Clinical Psychology, 17*, 237–242.

Festinger, L. (1945). A theory of social comparison processes. *Human Relations, 7*, 117–140.

Frankel, A., & Powers, B. (1971, April). *An S-R inventory of self-disclosure.* Paper presented at the Annual Meeting of the Western Psychological Association, San Francisco.

Freeman, H., & Giovannoni, J. (1969). Social psychology of mental health. In G. Lindzey & E. Aronson (Eds.), *Handbook of social psychology* (Vol. 5). Menlo Park, CA: Addison-Wesley.

Furnham, A. (1981). The choice of situation and medium as a function of the message. In

M. Argyle, A. Furnham, & J. A. Graham (Eds.), *Social situations*. London: Cambridge University Press.

Gibson, E. J. (1969). *Principles of perceptual learning and development*. New York: Appleton-Century-Crofts.

Goffman, E. (1959). *The presentation of self in everyday life*. Garden City, NJ: Anchor Books.

Goffman, E. (1963). *Stigma*. Englewood Cliffs, NJ: Prentice-Hall.

Goodstein, L. D., & Reinecker, V. M. (1974). Factors affecting self-disclosure: A review of the literature. In B. A. Maher (Ed.), *Progress in experimental personality research* (Vol. 7). New York: Academic Press.

Gouldner, A. W. (1960). The norm of reciprocity: A preliminary statement. *American Sociological Review, 25*, 161–178.

Grindler, J., & Bandler, R. (1976). *The structure of magic* (Vol. 2). Palo Alto, CA: Science and Behavior Books.

Grinker, R. R. (1967). *Toward a unified theory of human behavior* (2nd ed.). New York: Basic Books.

Hatfield, E., & Traupmann, J. (1981). Intimate relationships: A perspective from equity theory. In S. Duck & R. Gilmour (Eds.), *Personal relationships* (Vol. 1). New York: Academic Press.

Hatfield, E., & Walster, G. W. (1981). *A new look at love*. Reading, MA: Addison-Wesley.

Helson, H. (1964). *Adaptation-level theory*. New York: Harper.

Hemingway, E. (1952). *The old man and the sea*. New York: Scribner.

Hinde, R. A. (1976). On describing relationships. *Journal of Child Psychology and Psychiatry. 17*, 1–19.

Hinde, R. A. (1981). The bases of a science of interpersonal relationships. In S. Duck & R. Gilmour (Eds.), *Personal relationships* (Vol. 1). New York: Academic Press.

Horowitz, L. M. (1979). Cognitive structure of interpersonal problems treated in psychotherapy. *Journal of Consulting and Clinical Psychology, 47*, 5–15.

Huston, T. L., & Levinger, G. (1978). Interpersonal attraction and relationships. *Annual Review of Psychology, 1978, 29*, 115–156.

Huston, T. L., Surra, C. A., Fitzgerald, N. M., & Cate, R. M. (1981). From courtship to marriage: Mate selection as an interpersonal process. In S. Duck & R. Gilmour (Eds.), *Personal relationships* (Vol. 2). New York: Academic Press.

Ittelson, W., Proshansky, H. M., Rivlin, L., & Winkel, G. (1974). *An introduction to environmental psychology*. New York: Holt.

Jackson, D., & Weakland, J. (1961). Conjoint family therapy: Some considerations on technique and results. *Psychiatry, 24*, 30–45.

Jones, E. E., & Davis, K. E. (1965). From acts to dispositions. In L. Berkowitz (Ed.), *Advances in experimental social psychology* (Vol. 2). New York: Academic Press.

Jourard, S. M. (1959). Healthy personality and self-disclosure. *Mental Hygiene, 44*, 449–507.

Jourard, S. M. (1971). *The transparent self* (rev. ed.). New York: Van Nostrand Reinhold.

Jourard, S. M., & Landsman, M. J. (1960). Cognition, cathexis and the "dyadic effect" in men's self-disclosing behavior. *Merrill-Palmer Quarterly Journal of Behavioral Development, 6*, 178–186.

Kelley, H. H. (1979). *Personal relationships: Their structures and processes*. Hillsdale, NJ: Erlbaum.

Kelley, H. H., & Thibaut, J. W. (1978). *Interpersonal relationships: A theory of interdependence*. New York: Wiley.

Kleinke, C. L. (1979). Effects of personal evaluations. In G. J. Chelune (Ed.), *Self-disclosure*. San Francisco: Jossey-Bass.

Kohlberg, L. (1969). Stage and sequence: The cognitive-developmental approach to socialization. In D. A. Goslin (Ed.), *Handbook of socialization theory and research*. Chicago: Rand McNally, 1969.

Kon, I. S. (1981). Adolescent friendship: Some unanswered questions for future research. In S. Duck & R. Gilmour (Eds.), *Personal relationships* (Vol. 2). New York: Academic Press.

La Gaipa, J. J. (1981a). A systems approach to personal relationships. In S. Duck & R. Gilmour (Eds.), *Personal relationships* (Vol. 1). New York: Academic Press.

La Gaipa, J. J. (1981b). Children's friendships. In S. Duck & R. Gilmour (Eds.), *Personal relationships* (Vol. 2). New York: Academic Press.

Lerner, M. J., Miller, D. T., & Holmes, J. G. (1976). Deserving and the emergence of forms of justice. In L. Berkowitz & E. Walster (Eds.), *Advances in experimental social psychology*. New York: Academic Press.

Levinger, G. (1974). A three-level approach to attraction: Toward an understanding of pair relatedness. In T. L. Huston (Ed.), *Foundations of interpersonal attraction*. New York: Academic Press.

Levinger, G., & Snoek, J. D. (1972). *Attraction in relationship: A new look at interpersonal attraction*. Morristown, NJ: General Learning Press.

Levinson, D. J. (1978). *The seasons of a man's life*. New York: Knopf.

Mehrabian, A., & Diamond, S. (1971). Effects of furniture arrangement, props and personality in social interaction. *Journal of Personality and Social Psychology, 20*, 18–30.

Miller, G. R. (1976). Foreward. In G. R. Miller (Ed.), *Explorations in interpersonal communication*. Beverly Hills, CA: Sage.

Miller, L. C., Berg, J. H., & Archer, R. L. (1983). Openers: Individuals who elicit intimate self-disclosure. *Journal of Personality and Social Psychology. 44*, 1234–1244.

Minuchin, S. (1974). *Families and family therapy*. Cambridge, MA: Harvard University Press.

Mischel, W. (1973). Toward a cognitive social learning reconceptualization of personality. *Psychological Review, 80*, 252–283.

Mischel, W. (1977). On the future of personality measurement. *American Psychologist, 32*, 246–254.

Mischel, W. (1979). On the interface of cognition and personality. *American Psychologist, 34*, 740–754.

Morton, T. L., Alexander, J. F., & Altman, I. (1976). Communication and relationship definition. In G. R. Miller (Ed.), *Explorations in interpersonal communications*. Beverly Hills, CA: Sage.

Morton, T. L., & Douglas, M. A. (1981). Growth of relationships. In S. Duck & R. Gilmour (Eds.), *Personal relationships* (Vol. 2). New York: Academic Press.

Newman, H. (1981). Communication within ongoing relationships: An attributional perspective. *Personality and Social Psychology Bulletin, 7*, 59–70.

Patterson, M. L. (1976). An arousal model of interpersonal intimacy. *Psychological Review, 83*, 235–245.

Pawlby, S. J. (1981). Infant-mother relationships. In S. Duck & R. Gilmour (Eds.), *Personal relationships* (Vol. 2). New York: Academic Press.

Perlmutter, M. S., & Hatfield, E. (1980). Intimacy, intentional metacommunication and second order change. *American Journal of Family Therapy, 8*, 17–23.

Pervin, L. A. (1976). A free response description approach of person-situation interaction. *Journal of Personality and Social Psychology, 34*, 465–474.

Price, R. H. (1974). The taxonomic classification of behavior and situations and the problem of behavior-environment congruence. *Human Relations, 27*, 567–585.

Price, R. H., & Bouffard, D. L. (1974). Behavioral appropriateness and situational constraint as dimensions of social behavior. *Journal of Personality and Social Psychology, 30,* 579–586.

Reisman, J. M. (1981). Adult friendships. In S. Duck & R. Gilmour (Eds.), *Personal relationships* (Vol. 2). New York: Academic Press.

Rosenfeld, L. B., Civikly, J. M., & Herron, J. R. (1979). Anatomical and psychological sex differences. In G. J. Chelune (Ed.), *Self-disclosure.* San Francisco: Jossey-Bass.

Satir, V. (1967). *Conjoint family therapy* (rev. ed). Palo Alto, CA: Science and Behavior Books.

Schachter, S., & Singer, J. E. (1962). Cognitive, social, and physiological determinants of emotional state. *Psychological Review, 69,* 379–399.

Shields, M. M. (1981). Parent-child relationships in the middle years of childhood. In S. Duck & R. Gilmour (Eds.), *Personal relationships* (Vol. 2). New York: Academic Press.

Snyder, M. (1974). Self-monitoring of expressive behavior. *Journal of Personality and Social Psychology, 30,* 526–537.

Snyder, M. (1978). Self-monitoring processes. In L. Berkowitz (Ed.), *Advances in experimental social psychology* (Vol. 12). New York: Academic Press.

Taylor, D. A. (1979). Motivational bases. In G. J. Chelune (Ed.), *Self-disclosure.* San Francisco: Jossey-Bass.

Walster, E., Walster, G. W., & Berscheid, E. (1978). *Equity theory and research.* Boston: Allyn & Bacon.

Waring, E. M., & Chelune, G. J. (1983). Marital intimacy and self-disclosure. *Journal of Clinical Psychology. 39,* 183–190.

Waring, E. M., & Russell, L. (1981). Cognitive family therapy. *Journal of Sex and Marital Therapy, 6,* 258–273.

Waring, E. M., Tillman, M. P., Frelick, L., Russell, L., & Weisz, G. (1980). Concepts of intimacy in the general population. *Journal of Nervous and Mental Disease, 168,* 471–474.

Watzlawick, B., Weakland, J. H., & Fisch, R. (1974). *Change: Principles of problem formation and problem resolution.* New York: Norton.

Weiss, R. S. (1974). The provisions of social relationships. In Z. Rubin (Ed.), *Doing unto others.* Englewood Cliffs, NJ: Prentice-Hall.

Winch, R. F. (1958). *Mate-selection: A study of complementary needs.* New York: Harper.

CHAPTER 3

Human Motives and Personal Relationships

DAN P. MCADAMS

INTRODUCTION

This chapter articulates an approach to the understanding of personal relationships that emphasizes the role of two fundamental human motives—power and intimacy motives. Human motives occupy a special niche in the panoply of determinants mediating human behavior and experience. In the arena of personal relationships, such as romantic love and friendship, power and intimacy motives appear to inform thought, feeling, and behavior by conferring upon relationships a particular thematic meaning. In what follows, the idea of "motive" in personality and social psychology is briefly outlined, and consideration is given to psychologists' search for primary motives. Following Bakan's (1966) conceptualization of agency and communion as the two fundamental modalities in living forms, power and intimacy motives are presented as two basic motivational clusters in human lives that may shape and be shaped by significant interpersonal relationships. The measurement of power and intimacy motivation through content analysis of narrative responses is then described and selected research on the construct validity of the two motives reviewed. The bulk of the chapter then considers observed and hypothesized connections between power and intimacy motivation on the one hand and love and friendship on the other, via a review of empirical research on the topic and the presentation of some very new data concerning human friendships.

COMMUNICATION, INTIMACY, AND CLOSE RELATIONSHIPS

HUMAN MOTIVES

Persons and Environments

In his celebrated equation $B = f(P, E)$, Kurt Lewin (1935) formalized one of the few generally accepted "truths" in psychology, that behavior is a function of the person and the environment. One suspects that personal relationships, too, are functions of the persons involved and the environments in which the persons find themselves. Social psychologists have traditionally explored the environmental determinants of behavior and relationships, specifying the ways in which, for instance, room temperature, crowding, social class, the presence of strangers, and a host of other contextual factors impact upon a variety of aspects of interpersonal behavior. Though there are notable exceptions, personality psychologists have traditionally emphasized the internal person variables. Person variables have typically been divided between those relatively transient (state) factors such as mood, expectancies, and immediate goals, and those relatively enduring (dispositional) dimensions that assumedly remain with the person as he or she traverses a variety of situations over time. It is within this latter category of person variables—personality dispositions—that human motives of power and intimacy have traditionally been located.

In further delineating the place of human motives in personal relationships, it is instructive to consider a tripartite division of personality dispositions first proposed by McClelland (1951, 1981) many years ago. McClelland distinguishes among the personality *trait*, the *schema*, and the *motive*. The personality trait is typically a stylistic variable that indicates *how* an individual behaves or experiences his or her world. Traits are often couched in bipolar terms. Thus, a person may tend toward extraversion or introversion, depending upon his or her characteristic style of approaching life (i.e., in a characteristic outgoing or inward manner). A person may be friendly or unfriendly, serene or excitable, active or passive, dominant or submissive. Well-researched trait constructs include extraversion–introversion (Eysenck, 1960), dominance–submissiveness (Cattell, 1966), neuroticism (Eysenck, 1960), and Machiavellianism (Christie & Geis, 1970). The schema, on the other hand, is a cognitive frame imposed by the individual upon experience so as to make sense of that experience. The schema refers to *what* an individual characteristically "sees" (what inferences or conclusions he or she draws) when interacting with the world. The idea of schema casts a wide net, taking in such personality variables as characteristic roles, values, beliefs, attitudes, scripts, and even one's world view. With the popularity of cognitive constructs in personality and social psychology today, the list of schemata being studied is extremely long, but some of the more popular schema constructs include locus of control (Phares, 1976), dogmatism (Ehrlich, 1978), personal constructs (Kelly, 1955), psychological differentiation (Witkin, Goodenough, & Oltmann, 1979), and belief in a "just world" (Lerner & Miller, 1978).

Motives, on the other hand, reflect the *why* of behavior and experience. They refer to the underlying reasons for behavior, the internal "springs of action" as James (1890) put it. According to McClelland, the springs of action exist within the person as affectively-toned cognitive clusters centered around general experiential preferences. This is to say that constellations of ideas that refer to desired goal states (experiential preferences) come to be infused with emotion so as to form particular motive dispositions for a given individual. The motive dispositions serve to energize, direct, and select behavior and experience within the framework of constraints and opportunities afforded by the environment. For example, a person with a strong achievement motive (Atkinson & Raynor, 1974; McClelland, 1961) reveals a richer and more articulated network of associations (e.g., specific personal memories of success and failure, general attitudes and beliefs about "doing well") to an achievement cue (e.g., a challenging task) than does a person low on achievement motivation. The network of associations is laden with positive affect (joy, excitement, interest) such that opportunities for doing well, as they present themselves in daily living, come to be emotionally arousing and, thereby, consistently preferred. Consequently, the person high in achievement motivation may engage in challenging tasks with marked enthusiasm (the motive as energizer); he or she may choose to spend more time establishing and working towards the achievement of instrumental goals than, say, talking with friends, caring for children, or enjoying the arts (the motive as director); and he or she may attend more closely to achievement-oriented events and process more efficiently achievement-oriented information than events and information concerned with other goal states, such as intimacy or power (the motive as selector).

Primary Human Motives

Though most personality theorists have posited a circumscribed set of motivational constructs that energize, direct, and select human behavior and experience, questions concerning the exact nature and number of the fundamental human motives have traditionally evoked controversy. Occupying one end of a polemical continuum, James (1890) suggested that the number of human "instincts" (seen as unlearned "impulses" or motives) is very large, exceeding that for any other species. Included are motives of fear, sympathy, sociability, play, acquisitiveness, modesty, love, nurturance, and the hunting instinct. McDougall (1908) listed 12 instincts along with 5 "nonspecific innate tendencies." Murray (1938) put forth 20 "psychogenic needs" or motives detectable in the lives of men he studied. Murray's influential taxonomy included the needs for achievement, affiliation, aggression, dominance, exhibition, nurturance, succorance, and understanding. On the other end of the continuum are the theorists such as Rogers (1951) and Adler (1927), who posited a single primary need that may assume manifold form. For Rogers, all persons tend to actualize their own inherent potentialities; for Adler, the core tendency of personality is to strive toward superiority or perfection. Rogers' motive for self-actualization and Adler's will to power are the underlying springs of all action in their respective personality theories, the central organizing principles of all lives.

Occupying a middle position between James and Rogers are the dualistic conceptualizations of motivation that typically assert that two primary forces in the personality exist in a dialectical tension. Dualistic theories commonly imply that humans are, by their motivational nature, beset with conflict, and that the telos of development and therapy is reconciliation of opposites. Over the course of about 20 years, Freud (1900/1953, 1920/1955) moved from a twofold vision of motivation embodying the life-maintenance instincts (such as hunger) and the pleasure-inducing instincts (libido) to a more polarized view of life instincts (Eros) in conflict with death instincts (Thanatos). Rank (1936) maintained that the fear of life and the fear of death are the two supreme motives in human lives, while Angyal (1941) suggested the need for autonomy and the need for surrender. In a compelling dualistic synthesis, Bakan (1966) has argued that two fundamental "modalities" exist in all living forms. The first, *agency,* refers to the separation of the individual from others and from context; the second, *communion,* refers to the coming together of individuals and a merger with context. Bakan writes:

I have adopted the terms "agency" and "communion" to characterize two fundamental modalities in the existence of living forms, agency for the existence of an organism as an individual, and communion for the participation of the individual in some larger organism of which the individual is a part. Agency manifests itself in self-protection, self-assertion, and self-expansion; communion manifests itself in the sense of being at one with other organisms. Agency manifests itself in the formation of separations; communion in the lack of separations. Agency manifests itself in isolation, alienation, and aloneness; communion in contact, openness, and union. Agency manifests itself in the urge to master; communion in noncontractual cooperation. (1966, pp. 14–15)

As exceedingly broad and multidimensional tendencies in human living, agency and communion are best conceived as integrative themes in lives that encompass, among other things, dimensions of interpersonal style (traits), personal values and beliefs (schemata), and human motives. For instance, the theme of communion connects conceptually to stylistic personality traits such as sociability and friendliness (Guilford, 1959), belief and value clusters such as those centered around equality and a world at peace (Rokeach, 1973), and human social motives concerning warm and close interpersonal relations, such as the intimacy motive (McAdams, 1980). Agency connects thematically to traits such as dominance (Edwards, 1959) and Machiavellianism (Christie & Geis, 1970), beliefs and values concerning courage and a sense of accomplishment (Rokeach, 1973), and assertive human motives such as the need for achievement (McClelland, 1961) and the power motive (Winter, 1973).

Winter's (1973) construct, the power motive, appears to capture the lion's share of the motivational meaning attributed by Bakan to the general theme of agency. The power motive is a recurrent preference or readiness for experiences of having impact on one's environment and feeling *strong* (Winter, 1973; Winter & Stewart, 1978). Other motives proposed as tendencies toward separation or autonomy, such as McClelland's (1961) achievement motive and Rogers's (1951) self-actualization, fail to embody the agentic ideas of self-expansion and mastery of the surround to the extent that power motivation does. Similarly, McAdams's (1980) construct, the intimacy motive, was explicitly developed to capture the motivational meaning of communion (McAdams, 1980, 1982a; McAdams & Powers, 1981). The intimacy motive is a recurrent preference or readiness for experiences of close, warm, and communicative exchange with others—interpersonal interaction that is seen by the interactants as an end in itself, rather than a means to another end. In the following section, power and intimacy motives are presented as measurable, motivational prototypes of the more general themes of agency and communion as they exist in human lives and in human relationships.

Measuring Motives

Power and intimacy motives are assessed via thematic coding of imaginative stories that subjects write in response to a set of standard pic-

tures. This general method—the Thematic Apperception Test (TAT)—
was pioneered by Murray (1943) in his investigations of psychogenic
needs. McClelland and colleagues (McClelland, Atkinson, Clark, &
Lowell, 1953) formalized the approach to make it suitable for large-scale
empirical investigations of a single motive, the need for achievement.
The development of power (Veroff, 1957; Winter, 1973) and intimacy
(McAdams, 1980) constructs followed the basic procedural pattern established for achievement. Essentially, the scoring systems for each of
the motives were empirically derived by examining differences in content of stories written under specific arousal conditions (experimental
situations designed to arouse feelings of, say, power or intimacy) and
those written under neutral control conditions. The content categories
consistently differentiating between arousal and control stories were
then cross-validated in a new sample of stories coded by scorers blind to
the classification (arousal or control) of the storywriters. Those categories that continued to differentiate between arousal and control stories
upon blind cross-validation came to comprise the scoring system for a
given motive. Once the scoring system was established, then individual
differences in motivation manifested by subjects under neutral conditions were examined as indices of a relatively enduring motivational
trend in the persons studied. Construct validity for the motives began to
accumulate as subsequent studies linked differences in motivational
scores (among individuals writing stories under neutral conditions) and
motive-related behavior and experience (Atkinson, 1958; McAdams,
1980, 1982a; McClelland, 1961, 1971, 1975, 1980, 1981; McClelland et al.,
1953; Stewart, 1982; Winter, 1973; Winter & Stewart, 1978).

In the standard investigation of power or intimacy motivation, subjects are given 5 minutes to write a story in response to each of six
pictures projected on a screen. The stories are then coded by scorers
who have worked through one of the scoring manuals and its 210 practice stories (McAdams, 1981; Winter, 1973). After about 10 hours of
training for a given motive, a scorer's reliability (agreement with expert
scoring in manual) generally reaches acceptable levels for research. Typically, correlations between the scorer's and the manual's scoring of
practice stories are .85 (rho statistic) or better, with an 85% or better
agreement rate on the presence or absence of the "prime test" thematic
categories for each of the motive scoring systems (see Winter, 1973, and
the following discussion).

The scoring system for the power motive (Winter, 1973) consists of 11
thematic categories, one of which is termed a "prime test" of power
imagery and the other 10 are termed "subcategories." For each story,
the presence or absence of the prime test category is first determined.
This broad category refers to any instances in the story in which a

character shows power concerns through actions which in themselves express power (strong, forceful actions such as assaults, chasing or being chased, threats, or sexual exploitation; giving help or advice that has not been solicited by another character; trying to control another; or trying to impress another), through arousing strong positive or negative emotions in others, or through expressing concern about personal reputation or prestige. If an instance of the above is not found, the story receives a score of 0, and the scorer proceeds to the next story. If an instance of the above is found, however, the story receives a score of +1, and the scorer proceeds to examine the story for the presence or absence of each of the 10 subcategories. The story then receives a score of +1 or 0 for each of the 10 subcategories. Consequently, each scoring category receives a maximum of +1 for a given story, even if examples of the category appear many times in the story. Power motive subcategories include "instrumental activity" (overt or mental activity by a character to attain a power goal), "block in the world" (explicit obstacle or disruption to the attempt to reach a power goal), "positive goal anticipation" (a character looks forward to attaining the power goal), "positive goal state" (positive feelings result from attaining the power goal), and "effect" (a distinct response by someone to the power attempts or actions of a character). Scores on each category are summed to provide a total power score for the story, and the story scores for a given individual are summed to give the total power motivation score for the subject.

The scoring system for the intimacy motive (McAdams, 1981) consists of 10 thematic categories, of which 2 are prime tests and 8 are subcategories. The presence of at least 1 of the 2 prime-test categories in a story is a prerequisite for the scoring of the 8 subcategories. Below are brief descriptions of each of the scoring categories:

1. Relationship produces positive affect (Prime Test 1). An interaction between characters leads to love, liking, joy, excitement, happiness, or a feeling of peace. Example: "The people feel an emotional closeness."
2. Dialogue (Prime Test 2). Characters engage in verbal or nonverbal communication with each other that is reciprocal and noninstrumental. Example: "They talked about whatever crossed their minds."
3. Psychological growth and coping. A relationship facilitates the psychological growth, self-fulfillment, adjustment, self-esteem, or problem-solving abilities of a character. Example: "Bev is continually becoming better adjusted to everyday life and how to handle it because of Harry."
4. Commitment or concern. A character feels a sense of commitment

to or concern for another that is not rooted in guilt or begrudging duty. Example: "She is devoted to her husband."

5. Time–space. Two or more characters in the story are engaged in a relationship that transcends the usual limitations of time and/or space. This includes any explicit reference to the *enduring* quality of a particular relationship.

6. Union. Characters come together after being apart (psychologically or physically). This includes references to reunions and reconciliations.

7. Harmony. Characters find they are in harmony with one another. They are "on the same wavelength," their actions are in "synchrony," one "understands" the other, they find they "have something in common."

8. Surrender of control. A character finds that interpersonal relationships are subject to control that is in some way beyond him or her. He or she surrenders to this "outside" force (e.g., nature, fate, God, luck, society, inexorable passions).

9. Escape to intimacy. Characters actively or mentally escape from a nonintimate (not close, warm, or communicative) to an intimate situation.

10. Connection with outside world. Characters establish a relationship with their inanimate or nonhuman environments. Typically this takes the form of a communion with nature or the cosmos.

As in the case of power, scores on each category are summed to provide a total intimacy score for the story, and the story scores for a given individual are summed to give the total intimacy motivation score for the subject.

Correlates of the Motives

Winter and Stewart (1978) write, "the power motive predicts seeking and getting formal institutionalized social power by whatever means is most available to the person or most likely to be successful and within whatever situational constraints are operative" (p. 402). Winter (1973) found that officers in university student organizations scored higher in power motivation than nonofficers. Winter and Stewart (1978) have presented evidence suggesting that college students high in power motivation make themselves visible in a variety of ways so as to assure recognition and the opportunity to have impact. Power-motivated students are more likely to write letters to the university newspaper; they imagine themselves hostilely attacking prominent and high-status people; and they appear to take extreme risks in order to achieve public visibility (McClelland & Teague, 1975; McClelland & Watson, 1973). Fodor and Smith (1982) found that high-power leaders in decision-making groups tended to adopt more authoritative and less egalitarian leadership strategies than their low-power counterparts. McClelland (1975) reviews a number of studies documenting significant relationships between power motivation in men and (1) the collection of prestige possessions, (2) reading about sex and aggression, (3) participating in contact sports, and (4) impulsive, aggressive acts such as throwing objects around the room when angry, stealing towels from motels, and failing to show up for work "because they just don't feel like it" (p. 9) among working-class but not middle-class men. Finally, men and women high in power motivation described autobiographical recollections of personally meaningful events as having heightened physical or psychological strength, impact on others or on the environment, vigorous physical activity, and enhanced prestige or recognition from others (McAdams, 1982b).

A number of studies done in the late 1970s and early 1980s have documented the construct validity of the intimacy motivation scoring system. Sorority and fraternity members high in intimacy motivation were rated by their peers as significantly more "warm," "loving," "natural," "appreciative," and "sincere," and significantly less "dominant," "outspoken," and "self-centered," than members scoring low in intimacy motivation (McAdams, 1980). In an investigation of interpersonal behavior in a psychodrama, undergraduates high in intimacy motivation, assessed via a prior administration of the TAT, behaved in a warmer and more egalitarian manner with other group members, positioning themselves in closer proximity to others, encouraging others to get involved in the group activities, and engendering more positive affect in others, compared to subjects low in the motive (McAdams & Powers, 1981). Sampling behavior and experience naturalistically over the course of a week, McAdams and Constantian (1983) found that subjects high in intimacy motivation (1) spent more time thinking about people and relationships, (2) engaged in more conversational and letter-writing behavior, and (3) expressed more positive affect in interpersonal situations, than subjects scoring low in intimacy motivation. Other investigations have documented significant relationships between intimacy motivation and (1) themes of love and dialogue in autobiographical recollections of personally meaningful experiences (McAdams, 1982b), (2) memory for story themes concerning interpersonal interaction (McAdams, 1982a), (3) higher levels of ego development (Loevinger, 1976) and greater identity questioning with respect to religious ideology among students at a private, religiously oriented college (McAdams, Booth, & Selvik, 1981), and (4) better psychosocial adjustment in a cohort of middle-aged men studied longitudinally (McAdams & Vaillant, 1982).

Though a number of the previously mentioned studies concern themselves with interpersonal interaction of some kind (Fodor & Smith, 1982; McAdams, 1980; McAdams, & Constantian, 1983; McAdams & Powers, 1981), not one of them directly addresses the topic of significant interpersonal relationships such as those characterized by romantic love or friendship. The following discussion of studies of the motivational dimensions of love and friendship illustrates the value of an approach to significant relationships that considers the influences of power and intimacy motives. Recalling Bakan's (1966) dichotomy of agency and communion, a dual thesis is entertained: that the power motive confers an agentic meaning upon relationships, whereas the intimacy motive promotes relational communion.

POWER MOTIVATION AND PERSONAL RELATIONSHIPS

Romantic Love

Bakan (1966) suggests that the agentic mode of human existence is one in which the individual separates self out from an embedding context in an attempt to master context. This is to say that the agentic individual may seek to control his or her environment by either isolating or distinguishing himself or herself from that environment. Bakan argues that the self-expansive quality of unmitigated agency is virtually "field-independent," in that the self grows and moves without regard to the growth and movement of other elements in the "field" (environment). In romantic relationships, therefore, one might expect that the person high in power motivation would be more concerned with *controlling* his or her partner, whose own "growth and movement" is perceived either as unimportant (in that it does not impact upon the agentic striving of the high-power individual) or as a threat to the unimpeded growth and movement of the self, a threat to agency. Consequently, romantic relationships between persons high in power motivation should be more conflictual, leading to a higher incidence of breakups or divorce. A few studies have supported this hypothesis with high-power men but not high-power women.

Stewart and Rubin (1976) conducted a longitudinal investigation into the influence of power motivation upon relational expectations and outcomes in 63 dating couples living in the Boston area. The typical (modal) couple in the study was represented by a male junior in college dating a female sophomore for about 1 year. At the time of initial testing, high power motivation among the male members of the couples was significantly associated with greater expressed dissatisfaction with the relationship on the part of both members of the couple and greater anticipation of future serious problems in the relationship among the men. Important problem areas for the high-power males in the study included differences in attitudes and interests, "becoming bored with the relationship," conflict in attitudes toward sex, and "living too far apart." Power motivation scores among the female members of the couples failed to predict significantly satisfaction ratings and overall problem anticipations, although high-power women were more likely than low-power women to endorse the problem areas of pressure from parents and becoming bored with the relationship.

Two years after the initial testing session, Stewart and Rubin recontacted 59 of the 64 couples through the mail or by telephone in order to determine the stability of the relationships over time. Among men, power motivation was a potent predictor of instability whereas among the women the motive had no relation to the 2-year outcome assessment. In relationships in which the male was high in power motivation, 50% of the couples had broken up after 2 years and only 9% of the couples had married. In relationships in which the male was low in power motivation, only 15% of the couples had broken up and 52% had married over the 2-year span. Additionally, males high in power motivation were more likely to report that during the 2 years immediately preceding the start of this dating relationship, they had been seriously involved in a romantic relationship that eventually terminated. Stewart and Rubin (1976) concluded that men high in power motivation manifest marked instability in romantic relationships, moving from one serious involvement to the next in relatively rapid succession. Bolstering their claims are the findings of Winter (1973) in which power motivation among men was positively associated with number of sexual partners and frequency of sexual activity. According to Winter, the archetypal representation of the high-power-motive man in Western folklore is Don Juan, the expansive and profligate womanizer.

Winter, Stewart, and McClelland (1977) related power motive scores determined from TAT protocols collected in 1960 among undergraduate men to the career levels attained by these men's wives in 1974. Among the 51 husbands studied, power motivation assessed in 1960 was significantly and negatively related to wife's career level 14 years later. In other words, well-educated men high in power motivation were likely to be married to women without professional careers (over whom, presumably, they could exercise considerable influence and control). The authors entertained three possible interpretations of these results. First, it is possible that men high in power motivation tend to choose spouses who do not harbor career aspirations that would be seen as threatening the supremacy of the man's position as the source of instrumental control. Second, women who do not assume power positions in the occupational world may seek husbands who do, preferring men who cut the image of the strong and effective agent. A third possible explanation of the findings suggests that high-power men exert a stultifying influence upon career aspirations of their wives after marriage and that their wives eventually capitulate and take on traditional feminine roles.

A contrasting study undertaken with women (Winter, McClelland, & Stewart, 1981) found that well-educated women high in power motivation tended to marry successful men. Similarly, Veroff (1982) reports that power motivation in women is associated with marital satisfaction whereas other studies have associated power motivation in men with a higher divorce rate (McClelland, Davis, Kalin, & Wanner, 1972) and a greater degree of marital dissatisfaction (Veroff & Feld, 1970). At root of the high-power man's apparent dissatisfaction and instability in romantic heterosexual relations may be a latent fear of women and the control they may exert. Slavin (1972) has shown that men high in power motivation express more themes of feminine evil in fantasies than do men lower on the motive. These themes include females harming men through physical contact, females exploiting men, females rejecting men, females proving unfaithful in relationships, and females triumphing over men. In keeping with this image of feminine evil, Winter and Stewart (1978) report that men high in power motivation, when asked to draw pictures of women, produce sometimes frightening and bizarre sketches of females with exaggerated sexual characteristics.

Taken as a whole, the findings concerning the power motive and heterosexual dating and marital relationships suggest that the agentically-oriented male may encounter serious difficulties in his campaigns to exert control on this interpersonal front. Confronted with a partner perceived to have the capacity to exploit him, the high-power man may attempt to assure his preeminence by either choosing a relatively traditional wife harboring few career aspirations or actively subduing those aspirations in her and encouraging her to confine her own agentic strivings to the domestic scene. The attempts of the high-power man to exert control over the long run, however, appear in many instances destined for the disharmony and dissatisfaction that may presage eventual break-up. As Bakan (1966) has written, "unmitigated agency" may result in a self-protective interpersonal strategy and ultimately in "isolation, alienation, and aloneness" (p. 15).

Why power motivation is not associated with problems in romantic relationships among women is not readily apparent. McClelland (1975) has argued that power motivation may be expressed in a number of different ways and that pronounced sex differences in the motive's expression are to be expected. According to McClelland, women are more likely to fulfill strong power needs through giving and providing support, whereas men are more likely to adopt an aggressive and self-assertive orientation toward others. In fact, McClelland suggests that high power motivation *accentuates* the traditional sex-role stereotype of the giving female and the exploiting male: high-power women may be consummate givers, sources of support for others; high-power men may be the expansive, exploiting agents who master their environments. In both cases the high-power individual exerts a strong effect upon his or her world. He or she experiences the goal state of the power motive, which is to feel strong and have impact. In the context of romantic relationships, therefore, the feminine mode of power expression—that of giving and providing support—may tend not to lead to the conflict over control hypothesized to be related to high power motivation. The prototypical masculine form of power expression appears, then, closer in meaning to Bakan's (1966) "unmitigated agency" than does the feminine form. One might suggest that the classic feminine mode of power expression is inherently "mitigated" by communion in that giving and providing support suggest the union with others so characteristic of communion. In a related vein, Winter (1981) terms the characteristic masculine mode of power expression the "expansive, profligate" syndrome and argues that it arises developmentally by default in the lives of many high-power males who are not subject in childhood to the "socialization of responsibility" (training to develop a caring orientation toward weaker others). Such training, however, is more often a centerpiece of the female child's socialization experience.

Friendship

Two central themes of Bakan's (1966) conceptualization of agency are self-assertion and self-display. The agentic individual is a doer who makes things happen in his or her environment. Further, his or her doing is observed and remarked upon by others. Indeed, research on power motivation has shown that high-power individuals are active agents in their environments who assume dominant, influential positions (Fodor & Smith, 1982; Winter, 1973; Winter & Stewart, 1978), positions that, too, are highly visible (McClelland, 1975; Winter, 1973). One might expect, therefore, that persons high in power motivation would perceive friendships as arenas for self-assertion and display. Support for this general hypothesis is garnered from two very recent studies in which the intimacy and power motives were related to different patterns of friendship.

The first study is an exploratory investigation whose data are summarized for the first time in this chapter. In this investigation, 69 undergraduates (32 men and 37 women) attending Loyola University of Chicago in 1980–1981 provided detailed information concerning the history of their various friendships, focusing mainly on a single relationship with a best friend. The subjects' responses to a series of open-ended questions were content-analyzed and then compared to power and intimacy motive scores obtained from a prior administration of the TAT.

The second study (McAdams, Healy, & Krause) tests hypotheses concerning relationships between power and intimacy motives on the one hand and patterns of interactions with friends on the other. In this second investigation, 105 undergraduates (35 men and 70 women) attending Loyola University of Chicago in 1981–1982 (a completely different sample than that used in the first study) recalled 10 "friendship episodes" (interactions with friends lasting at least 15–20 minutes) that occurred in their lives during the previous 2 weeks. For each friendship episode, the subject provided information concerning time, place, number of people involved in the episode, major activity of the episode, contents of conversations occurring in the episode, major role he or she played in the episode, and emotional state at the time of the episode. Various content dimensions on the friendship episodes were then correlated with power and intimacy motive scores obtained from a prior administration of the Thematic Apperception Test (TAT).

Friendship Groups

A relatively consistent finding in the literature on the development of children's friendships is that boys tend to interact in groups, whereas girls generally maintain dyadic friendships (Laosa & Brophy, 1972; Waldrop & Halverson, 1975). In a longitudinal study of friendship patterns shown by 7–8-year-old boys and girls, Waldrop and Halverson (1975) factor analyzed data from 12 measures of children's relationships with their peers. Loading highly on the main factor extracted for the sample of boys were the variables "extensiveness" (participation in group activities), hours spent with more than one peer, and number of peers seen. Variables loading highly on the girls' factor were hours spent with one peer and intensity (importance of a best friend). Similarly, Eder and Hallinan (1978), in their study of sociometric choice among fifth- and sixth-graders, found a tendency for girls to have more exclusive friendship dyads than boys and for boys to participate more in nonexclusive triads than girls. Although less is known about sex differences in the structure of friendship groups among adults, Bell's (1981) research leads him to conclude that "women who have a variety of friends tend overwhelmingly to form dyadic relationships." Bell adds, "this is in contrast to many of the friendships of men, which do include three or more persons" (p. 64).

One would expect, however, that an agentic mode of friendship would more readily accommodate a larger group format for friendship interaction. Consequently, the person high in power motivation, regardless of his or her sex, should engage in more friendship scenarios set in large group contexts in that large groups provide more viable audiences for self-expansion and self-display. This prediction asserts that what has generally been considered a difference in friendship structure solely attributable to sex may be mediated by social motives that vary within as well as between the sexes.

Our data provide equivocal support for a connection between power motivation and large-group friendship interactions. When students were asked to describe in some detail 10 friendship episodes occurring within the last 2 weeks, (McAdams *et al.*, in press), those high in power motivation tended to describe significantly fewer episodes that were dyadic in structure $r(103) = -.23$, $p < .05$, than did those low in power. This relationship, however, was highly significant among the males ($r = -.52$) and nonexistent among the females. Power motivation was also positively associated with the number of friendship episodes reported in which the subject interacted with four or more other persons, ("large-group" episodes) $r = +.21$, $p < .05$. Again the relationship was quite marked among males ($r = +.42$) and nonexistent among the females. A two-way analysis of variance (sex by low versus high power motivation) showed that power motivation exerted a significant main effect upon the number of large-group friendship interactions reported whereas sex did not. Finally, males and females did not differ significantly on level of power motivation.

Helping: Doing

Most people would probably agree that friends will generally come to the aid of each other in times of distress. Some of the great stories of friendship—Damon and Pythias, David and Jonathan—dramatize this theme of helping as it manifests itself in acts of prodigious valor and sacrifice (Mohler, 1975; Reisman, 1979). Our data suggest that helping one's friend is a particularly agentic theme in the friendship worlds of many young adults. Helping—whether a heroic act or quiet counsel—is an active assertion of the self; it intervenes in the environment and effects a significant change. Helping temporarily transforms a relationship into one between relative unequals. For the moment, the helper is dominant; the helped is submissive. The relationship is hierarchical rather than egalitarian. With role reversals, helping relationships afford the opportunity for mutual self-assertion and self-display. Thus, this agentic theme of friendship need not imply exploitation of or subservience to the other. The agentic mode allows for the toleration of others' agentic strivings.

In describing a concrete incident in which they and their respective best friends grew closer, our students high in power motivation tended to highlight helping or being helped. One young man high in power motivation described in great detail how he had helped a younger friend of his get through his first year at the university by instructing him on what professors to avoid, what bars to hang out in, and what clothes not to wear to parties. "In thinking about how close we are," he adds, "I always come back to this incident." The biserial correlation between power motivation assessed on the TAT and the presence of a helping theme in subjects' accounts was $+.35$, $p < .01$. Students high in power motivation and low in intimacy were four times more likely to express the helping theme in their accounts than were students low in power motivation and high in intimacy. Among men, intimacy motivation, furthermore, was negatively associated with helping ($r = -.46$, $p < .02$). Men in general were no more likely to show helping than women.

If helping is a variation on the more general agentic themes of self-assertion and self-display, one might expect that power motivation would predict other forms of agentic striving in friendship experiences. In the study of friendship episodes occurring in the last 2 weeks (McAdams et al., in press), we developed a scoring category termed "agentic striving" that was defined as an active, assertive, or controlling role taken on by the subject in the friendship episode. Examples included taking charge of a situation, assuming responsibility, making a point in a debate or argument, helping another, giving advice, making plans, organizing activities, or attempting to persuade others. In these episodes, the subjects perceived their roles as dominant, guiding ones. They were actively *doing* something. Two independent coders scored responses to the question "what was your major role in the episode?" for the presence or absence of agentic striving. The results revealed a strong positive correlation between power motivation and number of episodes showing the agentic striving role, $r = +.43$, $p < .001$. Although men showed more agentic striving than women ($p < .05$), the relationship between power motivation and agentic striving was found in both sex subsamples. Intimacy motivation was unrelated to agentic striving. It appears, therefore, that males and females with a high power motive experience friendships in an agentic manner, understanding them in terms of opportunities to take on dominant, controlling, organizational roles. This is not to say that they are exploiting others. Rather, the world of friendship represents an extension of a generally agentic mode of interacting that may characterize other domains of human functioning as well (Bakan, 1966). In the agentic mode, relationships are apprehended in power terms. Self and other are understood as separate; neither is subsumed by an encompassing other (e.g., the relationship itself). The friends take advantage of various opportunities that may arise for self-display and self-expansion within the bounds of the relationship. Indeed, it may be the mutual appreciation of each other's agentic strivings that affirms and confirms the bond between them.

Friendship Stresses and Fears

Studies of power motivation and romantic love (McClelland et al., 1972; Stewart & Rubin, 1976; Winter et al., 1977, 1981) have linked a strong need for power in men and a higher incidence of problems or stresses in dating and marital relationships. Though our data on friendship do not support a parallel linkage, they do suggest that stresses in friendships are very common, even among best friends, and that the meaning attributed to these stresses may be partially a function of motives, for both men and women.

We asked students to describe in some detail a particular "low point" in the history of their relationship with their best friends. The low point was "a specific incident or episode in which you and your best friend had a fairly serious disagreement, and the bond between you was weakened or at least tested. This could be a time when you or your friend experienced jealousy, betrayal, anger, disappointment, a serious misunderstanding, or any other feeling that was decidedly unpleasant."

Male and female students high in power motivation tended to describe events in which one person violated a general norm of appropriate behavior applicable to virtually all forms of human interaction. The violation typically involved one person impacting on others in a way deemed inappropriate, noxious, disagreeable, or annoying. The transgressor in this case committed an action that violated the rights of others, or at least what others might see as their rights. Examples included fighting, boasting, and various forms of behavior that others saw as rude, boorish, or socially inappropriate. This theme was termed *inappropriate impact*. For both men and women (N = 69), power motivaton was significantly associated with the presence of inappropriate impact in low-point experiences, r = +.33, p < .05. Students high in power motivation and low in intimacy motivation were over four times as likely to show inappropriate impact as were students low in power and high in intimacy. Further, inappropriate impact appeared nearly twice as often in male reports of low points compared to female reports.

Inappropriate impact can be interpreted in part as an expression of concern over how one and one's friends appear in public. The boorish action of the friend may be seen as a humiliation that lowers the prestige of all involved. Consequently, a public display of self, reflected in the friends's public transgression, becomes an embarassment for the agentic individual who desires an approving audience to affirm self-display.

The agentic individual's concern for affirmation of agentic display is reflected in responses to another question provided by the students. The students were asked to recount some of their most disturbing fears they experience when with their best friends. Male and female students high in power motivation and low in intimacy motivation were over three times as likely to mention a fear of *conflict* with the friend, such as arguments or fights, as were students high in intimacy and low in power. Interestingly, males were no more likely to report this fear than were females.

In fearing conflict, the high-power student expresses concern over a possible clash between active agents. For agentic relationships to work well, the friends must tolerate, even condone, each other's agentic strivings, each other's ventures of self-expansion, self-assertion, and self-display. Conflict threatens the breakdown of equilibrium that had nurtured the agentic strivings of the friends. These findings are consistent with Winter's (1973) report that high-power men carefully tend to avoid the possibility of conflict in their relationships with peers.

INTIMACY MOTIVATION AND PERSONAL RELATIONSHIPS

Romantic Love

Bakan's (1966) communion implies a gentle and delicate approach to significant personal relationships. In communion, the self merges with another as boundaries between egos are blurred and each interactant surrenders manipulative control in the spontaneous process of relating. This theme of surrender of control has been captured as a scoring category in the thematic scoring system for the intimacy motive (McAdams, 1981). Moreover, it has manifested itself behaviorally in empirical studies in which men and women high in intimacy motivation have been seen by their peers as especially "nondominant" and "non-self-centered" (McAdams, 1980) while their behavior in laboratory settings has been rated as particularly *egalitarian*, behavior designed to de-emphasize the importance of self and involve all group members in friendly and reciprocal exchange (McAdams & Powers, 1981). Numerous theories of love and friendship state that a blurring of ego boundaries through a surrender of control is a hallmark of the harmonious and mature interpersonal relationship (Balint, 1979; Buber, 1970; Erikson, 1963; Guntrip, 1973; Maslow, 1968; Sullivan, 1953). Furthermore, intimacy motivation has been associated with peer ratings of "sincere" and "loving" (McAdams, 1980) and (1) more time thinking about people and relationships, (2) more conversation and letter-writing behavior, and (3) more positive affect in interpersonal situations (McAdams & Constantian, 1983). All of this strongly suggests that intimacy motivation should be associated with greater happiness and greater stability in romantic relationships. Two recent studies provide some direct support for this hypothesis.

McAdams (1980) re-analyzed Stewart and Rubin's (1976) data on dating couples, scoring TATs collected by the authors for intimacy motivation. Couples in which both members scored high on Rubin's (1973) "love scale"—a nine-item self-report measure assessing the intensity of love expressed and experienced in the relationship—scored significantly higher on intimacy motivation than did comparison students, most of whom were not involved in romantic relationships. In other words, individuals who reported a profound intensity of caring and love for their partners tended also to adopt a communal orientation on the TAT, which is to say they scored higher on intimacy motivation than other subjects who were not involved in intense romantic relationships.

In a study of marital satisfaction, McAdams and Vaillant (1982) re-analyzed longitudinal data collected between 1950 and 1967 on a cohort of men who graduated from Harvard College in the early 1940s. TAT stories written by 57 men in the early 1950s were coded for intimacy motivation, as well as other TAT-based motives such as power and achievement. In 1967, numerous indices of psychosocial adjustment were computed, including career advancement and success, constructive use of free time, alcohol and drug misuse, psychiatric visits, and marital enjoyment. Intimacy motivation, assessed in the early 1950s, significantly predicted overall psychosocial adjustment 17 years later, whereas power and achievement motivation did not. Furthermore, the correlation between intimacy motivation and the specific index of marital enjoyment was highly significant, $r(55) = +.38, p < .01$. Men high in intimacy motivation at age 30, therefore, were more likely to report happiness and stability in their marriages at mid-life. Power and achievement motivation were unrelated to marital enjoyment.

Friendship

Openness, contact, and union are earmarks of Bakan's (1966) communal mode of human existence. In surrendering active control in the process of relating, the communal individual focuses upon *being* over *doing* in a relationship (McAdams & Powers, 1981). He or she, therefore, is especially sensitive to the possibilities of reciprocal sharing with others, of the spontaneous kind of dialectic in relationships described by the philosopher Buber (1970) as the I–Thou encounter. According to Buber, in the I–Thou interaction, two individuals focus unswervingly on each other, each in turn making a "dialogical" offering to the other and each dialogical offering in turn shaping the next offering, the next contribution in dialogue that each partner is to make. The I–Thou unfolds naturally, according to a script that neither partner writes alone but that is written in process by the two partners together. The spontaneity endemic to this reciprocal, noninstrumental form of interpersonal communication should promote the sincere disclosure of the self on the part of both partners of the dyad. Indeed, Bakan (1966) suggests that genuine self-disclosure and the appreciation of the other's genuine self-disclosure in dyadic exchange is a theme of communion. One would predict, therefore, that persons high in intimacy motivation would (1) participate with their friends in more dyadic exchanges and (2) manifest more self-disclosure and listening to the other in these dyadic exchanges than would persons low in intimacy motivation. These hypotheses were evaluated in the two recent studies of motivation and patterns of friendship—the exploratory study of best friends whose data are being presented in this chapter for the first time and the study of 10 friendship episodes reported in McAdams *et al.* (in press).

Friendship Dyads

The significant relationship between power motivation and number of large-group friendship episodes among males (McAdams *et al.*, in press) suggests that a difference in the structure of friendship groups previously assumed to be largely a function of sex differences (Laosa & Brophy, 1972; Waldrop & Halverson, 1975) may be mediated by the social motive of power. Data from the same sample of students extends this possibility into the realm of intimacy motivation and dyadic friendship episodes. When the 105 students were asked to describe in some detail 10 friendship episodes occurring within the last 2 weeks, those high in intimacy motivation tended to describe significantly more episodes that were dyadic in structure, $r = +.20$, $p < .05$, than did those low in intimacy. This statistically significant but relatively weak correlation was reflected within both sex subsamples, though because of the reduced number of subjects the relationships failed to reach statistical significance within each subsample. A two-way analysis of variance (sex by low- versus high-intimacy motivation) showed that intimacy motivation exerted a significant main effect upon the number of dyadic friendship interactions reported, whereas sex did not. Males and females did not differ significantly on intimacy motivation. Finally, intimacy and power motivation, in this sample of 105 undergraduates, were not significantly related ($r = -.09$).

Combining these results with those for power motivation and large-group episodes, the low but significant correlations in the predicted directions suggest that social motives of power and intimacy may account for some of the variance in the structure of friendship interactions but that the great majority of the variance remains unexplained, undoubtedly due to a host of person and situation factors. Within each of the two sex subsamples, intimacy motivation was positively but nonsignificantly related to number of dyadic episodes, and it was only when the two subsamples were combined that the relationship reached statistical significance. The picture was more complex for power motivation. The motive was unrelated to number of large-group interactions among the females, but a strong and positive relationship was found in the male subsample ($r = .42$). Apparently power motivation has a marked influence on friendship patterns for men in that the high-power men tend to structure their friendship episodes along the large-group lines that other researchers (Waldrop & Halverson, 1975) have shown as characteristic of elementary-school and teen-aged boys. Low-power men appear to diverge from the male stereotype somewhat in that they report fewer large-group episodes and, furthermore, more dyadic interactions than their high-power peers. Interestingly, when levels of power and intimacy motivation are taken into consideration, significant sex differences with respect to dyadic and large-group friendship episodes do not appear. It is possible that social motives may have played the role of relatively covert mediating variables in some previous studies showing that males tend to interact in large friendship groups and females in dyads (Bell, 1981). Although motive scores were not significantly different for the two sexes in the present study, some other investigations have revealed that females occasionally score significantly higher than males on intimacy motivation, especially in environmental contexts in which traditional sex roles prevail (McAdams, 1982a). No consistent sex differences with respect to power imagery in the TAT, however, have appeared in the literature (Stewart & Chester, 1982).

Self-Disclosure: Being

Derlega and Grzelak (1979) write that "self-disclosure includes any information exchange that refers to the self, including personal states, dispositions, events in the past, and plans for the future" (p. 152). Today most would probably agree that one key function of close personal relationships such as friendships is to afford the exchange of personal information that is not generally revealed to others with whom one is not close. Conventional wisdom has it that close friends should feel comfortable enough with each other to reveal some of their secrets in their most intimate encounters. These revelations have been considered signs of a "healthy" or "mature" relationship (Altman & Taylor, 1973; Douvan, 1977; Maslow, 1968) and of the psychological health and sound personality functioning of the participants involved (Jourard, 1971; Rogers, 1961).

Since the early 1970s, personality and social psychologists have produced a plethora of empirical research on self-disclosure (Altman & Taylor, 1973; Chelune, 1979; Derlega & Chaikin, 1977; Jourard, 1971; Strassberg, Anchor, Gabel, & Cohen, 1978). According to Archer (1983), however, most of the studies have focused on the amount of information disclosed and the content of that information to the exclusion of personal and situational factors involved in the self-disclosure process. In his proposed attributional model of personal and situational factors involved, Archer includes perceiver variables such as dispositions and expectations as one set of factors. Similarly, Derlega and Grzelak (1979) propose that individual differences in a "need for intimate disclosure" (p. 175) may play a significant role in the regulation of privacy and disclosure, and thus "the value of self-disclosure may depend on a person's system of personal preferences" (p. 175). Our data suggest, in fact, that the intimacy motive exists as just such a "need for intimate disclosure" or recurrent "personal preference." The theme of self-disclosure turns out to be a pervasive motif in the communally oriented worlds of friendship manifested by students high in intimacy motivation.

We had students focus on the history of one special friendship in their lives. They were then asked to describe in some detail a concrete incident from that history in which the subject and his or her friend found that their friendship bond was strengthened. This could be seen as a high point or peak experience in the friendship history. Students high in intimacy motivation overwhelmingly described these high points as including some kind of personal revelation on the part of one friend and the acceptance of that revelation on the part of the other. When the 69 students' accounts were each coded for the presence (score +1) or absence (score 0) of self-disclosure on the part of one of the friends, the biserial correlation with TAT intimacy motivation was $+.47$, $p < .001$. The correlation was highly significant among the women ($r = +.61$) but failed to reach statistical significance in the sample of men. Among both males and females, subjects high in intimacy and low in power motivation were six times more likely to manifest a theme of self-disclosure in their accounts than were subjects low in intimacy and high in power motivation. Power motivation itself, however, was not significantly related to self-disclosure.

Our second window into self-disclosure in friendship comes from the study of friendship episodes occurring in the past 2 weeks (McAdams *et al.*, in press). In this study, each subject's response to the question "What in general was talked about?" during the episode was coded on a 0–2 scale for degree of self-disclosure by two independent coders. A score of 0 indicated no self-disclosure. A score of 1 indicated disclosure on the part of either subject or friend of personal feelings, emotions, needs, wants, fantasies, strivings, dreams, hopes, plans for the future, fears, or self-awareness. A score of 2 indicated a particularly intimate form of self-disclosure, in our view, termed "reflexive–relational." In this case the subject disclosed personal thoughts or feelings *about the present interaction* portrayed in the friendship episode or *about the relationship* in which the participants in the episode were involved. Scores were summed across the 10 reported episodes to arrive at a total self-disclosure score for each subject.

For all 105 students in the study, a very robust correlation was obtained between intimacy motivation and self-disclosure in friendship episodes ($r = +.49$, $p < .001$). The finding was equally strong in both sex subsamples. Power motivation was unrelated to self-disclosure scores. Contrary to other studies, which have shown that women tend to disclose more than men (Bell, 1981; Cozby, 1973), our data showed no significant sex differences when motive scores were taken into consideration.

Self-disclosure and listening are complementary phenomena in relationships. As the friend discloses information about the self, the other ideally assumes the role of listener. The listener does not actively assert the self in an agentic fashion. He or she has not been called upon to *do* anything—to engage in any kind of action. Rather, he or she is to *be* receptive, to hold agency in abeyance, as it were, and adopt a relatively passive role as the one who listens. We sought to investigate the role of listening in friendship episodes by coding responses to the question "What was your major role in the episode?" for the presence or absence of any mention of the role of listener. Our scoring for this theme was quite literal: the subject had to use the word "listening," "listener," etc., or a cognate. We found a strong correlation between intimacy motivation and number of episodes in which the subject reported listening ($r = +.43, p < .001$), and the association remained positive and statistically significant within the two sex subsamples. Power motivation was unrelated to listening. Again, sex differences in amount of listening reported in friendship episodes did not emerge.

The findings on self-disclosure and listening suggest that the person high in intimacy motivation is more apt to surrender control in the process of relating to the other (McAdams, 1982a), adopting the communal mode of interaction as he or she takes on the role of listener in interaction with friends. In the communal mode, relationships are understood as egalitarian. Two equals open up to each other, neither stifled by any fear of exposing vulnerabilities that may be exposed to others. Bakan states that the communal mode is characterized by "participation of the organism in some larger organism of which the individual is a part" (1966, p. 15). The "larger organism" in this case is the friendship itself—the relationship that partially subsume individuality as it spontaneously unfolds.

Friendship Stresses and Fears

Being high in intimacy motivation does not appear to guarantee that one's friendships will be free of strife and conflagration. Regardless of motivational profile, virtually all of the 69 students in the exploratory study of motives and best friends reported serious disagreements with their chums and confidants. Intimacy motivation did, however, appear to influence the meaning attributed by the students to these disagreements. Whereas subjects high in power motivation tended to portray the low point in their relationships with their best friends as instances of the friend displaying inappropriate impact, subjects high in intimacy focused on a *betrayal of trust*. As expected, students high in intimacy motivation tended to highlight incidents in their friendship histories in which one friend or the other violated an implicit rule or expectation *applicable to the particular relationship*. Rather than violating a norm of decent public conduct by being boorish or crude (inappropriate impact), the transgressor breaks a private and implicit norm of the relationship itself. Examples include breaking a promise, disclosing a secret to some third person, and failing to show warmth or understanding to the other. In a number of cases the violation involved a failure in candor.

Students high in intimacy motivation and low in power motivation were four times more likely to report betrayal of trust in low-point accounts than were students high in power and low in intimacy. For the entire sample, intimacy motivation was positively associated with the betrayal of trust theme, $r = +.36$, $p < .01$, though the relationship was stronger among women than men.

We also coded the responses for attribution of blame, noticing that in many accounts the subjects blamed themselves for the problem in the relationship whereas in many others the friend was blamed. Intimacy motivation was negatively associated with attribution of sole blame to the friend, $r = -.39$, $p < .01$. Power motivation was unrelated to attribution of blame. Furthermore, students high in intimacy motivation were more likely than students low in intimacy motivation to remark that the low point of the friendship history was followed by a reconciliation between the friends, and in some cases growth, biserial $r = +.40$, $p < .01$. Again, power motivation was unrelated to this theme. In assuming partial blame for the relational low point and in emphasizing the eventual reconciliation of the friends after a period of disagreement and stress, students high in intimacy motivation again personify communion's surrender of self and commitment to "some larger organism of which the individual is a part" (Bakan, 1966, p. 14).

Finally, this concern for the larger organism of the relationship appears to translate into a recurrent fear of *separation* from friend as reported by the high-intimacy-motive subjects when asked to describe fears experienced in friendships. Whereas fear of conflict was significantly associated with power motivation, students high in intimacy and low in power were twice as likely to indicate that they feared separation from their best friends either because of circumstances over which they had little control, such as moving or growing apart, or, in a few cases, death or injury, as were students high in power motivation and low in intimacy motivation. No sex differences in fear of separation were observed.

In fearing separation from the other, the person high in intimacy motivation expresses concern over the possibility of the dissolution of the friendship bond. Separation means that one is no longer "at one with the other" (Bakan, 1966, p. 14). As the friends part, each is wrenched away from the relational unity—Bakan's "larger organism"—to which each had heretofore surrendered. Interestingly, this finding raises the possibility that persons high in intimacy motivation may be more susceptible to loneliness when a close bond with another is severed. With the recent upsurge in interest among personality and social psychologists in the experience of loneliness (Hartog, Audy, & Cohen, 1980; Perlman & Peplau, 1981), this hypothesis appears ripe for testing.

CONCLUSIONS

The chapter has attempted to illustrate the fruitfulness of a motivational approach to significant personal relationships. It has been suggested that the power motive is linked to an agentic orientation toward love and friendship, an orientation emphasizing control, self-assertion, and self-display. The intimacy motive, on the other hand, is tied to a communal orientation toward relationships in which are underscored themes of self-surrender, communication, and union. Assessed via thematic coding of narrative responses to the TAT, power and intimacy motives capture a good deal of the motivational meaning in Bakan's (1966) fundamental modalities of human lives—agency and communion. As such, the two motives influence the ways in which individuals understand the most important relationships in their lives while energizing, directing, and selecting interpersonal behavior in ways commensurate with the desired goal states of feeling strong (for the power motive) and feeling close (for the intimacy motive).

In research on dating and marriage, power motivation in men has been associated with relational dissatisfaction and instability, a higher incidence of divorce, and marriages in which the wife assumes a relatively traditional, domestic role. Intimacy motivation, on the other hand, has been associated with reports of intense feelings of love in dating couples and marital enjoyment among middle-aged men. In the arena of friendship, power motivation is positively correlated with (1) a greater number of large-group interactions with friends (among men), (2) themes of helping and agentic striving (organizing, controlling, leading, persuading, planning) in reports of interactions with friends, (3) disagreements with friends concerning inappropriate public behavior, and (4) fears of conflict among friends. Intimacy motivation is related to (1) a greater number of dyadic friendship interactions, (2) a greater amount of self-disclosure and listening with friends, (3) disagreements with friends concerning betrayal of trust, and (4) fears of separation from friends. These findings come from a relatively small but growing literature on motivation and relationships. It is hoped that this chapter will prompt more researchers to adopt an approach to significant personal relationships that takes into consideration individual differences among persons in basic human motives of power and intimacy.

REFERENCES

Adler, A. (1927). *The practice and theory of individual psychology*. New York: Harcourt.
Altman, I., & Taylor, D. A. (1973). *Social penetration: The development of interpersonal relationships*. New York: Holt.
Angyal, A. (1941). *Foundations for a science of personality*. New York: Commonwealth Fund.
Archer, R. L. (1983). *Perceiving the intimacy of self-disclosure*. Unpublished manuscript, Southwest Texas State University.
Atkinson, J. W. (Ed.) (1958). *Motives in fantasy, action, and society*. Princeton, NJ: Van Nostrand.
Atkinson, J. W., & Raynor, J. O. (Eds.) (1974). *Motivation and achievement*. Washington, DC: Hemisphere.
Bakan, D. (1966). *The duality of human existence*. Boston: Beacon.
Balint, M. (1979). *The basic fault*. New York: Bruner/Mazel.
Bell, R. R. (1981). *Worlds of friendship*. Beverly Hills, CA: Sage.
Buber, M. (1970). *I and Thou*. New York: Scribner.
Cattel, R. B. (1966). *The scientific analysis of personality*. Chicago: Aldine.
Chelune, G. J. (Ed.) (1979). *Self-disclosure*. San Francisco: Jossey-Bass.
Christie, R., & Geis, F. L. (1970). *Studies in Machiavellianism*. New York: Academic Press.
Cozby, P. C. (1973). Self-disclosure: A literature review. *Psychological Bulletin, 79*, 73–91.
Derlega, V. J., & Chaikin, A. L. (1977). Privacy and self-disclosure in social relationships. *Journal of Social Issues, 33*(3), 102–115.
Derlega, V. J., & Grzelak, J. (1979). Appropriateness of self-disclosure. In G. J. Chelune (Ed.), *Self-disclosure*. San Francisco: Jossey-Bass.
Douvan, E. (1977). Interpersonal relationships: Some questions and observations. In G. Levinger & H. L. Rausch (Eds.), *Close relationships: Perspectives on the meaning of intimacy*. Amherst, MA: University of Massachusetts Press.
Eder, D., & Hallinan, M. T. (1978). Sex differences in children's friendships. *American Sociological Review, 43*, 237–250.
Edwards, A. L. (1959). *The Edwards Personal Preference Form*. New York: The Psychological Corporation.
Ehrlich, H. J. (1978). Dogmatism. In H. London & J. E. Exner, Jr. (Eds.), *Dimensions of personality*. New York: Wiley.
Erikson, E. H. (1963). *Childhood and society*. New York: Norton.
Eysenck, H. J. (1960). *The structure of human personality*. London: Methuen.

Fodor, E. M., & Smith, T. (1982). The power motive as an influence on group decision making. *Journal of Personality and Social Psychology, 42*, 178–185.

Freud, S. (1900/1953). The interpretation of dreams. In J. Strachey (Ed.), *The standard edition of the complete psychological works of Sigmund Freud* (Vols. 4, 5). London: Hogarth. (First German edition, 1900)

Freud, S. (1920/1955). Beyond the pleasure principle. In J. Strachey (Ed.), *The standard edition* (Vol. 18). London: Hogarth. (First German edition, 1920)

Guilford, J. P. (1959). *Personality.* New York: McGraw-Hill.

Guntrip, H. (1973). *Psychoanalytic theory, therapy, and the self.* New York: Basic Books.

Hartog, J., Audy, J. R., & Cohen, Y. A. (Eds.) (1980). *The anatomy of loneliness.* New York: International Universities Press.

James, W. A. (1890). *The principles of psychology* (Vols. 1, 2). New York: Holt.

Jourard, J. M. (1971). *Self-disclosure: An experimental analysis of the transparent self.* New York: Wiley (Interscience).

Kelly, G. (1955). *The psychology of personal constructs.* New York: Norton.

Laosa, L. M., & Brophy, J. E. (1972). Effects of sex and birth order on sex-role development and intelligence in kindergarten children. *Developmental Psychology, 6*, 409–415.

Lerner, M. J., & Miller, D. T. (1978). Just world research and the attribution process. *Psychological Bulletin, 85*, 1030–1051.

Lewin, D. (1935). *A dynamic theory of personality.* New York: McGraw-Hill.

Loevinger, J. (1976). *Ego development.* San Francisco: Jossey-Bass.

McAdams, D. P. (1980). A thematic coding system for the intimacy motive. *Journal of Research in Personality, 14*, 413–432.

McAdams, D. P. (1981). *Scoring manual for the intimacy motive.* Unpublished manuscript, Loyola University of Chicago.

McAdams, D. P. (1982a). Intimacy motivation. In A. J. Stewart (Ed.), *Motivation and society.* San Francisco: Jossey-Bass.

McAdams, D. P. (1982b). Experiences of intimacy and power: Relationships between social motives and autobiographical memory. *Journal of Personality and Social Psychology, 42*, 292–302.

McAdams, D. P., Booth, L., & Selvik, R. (1981). Religious identity among students at a private college: Social motives, ego stage, and development. *Merrill-Palmer Quarterly, 27*, 219–239.

McAdams, D. P., & Constantian, C. A. (1983). Intimacy and affiliation motives in daily living: An experience sampling analysis. *Journal of Personality and Social Psychology.*

McAdams, D. P., Healy, S., & Krause, S. (in press). Social motives and patterns of friendship. *Journal of Personality and Social Psychology.*

McAdams, D. P., & Powers, J. (1981). Themes of intimacy in behavior and thought. *Journal of Personality and Social Psychology, 40*, 573–587.

McAdams, D. P., & Vaillant, G. E. (1982). Intimacy motivation and psychosocial adjustment: A longitudinal study. *Journal of Personality Assessment, 46*, 586–593.

McClelland, D. C. (1951). *Personality.* New York: Holt.

McClelland, D. C. (1961). *The achieving society.* New York: Irvington, 1961.

McClelland, D. C. (1971). *Assessing human motivation.* Morristown, NJ: General Learning Press.

McClelland, D. C. (1975). *Power: The inner experience.* New York: Irvington.

McClelland, D. C. (1980). Motive dispositions: The merits of operant and respondent measures. In L. Wheeler (Ed.), *Review of personality and social psychology* (Vol. 1). Beverly Hills, CA: Sage.

McClelland, D. C. (1981). Is personality consistent? In A. I. Rabin, J. Aronoff, A. M. Barclay, & R. A. Zucker (Eds.), *Further explorations in personality*. New York: Wiley.

McClelland, D. C., Atkinson, J. W., Clark, R. A., & Lowell, E. L. (1953). *The achievement motive*. New York: Appleton-Century-Crofts.

McClelland, D. C., Davis, W. N., Kalin, R., & Wanner, E. (1972). *The drinking man*. New York: The Free Press.

McClelland, D. C., & Teague, G. (1975). Predicting risk preferences among power-related tasks. *Journal of Personality, 43*, 262–285.

McClelland, D. C., & Watson, R. I., Jr. (1973). Power motivation and risk-taking behavior. *Journal of Personality, 41*, 121–139.

McDougall, W. (1908). *Social psychology*. London: Methuen.

Maslow, A. H. (1968). *Toward a psychology of being*. New York: Van Nostrand.

Mohler, J. A. (1975). *Dimensions of love: East and West*. Garden City, NY: Doubleday.

Murray, H. A. (1938). *Explorations in personality*. New York: Oxford University Press.

Murray, H. A. (1943). *Thematic apperception test: Manual*. Cambridge, MA: Harvard University Press.

Perlman, D., & Peplau, L. A. (Eds.) (1981). *Loneliness: A sourcebook of current theory, research, and therapy*. New York: Wiley (Interscience).

Phares, E. J. (1976). *Locus of control in personality*. Morristown, NJ: General Learning Press.

Rank, O. (1936). *Will therapy and truth and reality*. New York: Knopf.

Reisman, J. M. (1979). *Anatomy of friendship*. Lexington, Massachusetts: Lewis.

Rogers, C. R. (1951). *Client centered therapy; its current practice, implications, and theory*. Boston: Houghton Mifflin.

Rogers, C. R. (1961). *On becoming a person*. Boston: Houghton Mifflin.

Rokeach, M. (1973). *The nature of human values*. New York: The Free Press.

Rubin, Z. (1973). *Liking and loving*. New York: Holt.

Slavin, M. (1972). *The theme of feminine evil: The image of women in male fantasy and its effect on attitudes and behavior*. Unpublished doctoral dissertation, Harvard University.

Stewart, A. J. (Ed.) (1982). *Motivation and society*. San Francisco: Jossey-Bass.

Stewart, A. J., & Chester, N. L. (1982). Sex differences in human social motives: Achievement, affiliation, and power. In A. J. Stewart (Ed.), *Motivation and society*. San Francisco: Jossey-Bass.

Stewart, A. J., & Rubin, Z. (1976). The power motive in the dating couple. *Journal of Personality and Social Psychology, 34*, 305–309.

Strassberg, D. S., Anchor, K. N., Gabel, H., & Cohen, B. (1978). Client self-disclosure in short-term psychotherapy. *Psychotherapy: Theory, Research, and Practice, 15*, 153–157.

Sullivan, H. S. (1953). *The interpersonal theory of psychiatry*. New York: Norton.

Veroff, J. (1957). Development and validation of a projective measure of power motivation. *Journal of Abnormal and Social Psychology, 54*, 1–8.

Veroff, J. (1982). Assertive motivations: Achievement *vs.* power. In A. J. Stewart (Ed.), *Motivation and society*. San Francisco: Jossey-Bass.

Veroff, J., & Feld, S. C. (1970). *Marriage and work in America*. New York: Van Nostrand-Reinhold.

Waldrop, M. F., & Halverson, C. F. (1975). Intensive and extensive peer behavior: Longitudinal and cross-sectional analysis. *Child Development, 46*, 19–26.

Winter, D. G. (1973). *The power motive*. New York: The Free Press.

Winter, D. G. (1981). *The power motive in women*. Paper presented at International Interdisciplinary Congress on Women, Haifa, Israel.

Winter, D. G., McClelland, D. C., & Stewart, A. J. (1981). *A new case for the liberal arts: Assessing institutional goals and student development*. San Francisco: Jossey-Bass.

Winter, D. G., & Stewart, A. J. (1978). The power motive. In H. London & J. E. Exner, Jr. (Eds.), *Dimensions of personality*. New York: Wiley.

Winter, D. G., Stewart, A. J., & McClelland, D. C. (1977). Husband's motives and wife's career level. *Journal of Personality and Social Psychology, 35,* 159–166.

Witkin, H. A., Goodenough, D. R., & Oltmann, P. K. (1979). Psychological differentiation: Current status. *Journal of Personality and Social Psychology, 37,* 1127–1145.

CHAPTER 4

Identities, Identifications, and Relationships[*]

BARRY R. SCHLENKER

INTRODUCTORY OVERVIEW

Identity is at the point of intersection between the individual and other people. Just as the scientist never approaches or experiences the world directly, but does so through the selective filters of a theoretical perspective, so, too, people never approach or come to know one another directly, but do so only through the selective filters of the identities they construct (e.g., Backman, in press; Hogan, 1982; McCall & Simmons, 1978; Schlenker, 1980, in press). *Identity* is a theory or schema of an individual, describing and interrelating his or her relevant features, characteristics, and experiences; it thereby provides the organizational structure for pertinent information about the individual (Schlenker, in press; see Epstein, 1973). It is honed through the actual or imagined consensual validation of the individual's characteristics and experiences, and provides a sense of autonomy, distinctiveness, and continuity over time (see Schlenker, in press). An actor's identity can be viewed from the perspective of the actor, in which case it refers to his or her conception of self (either in a particular relationship or across rela-

[*]Thanks are extended to Patricia Schlenker, Ruth Allis, Carl Backman, and Val Derlega for their valuable comments or assistance in the preparation of the chapter. The work on this chapter was supported by a Research Scientist Development Award (K02-MH00183) from the National Institute of Mental Health.

tionships, as a generalized theory of self), or from the perspective of another person, in which case it refers to the other's conception of the actor.

Identity not only organizes experiences, but also regulates them. Given that particular facets of identity (identity-images) are salient at a particular moment in time, they can act as a plan, script, or schema for channeling cognitions, affect, and actions (see Schlenker, in press). When a particular image is salient, people are more likely to notice, attend to, and recall image-relevant information, to process the information more easily and quickly, to organize and interpret supporting or ambiguous information in image-consistent ways, and to polarize attitudes to make them more supportive of the image (e.g., Cantor & Mischel, 1979; Judd & Kulik, 1980; Swann, in press; Tesser, 1978). The images also provide behavioral-prototype, or response-specifying, information and standards that indicate how such images should be symbolically expressed through actions (e.g., Carver, 1979; Hogan, 1982; Schlenker, 1980). For example, people who view themselves as independent should be less likely to agree with another's divergent opinion and, if they do happen to agree, interpret the behavior as "tact" rather than "conformity." People's images of others can have similar guiding effects. As examples, people reconstruct the biographies of friends and spouses to bring them in line with their images of them, interpret others' behaviors from the perspectives of the images they have assigned to them (e.g., physically attractive people do "good" things), and treat others in image-congruent ways (e.g., Backman, in press; Berscheid & Walster, 1974; Cantor & Mischel, 1979; Schlenker, 1980).

Given their regulatory effects, identities also can facilitate or impede actors' goal achievement in social life. To be regarded and treated a particular way (by self or others) requires that a particular combination of identity-images "exist" that would mediate the regard or treatment (e.g., Blau, 1964; Goffman, 1959; Jones & Pittman, 1982; Schlenker, 1980). If actors can construct, both for themselves and select others, the types of identities that permit them to achieve the goals that are important to them (e.g., obtaining respect, approval, support, status, monetary rewards), their self-satisfaction should be high. If they cannot do so, they will be continually frustrated in interpersonal relations. It follows that there are usually reasons for people to attempt to control the images of self that are presented to salient audiences, for by controlling the images, actors also control the reactions of the audiences (e.g., Goffman, 1959; Schlenker, 1980). The next section of this chapter examines the nature of the identification process in social life.

People are not equally sensitive to and concerned about the reactions of all others to them. When two people interact, they can be relatively indifferent to each other, hardly noticing or caring what the other is doing or saying, or they can hang on every word, phrase, and behavioral nuance as if their futures depended solely on the whims of the other. This continuum of concern for the reactions of the other is pertinent to all stages of relationships, from first meetings (e.g., "Oh, was he even at the party tonight?" to "I'll just die if he doesn't like me") to marriages (e.g., "She doesn't even notice I'm alive anymore" to "I'm nothing without her"). The goal of creating and maintaining a desired identity and/or type of regard from the other, which will be termed the motivation to impress the other, gives purpose to people's cognitive and behavioral activities. As the goal increases in importance, people's activities become increasingly marshaled in the service of goal accomplishment, ultimately influencing whether a relationship will begin and then whether it will prosper or degenerate.

The goal of creating or maintaining a desired impression does not always involve being perceived as attractive and being liked. Depending on the actor's personality and the situation, the actor might prefer to be viewed as, say, "tough," or "respected," or "irresponsible," or "disinterested," etc. (Jones & Pittman, 1982; Schlenker, 1980). People can attempt to impress others positively or negatively, and the type of impression that is desired by actors should have a guiding influence on the types of communications they employ in the relationship.

Being motivated to impress another person does not guarantee goal achievement, of course. Despite people's best efforts, they still can fail to secure the type of identity or regard they desire. As examples, people may be unsure of how to create a desired impression or generate a desired reaction (e.g., "I just don't know what he expects of me"), believe they cannot live up to the standards of conduct required to obtain the reaction (e.g., "She expects too much of me"), believe the other wants them to be something they are not (e.g., "She wants me to be a different type of person"), or believe they cannot rectify an undesired impression the other has already formed (e.g., "I just can't convince her I'm not as bad as she thinks"). The extent to which people feel and act indifferent, complacent, secure, challenged, or anxious in social interactions is proposed to be a joint function of the motivation to impress the other and the perceived likelihood of satisfactorily doing so (Schlenker & Leary, 1982). In combination, these factors influence a variety of cognitive, affective, and behavioral activities in interactions. As explored in the section entitled "Self-Presentational Concerns in Relationships," these factors have implications for loneliness, intimacy, and the types of identities people are able to construct in relationships.

Relationships develop when people's identities are or become interconnected. Relationships can represent preestablished associations over which actors have no control, as in the case of kinship; "forced" patterns of more or less frequent interactions, as in the case of a disliked co-worker at the office or an offensive neighbor; or voluntary interactions in which the parties find each other mutually attractive and rewarding. Over time, thought and behavior patterns develop that are intrinsic and unique to each relationship (Backman, in press). Based on the identities that have evolved in the relationship, the parties can anticipate how each will interpret situations, the evaluations and outcomes preferred by the other, and the actions the other will proffer. The closer the relationship, the greater the extent to which the evaluation of experiences and outcomes shifts from individual to joint criteria, the interests and needs of the other weigh more heavily as the actor can experience vicarious rewards and costs, and the behavioral plans that exist for a wide variety of situations are based on coordinated team performances, not solitary, individual acts (Backman, in press; Huston & Levinger, 1978). In especially close relationships, the other becomes an extension of one's own identity, as people come to define themselves partially in terms of their roles in the relationship and their associations with the other (e.g., James, 1890; Schlenker, 1980). If these interconnections and established patterns are destroyed by separation, divorce, or death, a partial disintegration of identity results (Levinger & Moles, 1979; Weiss, 1975). This interconnectedness is typified by the common lament of those whose long-time spouse has died: "I'm lost without him(her)."

Identities are constructed in relationships and must be accommodated by them for the parties to move toward intimacy and closeness. That is, the parties should receive from one another the support, validation, and enhancement of the identities they find desirable. If such support is not forthcoming, especially on the identity-images that most matter to the actors, dissatisfaction should result. Actors will be treated by the other as if they had qualities that they would rather not have. The interconnections that occur under such conditions can trap people into undesired patterns of future behaviors and outcomes in the relationship, at least for as long as the relationship survives. The final section of the chapter explores some of the ramifications of the accommodation of identities in relationships.

THE IDENTIFICATION PROCESS

Identities and Identifications

Identification is the process, means, or state of showing something to be a certain type of person or thing, thereby fixing its identity through definition, description, evidence, inference, analogy, or treatment.[1] Self-identification involves fixing and expressing one's own identity in the situation or relationship. Any cognitive or behavioral activity that serves to establish, maintain, clarify, or modify one's identity before an audience (oneself included) is a self-identification. The complementary process is identification of the other, wherein the actor attempts to establish the nature of the other in his or her own mind and in the relationship.

Self-identification is necessary for any types of dealings with the self, be they intrapsychic or interpersonal. To think about oneself requires that a self exists, something that must be defined and appraised. To interact with others requires that something is doing the interacting, something that others must define and appraise. The purpose of self-identification is to fix what this thing is: to specify its unique properties, its common properties, and therefore what it is like and how it should be treated. Once the self is fixed, at least more or less generally, all other dealings can follow (e.g., how the individual should act, feel, be treated), and these dealings can have some structure, order, and reason. Without this specification, nothing can follow.

The concept of identity is sometimes defined in the literature solely by a person's roles, or positions, occupations, and functions, in social groups. As used here, roles comprise only a portion, though an important one, of what is meant by the term. People's appearances (e.g., physical features, types of dress), backgrounds (e.g., ancestral lineage, schools attended), associates, friends, and relatives (people are judged by the company they keep, e.g., Sigall & Landy, 1973), perceived goals, motives, and personal characteristics (e.g., sociability, intelligence, feelings), performance settings (e.g., whether one frequents bars or church socials), and performances in general (e.g., job performance) also serve to identify people in social life and influence how actors are regarded and treated (Schlenker, 1980, in press). The present usage thus combines sociological emphases on roles and social structure with psychological emphases on the self and personal or physical attributes. Self-identifications include any activities relevant to fixing one's identity on such dimensions.

---

[1]Psychologists often think of identification in only one very limited sense, derived from psychoanalysis: a person identifying with someone else and trying to be like him or her. This is certainly one means of identifying oneself, because "I am like him" is an identification by means of analogy. But it is only one of the ways people can stipulate what they are (see also McCall & Simmons, 1978).

Identities represent a compromise between "wishes" and "reality," a merger of one's self-ideals with what appears to be true (e.g., McCall & Simmons, 1978; Schlenker, 1980, 1982, in press; Turner, 1968). They must be accommodated to the perceived evidence, but this accommodation is shaped by selective attention, recall, and interpretations that permit actors to construct personally beneficial views of themselves (e.g., Greenwald, 1980; Rosenberg, 1979; Schlenker, 1980, 1982, in press). The ability to construct reality from alternative perspectives, place different interpretations on the same characteristic or experience, and selectively evoke different combinations of facts provides latitude for constructing a view of self. The result is that with a certain amount of ingenuity, people can construct identities that are both *believable*, that is, are reasonably accurate construals of the evidence possessed or assumed to be possessed by salient audiences (oneself included), and *personally beneficial*, that is, facilitate the actors' goals by mediating desired outcomes, for example, respect, approval, and other rewards. Evidence can mount and limit the believable possibilities, but there is never one and only one way to specify what a person is. For present purposes, a *desirable identity* will be defined as one that, from the actor's perspective, is both believable and personally beneficial, facilitating his or her goals in the particular situation or relationship (see Schlenker, in press).

Not all aspects of identity can be salient at any single moment. The context of the situation, the pertinent audience, the actor's mood, the actor's goals, and so forth, cause particular facets of identity, or identity-images, to be salient or to appear especially relevant. Phrased differently, people cannot reveal everything about themselves, the information coming from all possible angles, in any single social interaction; their self-identifications therefore focus on information that is salient or appears to be relevant to the situation. Further, depending on the particular combinations of identity-images that are salient, the information that is revealed can be "packaged" in different ways (e.g., differentially weighted and interpreted) thereby symbolically expressing relevant identity-images or combinations of images.

One implication of such selectivity is that while people may recognize that they project somewhat different images of self in different situations and hence may have a variety of "social selves" (James, 1890), they still possess composite private identities that organize and regulate their experiences across social situations (e.g., Hogan, 1982; Schlenker, 1980, in press). A second implication is that personality factors, as represented by people's self-images and goals, and situational factors, as represented by such characteristics as norms, interaction rituals, and reward–cost structures should reciprocally interact to influence self-identifications at any point in time (Hogan, 1982; Schlenker, 1980). For example, in informal situations, such as a party among friends, people's self-identifications are guided largely by salient self-images. In more formal situations, such as a wedding or job interview, their self-identifications are guided largely by the salient interaction rituals or reward–cost demands. In situations in which reward–cost pressures are especially salient, people become more likely to exaggerate or even lie about their personal qualities, thereby constructing situated identities that they believe would facilitate their goals and be believable in the context of a short-term interaction (Jones & Wortman, 1973; Schlenker, 1980, 1982, in press).

Audiences

At least three types of audiences for people's self-identifications can be distinguished. First, there are immediate others with whom one is interacting; some of these may be significant or important to the actor and others may not. Second, there are imagined or fantasized audiences who, while perhaps not present in the immediate situation, can be evoked in thought and serve as internalized referents for regulating and evaluating conduct. These might include parents, best friends, spouse, etc., as well as fantasized others, as in the case of a little boy who tries to be like Superman or an adult male who uses James Bond as his prototype. Third, people can serve as their own audiences, employing internalized personal standards for the regulation and evaluation of conduct (e.g., Hogan & Cheek, 1982; Scheier & Carver, 1981; Schlenker 1980, 1982, in press; Snyder, Higgins, & Stucky, 1983).

When a particular audience is salient, it can influence cognitions, affect, and behaviors through the types of self-relevant information, conduct, and standards that are pertinent. For example, a member of a street gang that values toughness and censures emotional sensitivity may express the warm side of his identity when alone with a girl he likes who is sincere, sweet, and conventional. When the couple is in the presence of other gang members, though, he reverts to more insensitive and cold behavior toward her (visions of John Travolta's character in the movie *Grease* come to mind). Or, a housewife may do an unusually thorough job of housecleaning when her mother, a vanguard of traditional values, comes to visit. Different audiences are salient on different occasions, and attention may even fluctuate between them during the course of a single interaction (Snyder *et al.*, 1983). People who are inner-directed, privately self-attentive, not especially motivated to impress an immediate other (say, because the other is unattractive or low in status, see the following section), or focusing on a quality that is important and central to their private self-conceptions are more likely, in general, to use their private identity-images as guides for behavior and perform for internal audiences (Hogan & Cheek, 1982; Scheier & Carver, 1981; Schlenker, 1980, in press). Those who are other-directed, publicly self-attentive, motivated to impress an immediate other (e.g., because the other is especially attractive or powerful), or focusing on a quality that is unimportant to their private self-conceptions are more likely, in general, to perform for the immediate audience as their primary referent.

Self-Presentations

Self-identifications can vary in the extent to which they involve an attempt to control how audiences view the self. Control refers to the attempt to generate not just any impression, but a particular type or class of impressions; it is a goal-directed activity. As such, the desired impression-relevant reaction of the salient audience (self, internalized referent, or immediate other) is the criterion for assessing the effectiveness of the performance. If the performance meets the appropriate standard, that is, if it generates the desired reaction, it is successful and should produce satisfaction. If the performance fails to meet the standard, that is, it fails to generate the desired reaction, it is unsuccessful and should produce dissatisfaction. As examples, actors may attempt to present themselves in ways that will achieve self-verification, or liking, or respect, or fear, or nurturance, etc., or some combination of these (Jones & Pittman, 1982; Schlenker, 1980). The importance of the goal of creating desired impressions (i.e., ones that are both believable to the salient audience and personally beneficial) can vary considerably from time to time and audience to audience, and typically coexists with other goals in the situation. The more important the goal is, because of its subjective worth or ability to subsume and satisfy other goals, the more it will shape the actor's self-identifications, causing them to be "packaged" in ways that are perceived as likely to produce the desired impression and audience reactions (Schlenker, in press; Schlenker & Leary, 1982).

The term *self-presentation* refers to the conscious or nonconscious attempt to control identity-relevant images before audiences, oneself included, thereby influencing their reactions (Schlenker, 1980). Self-presentation is sometimes distinguished from self-disclosure, with the former regarded as calculated, superficial, and manipulative, and the latter regarded as spontaneous, expressive, and truthful. The distinction has some merit in identifying the opposite poles of a continuum of the importance of control relative to other goals at a particular time. The label "self-presentation" is often applied when the goal of creating a desired impression on an *immediate* audience is especially prominent and important; the label "self-disclosure" is often applied when such a goal is nonprominent and unimportant. Except at these extremes, however, the distinction has minimal usefulness.[2] People's self-presentations can be regulated by audiences other than an immediate other person, as when self-relevant information is "packaged" and expressed for consumption by imagined referents and the self (Hogan, 1982; Schlenker, 1980; Snyder *et al.*, 1983).[3] In addition, the goal of creating a desired impression can coexist with other goals, such as obtaining accurate feedback about the self, causing self-identifications to be "packaged" but not necessarily distorted. Further, over time, particular patterns of self-presentation become automatic, nonconscious, and modularized (Hogan, 1982; Schlenker, 1980). Thus, self-presentation is strategic in the sense that it has a particular goal. It is not strategic in the sense that it does not necessarily involve conscious planning, the inaccurate portrayal of self, the attempt to gain the approval of an immediate audience, or the attempt to build a public facade to cover the absence of an underlying structure.

SELF-PRESENTATIONAL CONCERNS IN RELATIONSHIPS
Self-Presentational Concerns: A Theoretical Perspective

People's self-identifications establish and maintain identity-images, thereby providing others with a basis for regarding and treating them. This is not to assume, though, that people are eternally vigilant in monitoring and controlling every movement. People are sometimes rela-

[2]Derlega and Grzelak (1979) take a slightly different perspective on the relationship between self-presentation and self-disclosure. They suggest that self-presentation "may represent a particular type of self-disclosure, emphasizing selective use of personal information to control outcomes in social relationships" (p. 160). Their analysis also leads to the conclusion that the distinction between the two may have minimal usefulness in many situations.

[3]The idea of "packaging" information for the self does not imply the existence of a little cognitive homunculus who censures and distorts that which it will allow the person to believe (see Schlenker, 1982). In any situation, there are alternative ways of attending to and combining the "facts" and alternative ways of conceptualizing and interpreting information to provide different shades of meaning. In short, there are alternative "truths." As

tively unconcerned about how they appear to others, as when they relax among friends; other times they are more concerned about how they appear, as when they are on an important first date; still other times they are excessively concerned to the point they are nearly paralyzed by social anxiety. Self-presentational concerns can vary along a continuum from low to high, and are hypothesized to arise from (1) the presence and importance of the goal of achieving a desired impression or generating a desired reaction from others, which will be termed the motivation to impress the other, and (2) the perceived likelihood that this goal can be satisfactorily achieved, which will be termed self-presentational outcome expectations (Schlenker & Leary, 1982). The combination of these factors should determine whether people are indifferent to an immediate other (low motivation to impress the other because, say, the other is regarded as unattractive or unimportant), complacent (the motivation to impress the other is nonsalient at the time because the actor is certain of the other's regard), secure (moderate to high motivation to impress the other and high self-presentational outcome expectations), challenged (high motivation to impress the other and moderate self-presentational outcome expectations), or anxious (high motivation to impress the other and low self-presentational outcome expectations).

People's goals give purpose to their cognitive and behavioral activities. When a particular goal exists, people evoke or develop plans to accomplish the goal, search out, attend to, and assess goal-relevant information, engage in a matching-to-standard process in which their performances are guided by their plans and periodically compared to the standards required for goal-accomplishment, and experience positive affect to the extent they have met or think they will meet the standards and negative affect when they do not (e.g., Carver, 1979; Miller, Galanter, & Pribram, 1960). The same types of cognitive, affective, and behavioral activities that have been previously associated with goal-directed behavior in general should also be pertinent to self-presentational behaviors in relationships.

When people are motivated to impress another person, it should produce several accompanying changes in their orientation toward the social interaction. Assume for the moment a situation in which such a goal is salient and actors anticipate a reasonable likelihood that they can achieve the goal. Such conditions should (1) prompt actors to seek out

---

information becomes more self-relevant, a self-assessment process should take place in which the possibilities are considered in terms of their believability and personal benefaction. Benefaction will tip the scales in favor of one reasonably believable explanation over others. Pertinent schemas may then play a part in further organizing and polarizing information around the more beneficial, yet believable, interpretations.

the other (e.g., Huston & Levinger, 1978); (2) increase actors' sensitivities to the characteristics, values, and opinions of the other, as the actors search for, attend to, and attempt to recall information about the other to achieve as clear an image as possible of what he or she is like and how he or she might act (e.g., Berscheid, Graziano, Monson, & Dermer, 1976); (3) cause the other's perceived characteristics, values, and opinions to play a larger role than they otherwise would in guiding and regulating the actors' self-presentations, that is, the actors perform more for *this* audience than other possible referents (e.g., Schlenker, 1980); (4) increase the actors' self-attention and self-assessment, focusing them on relevant abilities, attributes, and other information (e.g., Schlenker & Leary, 1982); (5) increase the actors' attempts at self-monitoring and control of their performances in order to meet the pertinent standards (e.g., Carver, 1979); (6) intensify the actors' sensitivities to the others' impression-relevant reactions, prompting the actors to interpret information in terms of its implications for their identities (e.g., Fenigstein, 1979; Schlenker & Leary, 1982); (7) intensify actors' affective reactions to the desired or undesired quality of the other's reactions (e.g., Fenigstein, 1979; Schlenker & Leary, 1982); and (8) generate nervousness to the extent their expectations of achieving the goal become lower (Schlenker & Leary, 1982). The more important the goal of creating or maintaining a desired impression and type of regard is to the actor, because of its subjective worth or ability to subsume and satisfy other goals, the more pronounced these effects should be. The importance of the goal at any particular moment can be influenced by the attributes of the audience (e.g., generally, it is more important to impress attractive or powerful others), the actor's personal characteristics (e.g., people who are other-directed are more oriented toward impressing immediate others), and the context of the situation (e.g., it is more important to impress an employer shortly before promotion decisions are made than at more mundane times) (see Schlenker & Leary, 1982, for a more complete review).

To illustrate the ramifications of the motivation to impress, picture an actor conversing at a party with a rather uninteresting, unappealing female who he is hardly motivated to impress positively. Although he tries to maneuver away, he becomes cornered. He asks few or no questions, barely manages to keep up his part of the conversation, is not interested in her thoughts on any topic, and does not even notice what she is wearing. His attention is elsewhere and, when she subtly hints that she finds him attractive, he misses the point. When she later makes her attraction to him clearer, it is met with affective indifference. Self-monitoring and control are minimal, and his actions are guided by habit, not concern. His behaviors may coincidentally impress her, but he makes no concerted effort to do so. In contrast, he seeks out the classmate whom he has admired from afar. Prior to the party he ruminated about what he might do and say if she were there, put on his best outfit, and even borrowed his roommate's more expensive car so he might be seen arriving in style. He is enthralled by her every word and phrase, tries to infer the implications of each verbal and nonverbal nuance, and even notices the ankle bracelet she is wearing. He monitors his actions to ensure that they are creating the right impression and takes the available opportunities to tell her about himself and his achievements. He especially stresses self-relevant information that he thinks she will find appealing, but he tries to introduce it in a way that avoids stepping over the line that might make him appear egotistical. He asks questions about her interests to find out more about her, and elaborates on common interests and opinions. When she hints she finds him attractive, his pulse quickens. Up until that point, he was thinking about how nervous he felt; now he feels more self-confident.

As illustrated in these anecdotal actions, the motivation to impress another person produces the types of verbal and nonverbal behaviors that demonstrate personal involvement with the other. Actors then appear committed to and involved with the interaction or relationship. The actors' attentions and actions are coordinated and focused on the other. If, as in the above example, actors are trying to generate liking, their nonverbal behaviors also should demonstrate high immediacy, by such actions as looking at and orienting their bodies toward the other's, maintaining closer interpersonal distances, and leaning toward rather than away from the other (Mehrabian, 1971; Schlenker, 1980). If the other's actions suggest mutual positive interest, the stage would be set for the development of a relationship. Even in established relationships, the frequency with which people are motivated to impress their partners positively and the importance of doing so should influence the amount of personal involvement they evidence at particular times. As people begin to feel increasingly secure in each other's regard, they can begin to present or disclose a wider variety of self-relevant information, establishing a basis for intimacy (e.g., Derlega & Chaikin, 1975).

As noted earlier, the goal of creating a desired impression does not always involve being perceived as attractive and being liked. Depending on personality and situational factors, people can attempt to be perceived as, say, intimidating, or helpless, or aloof, or dislikable (Jones & Pittman, 1982; Schlenker, 1980). For instance, if in the above example the unappealing female had persisted in her efforts beyond the actor's point of tolerance, he may have become motivated to impress on her his disinterest and perhaps dislike. In contrast to the state of indifference illustrated above, which is characterized by a lack of attention to the other, he then would marshal his verbal and nonverbal efforts to convey the desired impression. His actions would become personalistic and show "involvement" in the interaction, but the involvement would take the form of negative rather than positive communications. Thus, the motivation to impress another person in a particular way serves to channel activities toward a common goal, ultimately producing communications that can influence the course of the interaction or relationship.

The motivation to impress another person does not always generate facilitative patterns; it can have a darker side. When people's self-presentational outcome expectations fall below some critical level, thereby portending failure, the interpersonal consequences can become malignant. Schlenker and Leary (1982) proposed that the combination of high motivation to impress another person and expectations of unsatisfactory reactions from the other generates a state of social anxiety and ultimately produces the debilitation of social performance.

People who have low expectations of achieving a goal typically avoid the task if possible and, if they cannot avoid it, readily abandon it in the face of obstacles (Bandura, 1977; Carver, 1979). Similarly, people who anticipate interpersonal failures in situations where they would like to make a preferred impression usually attempt to avoid or withdraw from the other, either physically or psychologically, and experience negative affect (see Schlenker & Leary, 1982). In addition, people who anticipate such failure appear to become frozen or locked in assessments of self and the situation. Their minds race with thoughts about the unreachable goal and their inability to attain it. They become self-preoccupied and self-focused, continually reexamining their limitations in the situation (Carver, 1979; Schlenker & Leary, 1982). The combination of cognitive withdrawal from the difficult situation (e.g., fantasizing about more preferred activities or outcomes) and self-preoccupation produces distraction and further debilitates social performance. Information processing declines in effectiveness, reducing sensitivity to ongoing events, and self-monitoring and self-control worsen. The products are the types of behaviors that are associated with high social anxiety. These include jitteryness and nervousness (e.g., twitching hands and feet, nervous habits such as twirling one's hair), hesitant and awkward words and acts (e.g., stuttering, frequent use of "ahs" and "uhs," failure to complete one's sentences, clumsiness), reticence, slower and less frequent speech filled with long pauses, head nodding and other signs of acquiescence to others, minimal self-disclosure, and signs of withdrawal from the interaction (see Schlenker & Leary, 1982). Thus, the combination of the motivation to impress another and low self-presentational outcome expectations works to preclude effective social performances and the development of relationships.

Approaching Relationships: Attractions and Barriers in the Early Stages of Relationships

Combining ideas about reward with those about self-presentation, Blau (1964, p. 35) noted that "the reason a person is an attractive associate is that he has impressed others as someone with whom it would be rewarding to associate." In turn, a person "who is attracted to others is interested in proving himself attractive to them, for his ability to associate with them and reap the benefits expected from the association is contingent on them finding him an attractive associate and thus wanting to interact with him" (p. 20). Blau's statements summarize a part of the nature and implications of self-presentational concerns. People seek out those they believe will be rewarding, and must maintain their regard to continue to benefit.

In general, people who are physically attractive, powerful, expert, or high in status are especially sought out as companions (e.g., Berscheid & Walster, 1978; Tedeschi, 1974). As compared to their less-endowed counterparts, they can mediate material gains or losses (e.g., promotions, raises), their approval, respect, friendship, advice, and assistance are more valuable, their opinions are typically viewed as more diagnostic for self-verification purposes, and some of their qualities may generalize to their associates (e.g., Richardson & Cialdini, 1981; Schlenker, 1980; Sigall & Landy, 1973). Establishing a desired first impression on such people is especially important, since first impressions can act as schemas for interpreting and organizing subsequent information about the actor (e.g., Cantor & Mischel, 1979), and favorable first impressions stimulate others to try to learn more about the actor (e.g., Berscheid & Graziano, 1978), thereby increasing the likelihood that a relationship will develop.

As would be expected as a consequence of high motivation to impress such others, people who are interacting with more- rather than less-appealing others rely more on the others' preferences as guides for their own self-presentational activities (Jones & Wortman, 1973; Schlenker, 1980), conform more to the others' opinions and allow themselves to be cast into a role desired by the other (Jones & Wortman, 1973; Zanna & Pack, 1975), exaggerate their own strengths and minimize their weaknesses on dimensions that are expected to create the "best" impression

(Jones & Wortman, 1973), are more nervous in the other's presence (e.g., Jackson & Latané, 1981), engage in more face-saving behavior to protect their desired identities against possible threats (e.g., Garland & Brown, 1972), and display more extreme affective reactions to the others' interpersonal evaluations (e.g., Fenigstein, 1979).

One of the paradoxes of the initial stages of relationships is that the types of people who actors most want to impress are also more likely, in general, to generate lower self-presentational outcome expectancies. The importance of the goal of impressing them pulls actors forward, but the chances of failure can push actors back. If self-presentational outcome expectancies are sufficiently low, actors may avoid such others totally, or, perhaps worse from the actors' perspective, begin an interaction only to be overcome with anxiety, botching the performance so badly that an especially negative impression is formed of them.

The present analysis provides a self-presentational perspective on the hypothesis that liking for another leads to affiliation only insofar as a favorable response from the other is anticipated (e.g., Berscheid & Walster, 1978; Blau, 1964; Huston & Levinger, 1978). It is a special case of the more general hypothesis that people avoid specific others when they have the goal of creating a desired impression but doubt they can achieve the goal. Studies of dating choices (e.g., Berscheid, Dion, Walster, & Walster, 1971; Huston, 1973), information integration in a dating setting (Shanteau & Nagy, 1976), social anxiety (e.g., Curran, 1977; Schlenker & Leary, 1982), and affiliation (e.g., Sarnoff & Zimbardo, 1961) all indicate that people affiliate with others when they anticipate acceptance by them, but avoid others who they believe are likely to reject them. For instance, although physically attractive people are rated more positively than those who are less attractive, they are chosen as prospective dates only to the extent subjects believe the others will find them acceptable (e.g., Berscheid et al., 1971; Huston, 1973; Shanteau & Nagy, 1976). When people are not given explicit information about how others might regard them, they appear to assume that their chances of success are better with someone who is approximately equal to themselves in attractiveness. Thus, people tend to "match up" on the dimension of physical attractiveness in dating situations (Berscheid et al., 1971).

Creating a desired impression involves (1) knowing what to do (e.g., what images would create the desired impression), (2) how to do it (e.g., how to express symbolically those images through actions), and (3) having the self-presentation accepted by the other. Anticipated or perceived difficulties at any of these points can generate low self-presentational outcome expectations and produce barriers to the development of relationships.

Not knowing what to do or how to do it occurs when self-presentational guides for behavior are absent, ambiguous, or contradictory. Such uncertainty can arise when people are in novel or unstructured situations, such as at their first school dance; when people are interacting with others whose preferences are unknown or only vaguely appreciated, such as strangers or enigmatic others; or when people are unsure of how to go about creating a particular impression, such as at a formal dinner party where they want to look sophisticated but have no knowledge of the rules of etiquette or the prevailing fashionable customs. The result is an inability to formulate plans for goal achievement and the constant concern that rejection is but a moment away. Signs of some form of withdrawal from active participation are typically evidenced. Where possible, as at a party, people may attempt to hide in the crowd, making themselves as inconspicuous as possible (Jackson & Latané, 1981), and look to others to provide direction, thereby assuming a nondominant, noncommittal role in the setting (Schlenker & Leary, 1982). The tentative, cautious behaviors of people who are socially anxious appear to reflect in part the belief that it is better to be safe than sorry. Through minimal self-disclosures, the avoidance of contentious statements, and the presentation of an innocuous, inoffensive self, anxious people avoid immediate rejection at the risk of never really getting started in a relationship.

Even when people believe they know what to do and how to do it, they still may doubt that they can create the desired impression. They may know the rules, but believe they will not be able to translate them into goal achievement in the particular setting. On the one hand, there may be something about the other person that generates the belief they are unlikely to create the desired impression. For example, the other may appear especially snobbish or overly critical. On the other hand, people may believe they lack the skills, attributes, or resources to create a favorable impression on others. For example, their social or expressive skills may be regarded as poor and they may have no real accomplishments to present. Perceived or actual skills deficits have been viewed as major antecedents of the various forms of social anxiety, including dating anxiety, shyness, and speech reticence (e.g., Curran, 1977; Curran, Wallander, & Fiscetti, 1980).

Self-presentational concerns are a major barrier to the development of relationships for people who are either excessively motivated to impress others or who view themselves as having social deficits that impede the creation of desired impressions. People who are extremely high in the need for approval or high in the fear of negative evaluation, for example, appear to be overly concerned with the reactions of others to them; they seem to want to impress most others but doubt they can do so (Crowne & Marlowe, 1964; Schlenker, 1980; Schlenker & Leary, 1982; Watson & Friend, 1969). They conform more in groups, apparently trying to please others once they are in an interaction, but at the same time they usually avoid interactions whenever possible, do not go out of their ways to make friends, have higher levels of social anxiety in most situations, and are not especially successful in obtaining the regard of others or establishing friendships. The pattern illustrates the approach–avoidance conflict generated in those who experience self-presentational difficulties. Similarly, people who view themselves as shy or socially anxious seem to have excessively high chronic levels of the motivation to impress others and/or low chronic self-presentational outcome expectations (Leary & Schlenker, 1981; Schlenker & Leary, 1982). This is not to say they expect failure in every situation, but as compared to the average person, they are more likely to anticipate self-presentational difficulties and avoid or limit their participation in social life.

The personal consequences of the unwillingness to interact more fully with others are considerable, because they can preclude the development of relationships, hamper the acquisition of social skills, and result in debilitating attributions about one's social inadequacies. For example, even on those occasions when socially anxious people enter interactions, they usually restrict their participation to safe topics. By doing so, they impede the exchange of personal information that can lead to the perception of intimacy. Self-disclosures, especially those on private dimensions that the actor could choose not to reveal, lead to attributions of intimacy by others (e.g., Runge & Archer, 1981). Yet, this is precisely the type of information that people who fear they will create a negative impression are most likely to suppress, since it could make them vulnerable to negative attributions. Not surprisingly, then, social anxiety is highly correlated with self-reports of loneliness (Cheek & Busch, 1981).

Loneliness is "caused by the absence of an appropriate social partner who could assist in achieving important other-contingent goals, the belief that unavailability will endure, and the continuing desire for such contacts" (Derlega & Margulis, 1982, p. 155). The lack of an appropriate partner could arise for a variety of reasons, including high standards on the part of the lonely person. In many cases, however, it appears to arise from the fear of rejection (Cheek & Busch, 1981; Weiss, 1974). Lonely people are usually socially anxious—motivated to impress others but doubtful they can do so. Deprived of a supportive partner or group and especially hungry for acceptance, very lonely people might almost indiscriminately seek companionship with anyone who they anticipate would say a few kind words to them (Weiss, 1974). These predilections would make them easy targets for con artists, who may promise companionship in return for trust in their schemes.

At the opposite end of the spectrum are individuals who view themselves as especially skilled in social situations. A self-presentational analysis would suggest that such socially facile individuals usually have excellent social and expressive skills and also possess the sorts of characteristics that would cause others to seek them out and try to interact with them (e.g., physical attractiveness, expertise, high status, power). As a consequence of continued social interactions, their skills can further improve and they can develop high confidence in their abilities to create desired impressions across a wide range of social situations. Additionally, the acceptance they have received in the past would seem to make the acceptance of any particular other person less important to them. They can afford to be discriminating, and their motivation to impress others would, in general, be lower in any particular situation. This combination of a moderate motivation to impress others and confidence in one's ability to procure desired audience reactions should maximize self-presentational effectiveness. Indeed, people who have higher rather than lower social confidence are more successful in procuring the favorable regard of others (e.g., Jones & Panitch, 1971).

The Golden Mean: Self-Presentational Concerns in Established Relationships

Self-presentational concerns have implications for relationships throughout all their stages. As relationships progress to higher levels of intimacy and closeness, the parties can gain security and support. They will have mutually agreed on and accepted the identities each will have in the relationship, at least generally, and the regard each party has for the other is known or at least perceived to be known. Over time, habitual behavior routines develop and, secure in the other's regard, the parties can increasingly turn their attentions to achieving other goals in life, such as becoming successful in their careers or pursuing enjoyable hobbies. However, one of the challenges that exists in relationships, especially long-term ones such as marriages, is to maintain the interest and regard of the other. Unless the goal of maintaining that regard is occasionally salient, the effect on the relationship can be disastrous.

A common complaint heard by most marriage counselors is, "My spouse is taking me for granted." The spouse does not appear to notice what the neglected party is doing or wearing, does not listen to what he or she is saying, and no longer seems to care about his or her opinions or preferences. Concomitantly, the offenders allow their own appearances and actions to depart dramatically from what they once were, when they were on their best behavior trying to establish a good impression during the early stages of the relationship. The extreme case is, say, a man who, after 10 years of marriage, sits around in his underwear all weekend watching television, drinking beer, and building up a two-day growth of stubble on his face. Even if he noticed, which is by no means certain, that his wife walked into the room adorned in a provocative negligee, he is as likely to yawn as to do anything else. In brief, his motivation to maintain a desired impression on his wife has dwindled to the point of neglect. He is, as the spouse laments, literally not the man she married. His identity in her eyes has been altered by the inclusion of new images that now seem to describe him best (e.g., selfish, uncaring, fat) and the deletion of old images that are no longer appropriate (e.g., loving, caring, athletic, debonair). Inevitably, she nags and belittles him, attempting to change his behavior and get him back on the old path. For example, she tries charging him with some of the negative images that she hopes he will reject (e.g., screaming, "You're selfish"), trying to make him counter with a self-identification that will prompt him to modify his behavior (e.g., "No I'm not. Look, let's go out tonight so I can make up for this weekend"). Instead, he accepts the "new" image, and counters with a compensating attribute to quiet her down (e.g., "I may be selfish, but at least I'm a good provider"). Over time, his identity in the relationship, as perceived by both him and her, changes to incorporate these new images, and the spiral of nagging and countercharges intensifies. Needless to say, nagging and voicing complaints about one another have been found to be related to poor marital adjustment (Goode, 1956; Levinger, 1976; Markman, 1979), whereas supportive communications contribute to marital happiness (Markman, 1979). Much of the time, nagging appears to be related to dissatisfaction with the identity of one's partner and the attempt to change it, whereas supportive communications suggest satisfaction with the other's identity and the attempt to reinforce it.

The cognitive, affective, and behavioral consequences of taking another for granted are precisely what would be expected when people no longer have the goal of maintaining the regard of the other. Reexamine the list of concomitants of the motivation to impress another person and the pieces fall into place: people with low motivation are insensitive to the other's characteristics or opinions, do not monitor and control their actions for the other's benefit, are less concerned about the other's evaluations of them, and so forth. The question of why the actor no longer has or infrequently evokes the goal of maintaining the regard of the other is a separate issue. Perhaps the other became overly predictable and boring; perhaps the actor expected that the other would provide more support and rewards than turned out to be the case; perhaps the actor wants to establish a new identity in life, one that does not include the supports for the old identity that are associated with the spouse; etc. In any event, the other has lost his or her potency for serving as a significant audience for the actor.

At the opposite end of the spectrum are cases in which either (1) the actor remains overly motivated to impress the other or (2) begins to fear that he or she can no longer maintain the other's regard. If the motivation to impress another is too high, actors can become almost totally dependent on the other, bowing to the other's whims on most occasions and losing all sense of personal identity independent of the other. The actor's identity literally becomes anything the other wants it to be, as the actor conforms to whatever roles are demanded. The image evoked is the man or woman who meekly says, "Yes, dear," whenever the partner speaks. The relationship becomes one of master and slave. If the personalities of both parties are conducive to such arrangements and they willingly accede to the role each will play, the relationship can work out quite nicely (e.g., Carson, 1969). However, it becomes a problem for people who are excessively motivated to maintain the regard of another but do not want to become a slave. If they do not accede to the other's wishes, they fear the dissolution of the relationship. If they do, their identities in the relationship will probably become personally unsatisfactory, departing from the identities they desire and breeding discontent (see "The Accommodation of Identities in Relationships.")

Self-presentational outcome expectations usually recede into the background in established relationships because each party has an idea of how he or she is regarded by the other. They can become salient again, though, when some impediment arises to maintaining the other's regard. For example, people who view it as reasonably important to maintain the other's regard may begin to suspect that their partners are having a clandestine affair, or may begin to notice that their partner is interjecting derogatory remarks about them with some regularity. At such times of crisis, the others' regard can no longer be taken for granted, and people must again assess the relationship to develop clear goals, plans, and outcome expectations. The greater the impediment is perceived to be, the more intensive the reassessment of the relationship should be, as the actors struggle to resolve the dilemma.

People do not want to lose behavioral options, especially when they have already taken those options for granted. Reactance theory (Brehm, 1972) indicates that when the perceived threat to the relationship is great, people begin to focus on the attractive aspects of the option they might lose. This process produces selective attention to the benefits the other has to offer, while the other's liabilities are minimized. If they feel they have lost the other, that is, their outcome expectations are especially low, anxiety sets in, as does panic. As described earlier, the self-obsession and feelings of inadequacy that accompany low self-presentational outcome expectations further debilitate social performances and increase the likelihood that one cannot create a desired impression. The focus on the partner's positive qualities and one's own negative qualities generates feelings of marked dependence on the part of the actor. These feelings appear to be common in cases where people unwillingly go through separations or divorces while protesting their love for the other. Alternatively, the reassessment process might generate the expectation that the partner's regard can be maintained. In such cases, the crisis may actually prove beneficial for the relationship in the long run, because the reassessment of the relationship may have made the actor come to appreciate the unique benefits that are provided by the other and no longer take the other for granted. However, there is always the chance that the reassessment will lead to the conclusion that the actor is better off without, rather than with, the partner.

Between the preceding extremes are the more optimal states for relationships. Each party appreciates what the other has to offer, is motivated to maintain the regard of the other (not all the time, of course, but the goal is evoked with some frequency and has importance), and feels confident of the other's regard in return. Secure in each other's regard, the approval and respect of outsiders become less significant for them (Blau, 1964), and they can speak their minds more or less freely without worrying that it might jeopardize their standing in the relationship. Indeed, the perception that one can easily disclose personal information, including that which is negative, to the other differentiates "close" from "best" friends (La Gaipa, 1977). In these instances of the golden mean, neither party is taken for granted, neither is fettered by the whims of the other, and both can enjoy the security afforded by the acceptance of a significant other.

THE ACCOMMODATION OF IDENTITIES
IN RELATIONSHIPS
Interrelated Identities

Identities reflect relationships between people (e.g., Backman, in press; Carson, 1969; McCall & Simmons, 1978; Mead, 1934; Schlenker,

1980; Weinstein & Deutschberger, 1963). At one level, others provide referents for conduct. They can be both targets of one's performances and sources of comparison for them. At another level, others provide the templates into which people's own identities must fit. Simply because a person would like to have a particular identity in a given relationship does not ensure that it can be done. The other must recognize and bestow it, by tacitly or explicitly agreeing to view and treat the actor in the desired fashion. Although people often overestimate the extent to which others, especially friends, view them as they view themselves (e.g., Shrauger & Schoeneman, 1979), such congruence is not a "given" of social interaction.

Identity bargaining is the process of mutual accommodation to determine who each party will be in the relationship, including the roles they will enact and the characteristics they will be assumed to have (McCall & Simmons, 1978; Weinstein & Deutschberger, 1963). It involves the exchange of self-identifications, identifications of the other, and the attempt to resolve any problems or divergences that occur in the process of mutual identification. In cases in which potential disagreements exist, the parties can negotiate their differences, often trading concessions. For example, through his treatment of his date, a man may cast the woman into the traditional female role of being fragile, dependent, submissive, illogical, emotional, etc. In response, she can accede to the role, reject it in its entirety, attempt to compromise by accepting some elements while rejecting others, or attempt a trade-off where for one concession she extracts something in return (e.g., saying or implying. "I prefer to defer to your lead in public, but I expect you to treat me equally and consult me on all matters in our personal dealings").

Placing the other into a particular role or identity has been termed *altercasting* (Weinstein & Deutschberger, 1963) and can occur for a variety of reasons (see Backman, in press; McCall & Simmons, 1978). First, another may be altercast simply because the actor assumes or believes the identity-image is correct. For example, a person may be treated as incompetent or helpless because actors genuinely believe the other is, based on prevailing stereotypes, the other's reputation, or observed samples of the other's behavior. Second, another person may be altercast because, in order for the actor to enact his or her own desired identity in the relationship, the other must assume a corresponding stance. For example, a male who prefers the traditional male role cannot enact it unless a female assumes the traditional female role. Third, actors may attempt to superimpose on the other their own prototypic views of what the other should be like in the particular type of relationship. People have prototypes for best friends, spouses, children, secretaries, and others, and can attempt to get certain others to fit these prototypes through altercasting. Finally, altercasting can occur in order to influence the other's behavior in some personally preferred fashion irrespective of the long-term implications for one's own identity or the desired role for the other. It can thus be used as a symbolic reward or punishment designed to regulate the other's immediate actions. For example, a bois- terous party-goer might be asked, "What are you, some sort of trou- blemaker?" If he denies that image, he should calm down; if he accpets it, he should be ready to fight.

Relationships can progress when the identification process reaches mutually acceptable conclusions. To the extent the parties can agree, or at least perceive they agree, on how each will be identified and the type of relationship they should have, they will be able to coordinate their actions and work toward their goals. When they do not agree, the dis- crepancies can reduce the likelihood of harmonious interactions. In- deed, individuals who exhibit the greatest amounts of stress in their interpersonal relations also are found to have the greatest discrepancies between their views of self and the perceived or actual appraisals of themselves by others (Lundgren, 1978).

The identity that evolves for each party within the relationship should be a major determinant of satisfaction with the relationship. In essence, two questions must be answered by each party to determine whether a satisfactory accommodation has occurred: (1) "Am I who I want to be in this relationship?" and (2) "Is the other who I want him or her to be in this relationship?" The more affirmatively each party can answer each question, the more satisfied they should be with the relationship and the greater the likelihood the relationship will endure.

Each of the above questions can be addressed more precisely. People's satisfaction with their own identities in a particular relationship should be an inverse function of the discrepancy between their desired identifica- tions in the relationship across specific identity-dimensions and their perceived identifications in the relationship on those dimensions, weighted by the importance of each of the dimensions to them for the relationship. In other words, it is the discrepancy between the identities the actors desire and the identities they perceive they have or enact in the relationship that influences satisfaction. The discrepancy can arise for a variety of reasons, including: (1) actors may have acquired less than desired identity-images through the negotiation process or altercasting by the other; (2) the actors' desired identities may have changed over time as a consequence of mid-life crises or other events, yet they still maintain their "old," less-desired identites in the relationship; or (3) the actors may perceive that the other has never fully agreed with some of their self-identifications. In any event, to the extent that such a discrepancy exists, actors should be less than satisfied. The smaller the weighted discrepancy, the greater the actors' satisfaction.

Satisfaction with the other's identity in the relationship should be determined similarly. Satisfaction should be an inverse function of the discrepancy between the actor's perceptions of a prototypic partner in the relationship across specific identity-dimensions and the actor's perceptions of the other's standing in the relationship on those dimensions, weighted by the importance of each of the dimensions for the relationship. In other words, it is the discrepancy between the identity that actor would like the other to have and the identity he or she perceives the other to have in the relationship. The smaller this weighted discrepancy, the greater will be the actor's satisfaction with the other.

Murstein's (1971, 1976) theory of marital choice affords a prominent role to the similarity between people's ideal marriage partner and their perceptions of their partner. Although my definition of a prototypic identity for the other (see later discussion) and the definition of an ideal other differ slightly, there is a high degree of overlap between the two. Murstein contends that role fit in a relationship is not determined by the similarity or complementarity of the partner's roles, but by the extent to which the other matches one's ideal spouse. The data support his reasoning. Huston and Levinger (1978), for example, concluded that courtship progress is poorly predicted by similarity or complementarity of needs or personality fit. Rather, the more promising approaches emphasize the extent to which the parties "understand" each other and "agree in their definition of their relationship" (p. 142). Understanding one another and agreeing on who each will be in the relationship involve, in large part, supporting one another's desired identity.

Desired Identities

As discussed in an earlier section, identities are desirable to the extent that they are believable and personally beneficial (see also Schlenker, in press). When considering actors' own identities, the identities must portray something the actors think they *can* be. These identities may not be something the actors believe they actually are at the moment, but the perception must exist that the actors could live up to the requirements of the identities if they really tried, and if they were in the right environment or relationship, for instance, they could perform the requisite role behaviors with success. A desired identity is one that the self could be, at least at its best, as perceived by the actor.

Many theorists have discussed the ideal self—the self as the actor would fantasize it to be—and have posited strivings to reach such an ideal (see Rosenberg, 1979; Wylie, 1979). Without trying to make too much of the distinction, since the concepts are probably correlated highly, there is undoubtedly a difference between the things people have pretensions of being (James, 1980) and what they might ideally like to be. Pretensions refer to potentialities: what one might be at one's best. Ideals suggest unreachable heights: what no one could possibly hope to be.

People do not want others to view them as Supermen or Wonderwomen. To be viewed in this fashion is to confront perpetual frustration in social life, as the "beneficiary" of the identification would continually fail. People want others to bring out the best in them, not impose standards on them that are unreachable. Indeed, people reject excessive praise when it commits them to perform up to standards that they do not believe they can reach (e.g., Jones, 1973).

People who insist that they literally have ideal characteristics are regarded as remarkably egotistical. People who insist that their partner is literally ideal are viewed as remarkably naive or insipid. People want support from relationships, but they want support that they can perceive as both sincere and believable. Being told one is a "god" on every conceivable dimension and that one can do no wrong may flatter one's ego for a few days, but after a while one must begin to wonder about the insight, intelligence, and credibility of the source of such excessive praise. Praise that comes from noncredible sources is discounted and worthless to the receiver except where it might coincidentally agree with receiver's own perceptions of self (e.g., Mettee & Aronson, 1974). Once the support of a partner begins to appear noncredible and continues as such despite the evidence, the partner's significance as a referent and source of self-validation declines (e.g., Mettee & Aronson, 1974; Swann, in press).

In an analogous fashion, a prototypic partner in a relationship is not necessarily an ideal of perfection. It is the best type of person with whom people think they could sustain a relationship if all went well. A meek, shy, homely, and poor man might fantasize about a Marilyn Monroe type and rate her extremely positively in the abstract. Indeed, if he could be assured such an ideal person would accept and treat him exactly as he wanted, that might be his choice. His own limitations, however, place constraints on the best type of person he could possibly hope to attract and keep attracted. An ideal other would introduce considerably inequity into a relationship and generate less satisfaction and happiness than one who had some such qualities but reflected a more realistic representation of one's potentialities (see Blau, 1964; Walster & Walster, 1978). Thus, a prototypic partner is one who represents a compromise between one's wishes and reality—the best type of person with whom one could reasonably hope to associate. This prototype should form the standard against which others are compared.

Support from Relationships

The perceived discrepancy between the identity one perceives or enacts in a relationship and one's desired identity can be exacerbated or attenuated by the criticism or support of others. When desired identities are supported by others, interpersonal tensions are minimized, the actors' goals in the relationship are facilitated, and a predictable, familiar, and uncertainty-reducing environment is created (e.g., Secord & Backman, 1965; Schlenker, 1980; Swann, in press). It is therefore proposed that people seek out, prefer to interact with, and are most satisfied in relationships with others who they believe support, validate, enhance, or elicit desirable identity-images.

Two points of clarification, each drawing on issues that were mentioned earlier, are necessary. First, the identity-images that form the basis for actors' self-identifications in any particular situation may or may not correspond precisely with the actors' private self-images elicited in the absence of the particular immediate audience or situational pressures. Situational pressures and potent immediate audiences can cause self-relevant information to be packaged differently for public self-presentations, including the use of different identity-images than might be privately employed. Actors may exaggerate their qualities or even lie about them to create situated identities that will facilitate their immediate goals and that they think can be believably maintained for an immediate audience during the length of a short-term interaction (e.g., Jones & Wortman, 1973; Schlenker, 1980, 1982). Thus, their private self-images could diverge from their desired identity-images in the situation.

In enduring relationships, where the parties have had the opportunity to interact and observe one another across a wide range of situations, it becomes more likely that the person's privately perceived self-images and desired identity-images will correspond. Even here, though, some divergence is possible. Actors may feel they have been trapped or locked into identities that are less than desirable. Unhappily married couples, for example, often complain that their relationship does not let them fulfill themselves, that is, express the identities they think they should and could be expressing. Their *current* self-images, which have been partially shaped by their roles in the relationship, indicate they *now are* one type of person, but their desired identity-images indicate that they *should* be another type of person. The above proposition, then, suggests that people want to obtain support and validation of desired identity-images. These may or may not correspond precisely with private self-conceptions. This point distinguishes the proposition slightly from similar ones suggesting that people want to maintain congruence with their self-concepts (e.g., Secord & Backman, 1965; Swann, in press).

Second, it is worth reiterating that desired identity-images are ones that are both personally beneficial and believable. Desired identity-images are held in check by their believability; this pertains to both public identities that are maintained before specific immediate audiences (e.g., Baumeister & Jones, 1978; Goffman, 1959; Schlenker, 1975, 1980), and privately perceived identities that are maintained for the self (e.g., Greenwald, 1980; Schlenker, 1980, in press). Thus, people do not act simply to maximize their self-esteem without bounds; they do so within the confines of the images they think they can reasonably maintain. People will reject overly positive information about the self if it exceeds these confines (Carson, 1969; Jones, 1973).

Given the preceding, the present proposition provides an integrating perspective on the debate between consistency or congruency theories (e.g., Secord & Backman, 1965; Swann, in press), which propose that people want to receive feedback that verifies their self-conceptions, and esteem enhancement theories (e.g., Jones, 1973), which propose that people want to receive feedback that maximizes their self-esteem.[4] Each of these theories approaches the issue from a different angle and addresses different parts of the process, with esteem theories focusing largely on the extent to which information is personally beneficial, and congruency theories focusing on the extent to which information is believable. Not surprisingly, each theory has introduced qualifiers to explain phenomena that are more readily handled by the other theory. For

---

[4]Backman (in press) has rejected the exclusive emphasis on consistency that was taken in the earlier version of congruency theory and now emphasizes the importance of attempting to create support for the fantasized or ideal self. Such attempts often appear to reflect what could be termed self-enhancing tendencies. His more recent position thus is very close to the one presented here, emphasizing the attempt to construct and maintain a desirable identity.

example, it has been suggested by esteem theorists that when people anticipate making important choices that demand veridical perceptions of self-attributes and when they anticipate that their past or future behaviors would publicly repudiate an overly enhanced self-image, they prefer congruent feedback (Jones, 1973). In short, people avoid esteem enhancement when the relevant images are no longer desirable because they are not believable to the pertinent audience (self or others). In contrast, congruency theorists have suggested that when people are uncertain of their standing on a particular dimension, which is said to be typically the case when people rate themselves poorly on a dimension, they prefer esteem-enhancing feedback (e.g., Swann, in press). In short, people avoid congruency in favor of personally beneficial information when they expect they can believably construct and maintain more desirable identity-images. Given these qualifications, the two theories converge in their predictions; it is doubtful they could be empirically separated.

By refocusing the issue on the nature of desired identity-images, the self-identification approach provides an integrating theme for the literature. The audience that is salient at a particular point in time, the actors' private self-images, and the context of the situation (including salient reward–cost pressures) reciprocally interact to determine the desirability of particular identity-images in the situation or relationship. These identity-images then guide people's self-identifications and their reactions to self-relevant feedback from others.

Support as an Active Process

Obtaining support for and validation of desired identity-images is an active process on the parts of both the actor and the other(s)—neither actors nor immediate audiences idly sit by and passively allow events to transpire around them. In an excellent analysis of self-verification processes, Swann (in press) describes how people attempt to "create—both in their actual social environments and their own minds—a social reality that verifies and confirms their self-conceptions." Although I would substitute the phrase "desired identity-images" for "self-conceptions," the underlying theme remains that people actively build and attempt to obtain support for their identities, both privately and interpersonally. Through (1) displays of the signs and symbols of their identities (e.g., style of dress, house furnishings), (2) selective performance of jobs or tasks that permit identities to be built and maintained, including one's selection of an occupation and hobbies, (3) selective affiliation with others whose appraisals are supportive, (4) interpersonal behaviors designed to shape others' responses, and (5) cognitive activities such as selective attention, recall, and interpretation of self-relevant information, people shape the information and appraisals they encounter (Backman, in press; Schlenker, 1980; Secord & Backman, 1965; Swann, in press).

In relationships, especially close ones, the support people give to their partners can also be a rather creative activity. Support goes beyond simply nodding one's head at the other's self-identifications. Partners can shape each other's identities in the same sorts of ways that they can shape their own. This, of course, can be to the benefit or detriment of the partner in the relationship. First, individuals can influence the signs and symbols of their partner's identity through gifts or encouragements to wear, display, or purchase certain types of things. For example, a wife who receives presents such as sexy lingerie or expensive perfumes from her husband is likely to feel and respond differently in the relationship than one who receives long woolen nighties and kitchen appliances from her husband. Second, they can influence the types of jobs or tasks that their partners perform, including occupations and hobbies. As examples, people can encourage their spouses either to remain in or leave certain occupations, thereby encouraging a trap or an opportunity for the others' identities; or they can encourage certain types of joint activities, such as giving frequent parties or going to certain types of functions (e.g., dances, athletic contests), that will bring out the best or worst aspects of their partners' identities. Third, they can jointly determine the people with whom their partners associate, thereby influencing the interpersonal appraisals received by the partners from those outside the relationship. For example, people's relatives or friends might not be persons with whom their partners otherwise would elect to associate. People have some latitude in determining the frequency and extent to which their partners are brought into contact with those whom the partners like versus those they detest, and who will therefore bring out the best or worst in the partners.

Finally, through their own creative cognitive processes, people can provide others with evaluations that support or demean the others' desired identities. Partners can even go beyond each others' expressed self-identifications by amplifying, elaborating, or reinterpreting information, thus influencing the dimensions on which the others' identity is evaluated, the others' standing on the dimensions, and the standards that are relevant to a satisfactory evaluation. In some relationships, each partner will assist the other in converting weaknesses to strengths and further intensifying existing strengths; in other relationships, each will condemn the other by converting strengths to weaknesses and further intensifying existing weaknesses. For example, a person who has viewed himself as nonassertive, a quality he regards unfavorably, might discuss the matter with his wife. She might reply with analyses such as: "I've never thought of you like that. I think it's just that you're tactful and skilled at getting your way without creating hostility"; or "Maybe about trivial things, but not about the things that really matter"; or "The same qualities that you regard as evidence of nonassertiveness also make you sensitive, caring, and open, and that's why I fell in love with you"; or "It's a minor flaw at worst compared to your strengths." The list could continue almost indefinitely and contain remarks that disparage rather than benefit the actor. Thus, people can do more than simply support or disparage others' identities. They can, for instance, desirably enhance others' identities without committing the others to impossible ideals. People truly can bring out the best or worst in each other.

SUMMARY

The identification process, that is, the process of fixing one's own and others' identities in social interactions, is central to the genesis and ultimate fate of relationships. People's identities permit them to interrelate, providing a basis for regulating interpersonal conduct and mediating the regard and treatment they receive from one another. Through the exchange of self-identifications and identifications of the other, people construct identities that provide them with opportunities and constraints in the relationship. Consequently, a premium is placed on controlling the images of self and other that are established and maintained in any relationship. The identity-analytic approach that was presented examined some of the implications of the identification process, particularly the self-presentational aspects. Self-presentational concerns, arising from the motivation to impress a particular other and the perceived likelihood of doing so, affect the orientation with which people approach specific interactions, prompting them to be indifferent, complacent, secure, challenged, or anxious. These concerns influence people's cognitive, affective, and behavioral activities in social interactions and can facilitate or impede the development and maintenance of relationships. People's satisfaction in relationships appears to be predicated in large part on the orientations they assume toward the other and on the extent to which the relationship supports their own desired identities and their prototypic identity for the other.

REFERENCES

Backman, C. W. (in press). Towards an interdisciplinary social psychology. In L. Berkowitz (Ed.), *Advances in experimental social psychology*. New York: Academic Press.

Bandura, A. (1977). Self-efficacy: Toward a unifying theory of behavioral change. *Psychological Review, 84*, 191–215.

Baumeister, R. F., & Jones, E. E. (1978). When self-presentation is constrained by the target's knowledge: Consistency and compensation. *Journal of Personality and Social Psychology, 36*, 608–618.

Berscheid, E., Dion, K., Walster, E., & Walster, G. W. (1971). Physical attractiveness and dating choice: A test of the matching hypothesis. *Journal of Experimental Social Psychology, 7*, 173–189.

Berscheid, E., & Graziano, W. (1978). The initiation of social relationships and interpersonal attraction. In R. L. Burgess & T. L. Huston (Eds.), *Social exchange in developing relationships*. New York: Academic Press.

Berscheid, E., Graziano, W., Monson, T., & Dermer, M. (1976). Outcome dependency: Attention, attribution, and attraction. *Journal of Personality and Social Psychology, 34*, 978–989.

Berscheid, E., & Walster, E. (1974). Physical attractiveness. In L. Berkowitz (Ed.), *Advances in experimental social psychology* (Vol. 7). New York: Academic Press.

Berscheid, E., & Walster, E. H. (1978). *Interpersonal attraction* (2nd ed.). Reading, MA: Addison-Wesley.

Blau, P. M. (1964). *Exchange and power in social life*. New York: Wiley.

Brehm, J. W. (1972). *Responses to loss of freedom: A theory of psychological reactance*. Morristown, NJ: General Learning Press.

Cantor, N., & Mischel, W. (1979). Prototypes in person perception. In L. Berkowitz (Ed.), *Advances in experimental social psychology* (Vol. 12). New York: Academic Press.

Carson, R. C. (1969). *Interaction concepts of personality*. Chicago: Aldine.

Carver, C. S. (1979). A cybernetic model of self-attention processes. *Journal of Personality and Social Psychology, 37*, 1251–1281.

Cheek, J. M., & Busch, C. M. (1981). The influence of shyness on loneliness in a new situation. *Personality and Social Psychology Bulletin, 7*, 572–577.

Crowne, D. P., & Marlowe, D. (1964). *The approval motive*. New York: Wiley.

Curran, J. P. (1977). Skills training as an approach to the treatment of heterosexual-social anxiety. *Psychological Bulletin, 84*, 140–157.

Curran, J. P., Wallander, J. L., & Fischetti, M. (1980). The importance of behavioral and cognitive factors in heterosexual-social anxiety. *Journal of Personality, 48*, 285–292.

Derlega, V. J., & Chaikin, A. L. (1975). *Sharing intimacy: What we reveal to others and why*. Englewood Cliffs, NJ: Prentice-Hall.

Derlega, V. J., & Grzelak, J. (1979). Appropriateness of self-disclosure. In G. J. Chelune (Ed.), *Self-disclosure*. San Francisco: Jossey-Bass.

Derlega, V. J., & Margulis, S. T. (1982). Why loneliness occurs: The interrelationship of social-psychological and privacy concepts. In D. Perlman & L. A. Peplau (Eds.), *Loneliness: A sourcebook of current theory, research and therapy.* New York: Wiley (Interscience).

Epstein, S. (1973). The self-concept revisited: Or a theory of a theory. *American Psychologist, 28,* 404–416.

Fenigstein, A. (1979). Self-consciousness, self-attention, and social interaction. *Journal of Personality and Social Psychology, 37,* 75–86.

Garland, H., & Brown, B. R. (1972). Face-saving as affected by subjects' sex, audiences' sex, and audience expertise. *Sociometry, 35,* 280–289.

Goffman, E. (1959). *The presentation of self in everyday life.* Garden City, NY: Doubleday Anchor.

Goode, W. J. (1956). *After divorce.* Glencoe, IL: Free Press.

Greenwald, A. G. (1980). The totalitarian ego: Fabrication and revision of personal history. *American Psychologist, 35,* 603–618.

Hogan, R. (1982). A socioanalytic theory of personality. In M. Page & R. Dienstbier (Eds.), *Nebraska symposium on motivation.* Lincoln: University of Nebraska Press.

Hogan, R., & Cheek, J. (1982). Identity, authenticity, and maturity. In T. R. Sarbin & K. E. Scheibe (Eds.), *Studies in social identity.* New York: Praeger.

Huston, T. L. (1973). Ambiguity of acceptance, social desirability, and dating choice. *Journal of Experimental Social Psychology, 9,* 32–42.

Huston, T. L., & Levinger, G. (1978). Interpersonal attraction and relationships. In M. R. Rosenzweig & L. W. Porter (Eds.), *Annual review of psychology* (Vol. 29). Palo Alto, CA: Annual Reviews.

Jackson, J. M., & Latané, B. (1981). All alone in front of all those people: Stage fright as a function of number and type of co-performers and audience. *Journal of Personality and Social Psychology, 40,* 73–85.

James, W. J. (1890). *The principles of psychology.* New York: Holt.

Jones, E. E., & Pittman, T. S. (1982). Toward a general theory of strategic self-presentation. In J. Suls (Ed.), *Psychological perspectives on the self* (Vol. 1). Hillsdale, NJ: Erlbaum.

Jones, E. E., & Wortman, C. (1973). *Ingratiation: An attributional approach.* Morristown, NJ: General Learning Press.

Jones, S. C. (1973). Self- and interpersonal evaluations: Esteem theories vs. consistency theories. *Psychological Bulletin, 79,* 185–199.

Jones, S. C., & Panitch, D. (1971). The self-fulfilling prophecy and interpersonal attraction. *Journal of Experimental Social Psychology, 7,* 356–366.

Judd, C. M., & Kulik, J. A. (1980). Schematic effects of social attitudes on information processing and recall. *Journal of Personality and Social Psychology, 38,* 569–578.

La Gaipa, J. J. (1977). Testing a multidimensional approach to friendship. In S. Duck (Ed.), *Theory and practice in interpersonal attraction.* London: Academic Press.

Leary, M. R., & Schlenker, B. R. (1981). The social psychology of shyness: A self-presentational model. In J. T. Tedeschi (Ed.), *Impression management theory and social psychological research.* New York: Academic Press.

Levinger, G. (1976). A social psychological perspective on marital dissolution. *Journal of Social Issues, 32,* 21–47.

Levinger, G., & Moles, O. C. (Eds.) (1979). *Divorce and separation: Context, causes and consequences.* New York: Basic Books.

Lundgren, D. C. (1978). Public esteem, self-esteem, and interpersonal stress. *Social Psychology, 41,* 68–73.

McCall, G. J., & Simmons, J. E. (1978). *Identities and interactions* (2nd ed.). New York: Free Press.

Markman, H. J. (1979). Application of a behavioral model of marriage in predicting relationship satisfaction of couples planning marriage. *Journal of Consulting and Clinical Psychology, 47*, 743–749.

Mead, G. H. (1934). *Mind, self, and society*. Chicago: University of Chicago Press.

Mehrabian, A. (1971). Nonverbal communication. In J. K. Cole (Ed.), *Nebraska symposium on motivation*. Lincoln: University of Nebraska Press.

Mettee, D. R., & Aronson, E. (1974). Affective reactions to appraisal from others. In T. L. Huston (Ed.), *Foundations of interpersonal attraction*. New York: Academic Press.

Miller, G. A., Galanter, E., & Pribram, K. H. (1960). *Plans and the structure of behavior*. New York: Holt.

Murstein, B. I. (1971). *Theories of attraction and love*. New York: Springer-Verlag.

Murstein, B. I. (1976). *Who will marry whom?* New York: Springer-Verlag.

Richardson, K. D., & Cialdini, R. B. (1981). Basking and blasting: Tactics of indirect influence. In J. T. Tedeschi (Ed.), *Impression management theory and social psychological research*. New York: Academic Press.

Rosenberg, M. (1979). *Conceiving the self*. New York: Basic Books.

Runge, T. E., & Archer, R. L. (1981). Reactions to the disclosure of public and private self-information. *Social Psychology Quarterly, 44*, 357–362.

Sarnoff, I., & Zimbardo, P. G. (1961). Anxiety, fear, and social affiliation. *Journal of Abnormal and Social Psychology, 62*, 356–363.

Scheier, M. F., & Carver, C. S. (1981). Private and public aspects of self. In L. Wheeler (Ed.), *Review of Personality and Social Psychology*. Beverly Hills, CA: Sage.

Schlenker, B. R. (1975). Self-presentation: Managing the impression of consistency when reality interferes with self-enhancement. *Journal of Personality and Social Psychology, 32*, 1030–1037.

Schlenker, B. R. (1980). *Impression management: The self-concept, social identity, and interpersonal relations*. Monterey, CA: Brooks/Cole.

Schlenker, B. R. (1982). Translating actions into attitudes: An identity-analytic approach to the explanation of social conduct. In L. Berkowitz (Ed.), *Advances in experimental social psychology* (Vol. 15). New York: Academic Press.

Schlenker, B. R. (in press). Identity and self-identification. In B. R. Schlenker (Ed.), *The self and social life*. New York: McGraw-Hill.

Schlenker, B. R., & Leary, M. R. (1982). Social anxiety and self-presentation: A conceptualization and model. *Psychological Bulletin, 92*, 641–669.

Secord, P. F., & Backman, C. W. (1965). Interpersonal approach to personality. In B. H. Maher (Ed.), *Progress in experimental personality research* (Vol. 2). New York: Academic Press.

Shanteau, J., & Nagy, G. (1976). Decisions made about other people: A human judgment analysis of dating choice. In J. Carroll & J. Payne (Eds.), *Cognition and social behavior*. Hillsdale, NJ: Erlbaum.

Shrauger, J. S., & Schoeneman, T. J. (1979). Symbolic interactionist view of self-concept: Through the looking glass darkly. *Psychological Bulletin, 86*, 549–573.

Sigall, H., & Landy, D. (1973). Radiating beauty: Effects of having a physically attractive partner on person perception. *Journal of Personality and Social Psychology, 28*, 218–224.

Snyder, C. R., Higgins, R. L., & Stucky, R. J. (1983). *Excuses: Masquerades in search of grace*. New York: Wiley (Interscience).

Swann, W. B., Jr. (in press). Self-verification: Bringing social reality into harmony with the self. In J. Suls & A. G. Greenwald (Eds.), *Psychological perspectives on the self* (Vol. 2). Hillsdale, NJ: Erlbaum.

Tedeschi, J. T. (1974). Attributions, liking, and power. In T. Huston (Ed.), *Foundations of interpersonal attraction.* New York: Academic Press.

Tesser, A. (1981). Self-generated attitude change. In L. Berkowitz (Ed.), *Advances in experimental social psychology* (Vol. 11). New York: Academic Press.

Turner, R. H. (1968). The self-conception in social interaction. In C. Gordon & K. J. Gergen (Eds.), *The self in social interaction.* New York: Wiley.

Walster, E., & Walster, G. W. (1978). *A new look at love.* Reading, MA: Addison-Wesley.

Watson, D., & Friend, R. (1969). Measurement of social-evaluative anxiety. *Journal of Consulting and Clinical Psychology, 33,* 448–457.

Weinstein, E. A., & Deutschberger, P. (1963). Some dimensions of altercasting. *Sociometry, 26,* 454–466.

Weiss, R. S. (1974). *Loneliness: The experience of emotional and social isolation.* Cambridge, MA: MIT Press.

Weiss, R. S. (1975). *Marital separation.* New York: Basic Books.

Wylie, R. C. (1979). *The self-concept: Theory and research on selected topics* (Vol. 2, rev. ed.). Lincoln: University of Nebraska Press.

Zanna, M. P., & Pack, S. J. (1975). On the self-fulfilling nature of apparent sex differences in behavior. *Journal of Experimental Social Psychology, 11,* 583–591.

CHAPTER 5

Intimacy, Social Control, and Nonverbal Involvement: A Functional Approach

MILES L. PATTERSON

The study of nonverbal behavior in interaction is important because this behavior touches on a wide variety of interpersonal issues. Most research in this area focuses either on the expressive or on the exchange role of nonverbal behavior. Although these two aspects of nonverbal behavior are not completely independent, they do represent distinctly different emphases. The expressive role may be seen in the manner in which nonverbal behavior serves to express or represent specific feelings or reactions. In contrast, the exchange role may be seen in the manner in which nonverbal behavior relates to the structure and meaning of interaction. A comparison between the expressive and the exchange roles of nonverbal behavior should facilitate an appreciation of the diversity of this research. More specifically, a comparison of the expressive and exchange aspects and their related methodologies should provide a useful context for this chapter's discussion.

EXPRESSIVE AND EXCHANGE PROCESSES

A number of issues dealing with expressiveness and various subjective states have been investigated in recent research. A sampling of these should serve to represent the expressive focus in research and

COMMUNICATION, INTIMACY,
AND CLOSE RELATIONSHIPS

105

provide a contrast to the research on nonverbal exchange. One major issue in this research is the question of the universality of emotional expressions. Ekman and Oster (1979) noted that basic emotional states (happiness, sadness, anger, fear, and disgust) seem to be encoded and decoded similarly across widely discrepant cultures. However, cultural "display rules" may require that, on certain occasions, facial responses be masked (Ekman, 1972). That is, the facial display shown is designed to cover the real feeling state experienced. A second active area of research on the expressive role of nonverbal behavior focuses on the role of bodily feedback in determining an individual's emotional response. James (1890/1950) first proposed that feedback from bodily movement helps to define specific feeling states. The relationship of bodily movement in general, and facial expression in particular, to the initiation of feeling states is still a matter of considerable controversy (see Buck, 1980). A third area of extensive research on expressive behavior has examined individual differences in the encoding and decoding of affect. A primary concern of this research is identifying those factors affecting accuracy in encoding and decoding affect (Rosenthal, 1979). A fourth emphasis area in research on expressive behavior deals with the patterns of various verbal and nonverbal cues in detecting deception (Ekman & Friesen, 1974; Kraut, 1978). A fifth and final emphasis area deals with the impressions created by various patterns of expressive behavior. Schneider, Hastorf, and Ellsworth (1979, Chap. 6) propose that judgments made about others from their nonverbal behavior may be either reactive or purposive. A reactive attribution is based on the assumption that the behavior represents a spontaneous, uncontrolled reaction, whereas a purposive attribution is based on the assumption that the individual's behavior was controlled or managed. Reactive behavior provides a basis for inferring something about a person's "true" personality or motivation, but purposive behavior may be discounted as not representative of a person's true characteristics.

Research that takes an expressive perspective is basically concerned with the relationship between particular nonverbal displays and judgmental reactions. When the judgments (or the affective stimuli precipitating them) are manipulated by the experimenter, and the individual either spontaneously or deliberately initiates a behavioral reaction, that methodology may be described as an encoding strategy. That is, various traits or states (e.g., happiness, sadness, friendliness, dominance) may be manipulated directly or indirectly and then the encoded behavioral presentations compared. In contrast, a decoding methodology would manipulate standardized behavioral presentations and then compare the judgments made of those presentations.

A focus on the exchange process involves an analysis of the interactive consequences of various behavioral patterns over the course of some encounter. That is, how does the behavior of one individual relate to the subsequent behavior of his or her partner? This interactive strategy may either involve the use of a confederate (whose behavior toward a subject is manipulated in some specific fashion) or involve the spontaneous interaction between two or more naive subjects. In either case, the goal is to understand the development of behavioral changes over time and across individuals. The interactive strategy may be supplemented by rated impressions (as in the decoding methodology), but the primary concern is the analysis of the interaction sequence. Thus, ratings of self, other, or the situation would be useful to the extent that such information might help to explain the patterns of nonverbal exchange.

The purpose of this chapter is to analyze nonverbal exchange from a functional perspective. Although the pursuit of that goal requires a primary emphasis on the exchange role of nonverbal behavior, expressive concerns will also be identified in some of the functional categories. The theme of this book emphasizes the role of intimacy in social interaction. However, the functional approach described here stresses that other motives may also mediate social behavior in close relationships. Before discussing this functional framework for the analysis of nonverbal behavior, it may be useful to review briefly two previous intimacy-based models of nonverbal exchange.

INTIMACY MODELS OF NONVERBAL EXCHANGE

Equilibrium Theory

Argyle and Dean's (1965) equilibrium theory was the first developed explanation for the dynamics involved in intimacy exchange. Argyle and Dean proposed that interpersonal intimacy was manifested by interpersonal distance, eye contact, smiling, and possibly other behaviors. Equilibrium theory assumes that, in any given interaction, a comfortable or appropriate level of intimacy exists between individuals. To the extent that the coordinated behavior of the pair approximates the appropriate level of intimacy, a state of equilibrium exists. When one or more behaviors deviate enough from the appropriate level of intimacy, a condition of disequilibrium is precipitated. Subsequently, an adjustment by one person would be required to restore the intimacy equilibrium. For example, a too-close approach by one person may increase intimacy beyond the comfortable level. When that happens, the partner may decrease gaze or orient away from the other person so that the intimacy is decreased. Although comfortable levels of intimacy vary across people and situations, the predicted compensatory adjustment in response to disequilibrium remains constant. That is, when there is too little or too much behavioral intimacy initiated by one person, adjustments by the other person should help to restore intimacy to a more comfortable level.

Most of the research on equilibrium theory has been generally supportive of its predictions (see Cappella, 1981; Patterson, 1973, for reviews of that work). However, some critical, opposing results (e.g., Breed, 1972; Chapman, 1975; Jourard & Friedman, 1970) present a considerable problem for the predicted compensation process. In those few published studies, a response pattern of matching or reciprocity was found following an increase in behavioral intimacy. Thus, an initial increase in intimacy produced a further increase in intimacy, in contrast to the decrease predicted by equilibrium theory. Although the dominant trend in the research was that of compensation, it seemed likely that reciprocation of intimacy was, in fact, a common trend in everyday life. Specifically, interactions between parent and child, loved ones, or good friends are probably characterized by a pattern of reciprocity. Because most of the published research examined interactions between strangers in unusual laboratory or field settings, it is probably not surprising that compensation commonly occurred. That is, the typical response to increased intimacy by a stranger in the laboratory or field settings usually involved compensation. A consideration of these relational and situational variables was a major component of a theory designed to account for both compensatory and reciprocal changes (Patterson, 1976).

Intimacy–Arousal Model

An alternate explanation encompassing both compensation and reciprocal adjustments would require a more general mechanism that might mediate behavioral adjustments. One factor that had been linked to increased intimacy was arousal (Gale, Lucas, Nissim, & Harpham, 1972; Kleinke & Pohlen, 1971; McBride, King, & James, 1965; Nichols & Champness, 1971). If arousal precipitates a cognitive labeling process as Schachter and Singer (1962) suggest, then the resulting emotional state may direct one's behavioral adjustment. That is, the combined arousal-labeling mechanism determines one's feeling state, and that, in turn, specifies the type of adjustment. Figure 5.1 provides a diagram of the

intimacy–arousal model. In general that model proposes that sufficiently large changes in one person's behavioral intimacy precipitate
arousal change in the other person. If that arousal change is positively
labeled (e.g., liking or love), then that person reciprocates the first person's change in intimacy. For example, an affectionate greeting (high
intimacy) by a loved one might produce increased arousal that is labeled
as love. That positive feeling state then facilitates a reciprocation of the
high intimacy, perhaps in the form of a hug and kiss. In contrast, a close
approach and touch by a stranger may increase arousal and result in a
negative feeling state such as fear. The fear, in turn, facilitates a compensatory response that serves to decrease the behavioral intimacy of the
stranger. Thus, a common arousal-labeling process provides the means
for explaining contrasting patterns of behavioral adjustment.

In general, recent research on the intimacy–arousal model is moderately supportive of its predictions. For example, several studies have
shown contrasting patterns of behavioral adjustments and/or affective
judgments as a function of the positive or negative context surrounding
an increase in behavioral intimacy (Foot, Chapman & Smith, 1977; Foot,
Smith & Chapman, 1977; Storms & Thomas, 1977; Whitcher & Fisher,
1979). That is, when the relationship or circumstances were positive,
increased intimacy was usually reciprocated. In contrast, when the relationship or circumstances were negative, increased intimacy usually
precipitated a compensatory adjustment. Research in our own laboratory has not been so supportive of the intimacy–arousal model (Ickes,
Patterson, Rajecki, & Tanford, 1982; Patterson, Jordan, Hogan, &
Frerker, 1981; Patterson, Roth, & Schenk, 1979). Later, I discuss some of
the results of these studies in detail, but at this point it is probably
sufficient to note that those results provided the impetus for a new,
more comprehensive model of nonverbal exchange. The foundation of
that functional model rests on a distinction between the constructs of
intimacy and nonverbal involvement.

INTIMACY AND NONVERBAL INVOLVEMENT

The construct of intimacy has been a central one in research on the
exchange role of nonverbal behavior. In that research, intimacy has had
two separate, but related, referents. One referent has focused on intimacy as the underlying motivation determining one's behavior toward
another person. In this sense intimacy may be manifested in liking, love,

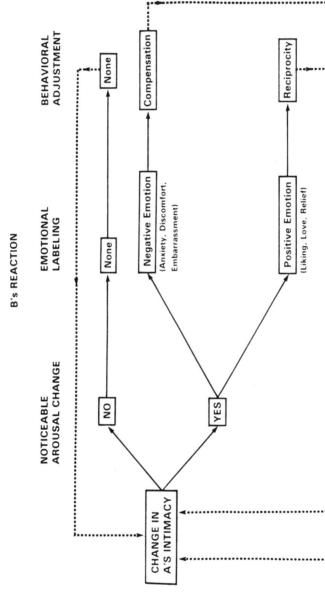

Figure 5.1 Diagram of the arousal model of interpersonal intimacy. From Patterson M. L. An arousal model of interpersonal intimacy. *Psychological Review*, 1976, *83*, 235–245. Copyright 1976 by the American Psychological Association. Reprinted/Adapted by permission.

or more general affiliative tendencies. In effect, intimacy as a motive describes one general function of interaction. A second usuage of intimacy is in describing the set of behaviors that reflect the underlying affective (i.e., intimacy as a motive) reaction towards another person. Both equilibrium theory (Argyle & Dean, 1965) and the intimacy–arousal model (Patterson, 1976) use the term "intimacy" interchangeably to refer to a function and to its behavioral representation. At the same time both theories recognize that the "intimacy behaviors" can also serve other functions. However, one likely result of that dual usage is a decreased sensitivity to alternative functions served by the same behaviors. One means of clarifying the terminology surrounding the focal behaviors and the functions served by them is to adopt distinct terms.

In introducing my functional model (Patterson, 1982) I proposed that the term *nonverbal involvement* be used to describe a set of behaviors that serve to define the degree of involvement manifested between individuals in a social setting. Thus, nonverbal involvement is a lower-level, behaviorally linked construct that is distinct from higher-order functional constructs such as intimacy. In addition, I suggested that the range of behaviors contributing to nonverbal involvement is wider than that included in either the intimacy (Argyle & Dean, 1965) or immediacy cues (Mehrabian, 1969). A listing of the involvement behaviors would include the following: (1) interpersonal distance, (2) gaze, (3) touch, (4) body orientation, (5) lean, (6) facial expressiveness, (7) duration of talking, (8) interruptions, (9) postural openness, (10) relational gestures, (11) head nods, and (12) paralinguistic cues such as intonation, speech rate, and pauses.

A number of other nonverbal behaviors probably fall outside of this involvement category because they are less salient to the dynamics of exchange. Many of these noninvolvement cues relate to a relaxation–tension dimension. For example, rocking leg or foot movements, object manipulations (e.g., spinning a ring or keys), and arm position symmetry seem to be indicators of stress (Mehrabian, 1970; Mehrabian & Ksionzky, 1972). In addition, self-manipulations or "self-adaptors" (Ekman & Friesen, 1969) seem basically to be outside of the interactive process. That is, behaviors such as rubbing, scratching, wringing one's hands, or covering the eyes seem to serve a personal rather than an interpersonal need (Ekman & Friesen, 1969).

The contrast between the behaviors of interest and the functions served by them provides the foundation for the functional classification described in the next section. In general it is assumed that comparable levels and forms of nonverbal involvement may serve very different functions in an interaction.

A FUNCTIONAL CLASSIFICATION OF NONVERBAL BEHAVIOR

The functional classification proposed here overlaps with previous systems such as those by Argyle (1972) and Ekman and Friesen (1969). Common to these systems and most others are the categories of (1) communication, (2) regulating interaction, and (3) expressing intimacy. Although these three functions are included in the present classification, the addition of other functional categories makes this classification potentially more discriminating. Before each of the categories is described, a general distinction among the functional categories can be proposed. Specifically, it is suggested that the first two categories—providing information and regulating interaction—refer to functions of isolated behaviors, for example, a discrete smile, a touch, a brief glance. In contrast, the last three functions—expressing intimacy, social control, and the service-task function—refer to the goals underlying the behavioral patterns over the course of an exchange. Conceptually, this functional structure may be represented by a 2 (molecular) × 3 (molar) matrix. That is, a determination of the molecular versus molar functions is a relatively independent matter.

Providing Information

In a general sense all nonverbal behavior is potentially informative. That is, everything an actor does can provide information to the decoder. Although such a description does not suggest a very discriminating functional category, a distinction between types of informative behavior is both discriminating and useful. I would like to propose a contrast between informative behavior that is *communicative* and that which is *indicative*. This distinction is based on MacKay's (1972) discussion of communication, one that is similar to Ekman and Friesen's (1969) position. Specifically, MacKay (1972) proposed that communicative behavior is purposive, whereas indicative behavior is not. Because communicative behavior is purposive, an evaluation of the intended consequences would be a part of a communicative sequence. That is, if turning away, avoiding gaze, and "wearing a frown" were part of a routine to discourage interaction, then when the unwanted party left those specific behaviors should cease. Ekman and Friesen (1969) made a similar distinction, but emphasized the requirement of awareness of an explicit intention underlying some nonverbal routine. It should also be noted that the indicative–communicative contrast is analogous to the Schneider *et al.* (1979, Chap. 6) distinction between reactive and purposive cues. That is, the spontaneous, indicative (reactive) cues provide a basis for inferring something about a person's trait, state, or motivation, whereas managed, communicative (purposive) cues may be discounted as not representative of those characteristics. The contrast between communication and indication will be salient in the later discussion of intimacy and social control.

Regulating Interaction

Although all nonverbal behaviors are potentially informative, in many instances various behaviors also serve a more specific function of regulating interaction. Consequently, in those instances such behaviors will be categorized as regulating interaction. In interactions, behaviors such as regulating interpersonal distance, orientation, and posture provide a behavioral framework within which more subtle and variable cues (e.g., gaze, facial expressiveness, head nods) direct the momentary changes in conversations. Argyle and Kendon (1967) have termed the former behaviors "standing features" and the latter behaviors "dynamic features". Considerable research has documented the importance of a variety of nonverbal cues in coordinating listener and speaker roles in conversation (see, Feldstein & Welkowitz, 1978; Rosenfeld, 1978 for reviews of that work).

Expressing Intimacy

Although much of the research on nonverbal exchange has been interpreted from an intimacy perspective, differences in the meaning of intimacy affect a description of this function. Argyle and Dean (1965) seem to use intimacy in a rather general way to refer to broad affiliative needs. In contrast, McAdams (McAdams, 1980; McAdams & Powers, 1981) has proposed that intimacy can be distinguished from affiliation. For example, the affiliative motive might be reflected in attempts to initiate, maintain, or restore positive relationships with others, whereas intimacy focuses on the experience and quality of a relationship. Intimate exchanges would be characterized by openness, receptivity, harmony, concern for the other person, and a surrender of manipulative control over the other person (McAdams & Powers, 1981).

The latter conception of intimacy describes a more focused and intense relationship than that implied by the former conception of intimacy. Common to both seems to be an affective or evaluative reaction toward another person or the relationship. Practically, this would identify liking, love, concern for, or commitment to the other person as a basic component in intimacy. That affective reaction should, in turn, lead to a relatively spontaneous initiation of high nonverbal involvement. In terms of the earlier discussion, a high level of nonverbal involvement would *indicate* high positive intimacy. Thus, to the extent that intimacy (positive or negative) determines an interaction, nonverbal involvement should approximate that intimacy. An example of this intimacy–involvement link is Rubin's (1970) finding that couples scoring higher on a romantic love scale had higher levels of mutual gaze than those scoring lower. The nature of the intimacy function should become clearer as the contrasting social control function is described.

Social Control

When nonverbal involvement is not the simple product of an affective reaction toward another person, a social control function may be operating. Specifically, social control may be described as the managed involvement of one person that is designed to change the behavior of another person. Most analyses of interactive behavior have ignored the managed, social control goals evident in some situations. Exceptions to this trend include Henley's (1973, 1977) analysis of nonverbal correlates of status and power differences and Goffman's (1967, 1972) self-presentation perspective on social behavior.

Social control motives may be stimulated not only by specific goals of influencing others but also by a more general concern about being evaluated. As a given situation is more structured and more important to the individual, nonverbal involvement may be managed to achieve a desirable presentation. Consistent with the earlier distinction, such managed, purposeful behavior would be classified as *communicative*.

Service—Task

This last category identifies a function that is "objectively" irrelevant to interpersonal attributions. That is, the specific level of involvement required in various service and task relationships is independent of the personal relationships between individuals. Heslin (1974) identified service relationships such as physician–patient and barber–customer in which touch is appropriate and necessary to complete the specific service. Various solitary task requirements such as studying or writing may require very low levels of nonverbal involvement. In contrast, cooperating on the assembly of some item or simply sharing materials may necessitate relatively high involvement. Because involvement is constrained by the task or setting norms, dispositional inferences about the other person's behavior should be minimal. Of course, if one party is unaware of those norms, the behavior of the other may be misattributed to some dispositional factor.

THE SEQUENTIAL FUNCTIONAL MODEL

The classification of functions presented in the last section provides the foundation for a sequential functional model of nonverbal exchange (Patterson, 1982). That model attempts to explain and predict the development of different patterns of nonverbal exchange from a functional perspective. This functional analysis of nonverbal behavior stresses that comparable overt patterns of behavior may serve different purposes and lead to different exchange outcomes. That judgment has important consequences for understanding intimacy in interactions. In particular, this functional view emphasizes that the level of imtimacy between individuals in an interaction cannot be uniformly inferred from their behavioral involvement. A general summary description of the functional model should facilitate a more detailed analysis of intimacy in social exchanges. The component elements of the theory and their relationships to one another can be seen in Figure 5.2.

Antecedent Factors

The antecedent factors describe sets of variables that determine the mediating influences on the functions of nonverbal involvement. The

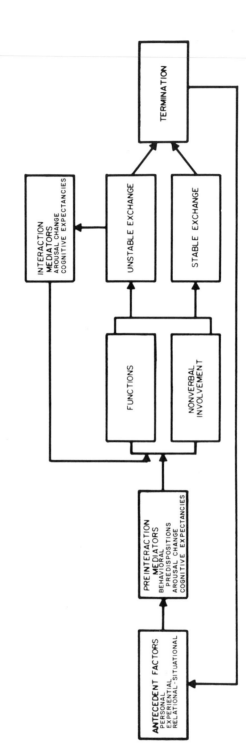

Figure 5.2 A diagram of the sequential functional model. From Heslin, R. & Patterson, M. L., *Nonverbal Behavior and Social Psychology*. New York: Plenum, 1982.

three classes of antecedent factors are *personal, experiential,* and *relational-situational* variables. The more important personal factors include culture, gender differences, and personality. These individual and group difference variables are related to stable tendencies in the way that people initiate nonverbal involvement with others.

The experiential factors describe recent events or events similar to the impending exchange that determine preferred involvement levels. A homeostatic process such as Milgram's (1970) overstimulation model would predict compensatory-like adjustments in involvement preferences over time. For example, following an intense, highly involved interaction, an individual would probably prefer some isolation or at least an interaction with less involvement. A contrasting adaptation-level process (Helson, 1964) applied to interactional involvement would predict that continued deviations from the previous adaptation level (AL) for nonverbal involvement are incorporated into the formation of a new AL. The result is that the same extreme "objective levels" of involvement would, in fact, be experienced as less extreme. Presumably, less of an adjustment would then be required to the repeated extreme levels of involvement.

The relational–situational factors identify the converging influences of relationships and settings or activities. That is, different patterns of involvement are a product not only of the relationship, but also the setting in which the exchange takes place. For example, a superior and a subordinate may interact in a relatively formal manner, with minimal involvement, in the office setting, but be more friendly and highly involved as they go out for a cocktail.

Preinteraction Mediators

The effects of the antecedent factors on nonverbal exchange are produced through the preinteraction mediators. Prior to the start of an interaction these mediators identify the specific mechanisms through which nonverbal involvement is initiated and functional expectancies develop. The first mediator, *behavioral predispositions,* describes the relatively stable pattern of involvement characteristic of each person. That is, the contributing effects of the personal factors are manifested in habitual levels of nonverbal involvement initiated over time. It is assumed that these behavioral predispositions are usually initiated without cognitive awareness. For example, the tendency for females to interact with higher levels of involvement than males is an habitual pattern for each, requiring little or no cognitive representation. Awareness of one's preferred level of involvement may develop only when it is violated in an interaction.

Arousal change is a second mediating factor. There is considerable evidence that extreme or inappropriate levels of nonverbal involvement can produce arousal change (Gale, Lucas, Nissim, & Harpham, 1972; Kleinke & Pohlen, 1971; Nichols & Champness, 1971; Whitcher & Fisher, 1979). Arousal change may be the stimulus that initiates the third mediating factor—*cognitive expectancies*—or the sequence may be just the opposite. That is, arousal change may stimulate some cognitive evaluation or meaning analysis (Mandler, 1975, Chap. 4), or the expectancy may be primary and lead to arousal change. The cognitive activity may be as minimal as some vague good or bad judgment or as detailed as a schema (Markus, 1977) or script (Abelson, 1981).

Interaction Phase

The preinteraction mediators provide structure to the interaction by affecting both the initiation of specific involvement levels and the course of functional expectancies. In general, as an impending interaction is seen as more formal or more highly evaluative, expectancies may develop around a social control function. For example, a job applicant would probably attempt to impress a personnel manager in his or her interview. When such detail is unknown about the impending interaction, habitual involvement levels may determine a person's initial level of involvement and provide a kind of standard against which the other person's behavior may be judged. Thus, a person whose preferred involvement level is low would react more strongly to a close approach and touch than would a person whose preferred involvement level is high. When the discrepancy between the expected and the real level of involvement initiated by the other becomes too great, the exchange may be described as unstable. Instability should lead to additional cognitive-arousal activity that, in turn, should mediate further behavioral adjustments. One form of the cognitive reaction is an assessment of the function of the exchange. This type of functional assessment is more likely as the discrepancy between the expected and real levels of involvement increases.

Accurate functional assessments should facilitate behavioral adjustments that promote stability in an exchange. For example, if two people have contrasting functional attributions about the exchange, the opportunity for one or both misinterpreting each other's behaviors is considerable. Shared accurate functional assessments do not necessarily result in a stable and comfortable exchange. For example, although two adversaries may share accurate, competitive views of their exchange, that would obviously not promote a stable and pleasant interaction. However, predictability would probably increase as each person's functional assessment approximates an accurate judgment of the interaction.

In summary, the preinteraction mediators structure preferred levels of involvement and functional judgments specific to each interaction context. When the functional expectancies are dominant (e.g., I want to impress her, or I'm looking forward to seeing my son again), nonverbal involvement is structured by those expectancies. In contrast, when functional expectancies are not developed, habitual involvement levels may determine the behavioral involvement at any time. In that case, functional assessments may develop only as a result of the developing patterns of nonverbal involvement. Finally, continued behavioral adjustments are likely to be cycled through the arousal and cognitive mediators until stability is achieved. If repeated adjustments do not resolve the instability, the interaction might terminate sooner than normal.

IMPLICATIONS OF THE FUNCTIONAL MODEL

The functional perspective described in this chapter stresses a distinction between the overt behavioral manifestation of involvement and the functional motives underlying that behavioral involvement. In the past, the term *intimacy* has been used to describe both the overt behavioral involvement and the covert motive of liking, loving, or attachment to another person. By substituting the term *nonverbal involvement* for behavioral intimacy, the critical emphasis is placed on intimacy as one function of nonverbal involvement. The clear implication is that, on some occasions, variable behavioral involvement (high or low) serves purposes other than expressing intimacy toward another person. In order to appreciate the variable purposes served by nonverbal involvement, a closer analysis of the social control function is required. Some, and perhaps many, instances of high (and low) nonverbal involvement are the result of relatively deliberate attempts to influence another person, and not the spontaneous result of liking or loving that person. A purposeful and managed behavioral routine, even one of high involvement, does not constitute intimacy, but rather a social control function. In reality it seems likely that specific interactions are not solely the product of one or another function, but the blend of two or more. An affectionate

exchange between a parent and child may be primarily a result of intimacy. However, that exchange may also provide the context for managing one's involvement behavior to manipulate the reactions of the other
person. Thus, intimacy might be primary and social control secondary in
that exchange.

The present view of the intimacy function stresses the consistency
between the underlying motive and its spontaneous behavioral manifestation. That is, it is assumed that behavioral involvement is propor-
tionate to the valence and intensity of the intimacy felt toward another—
within the constraints of situational norms. For example, nonverbal involvement should spontaneously decrease as one interacts in succession
with (1) a loved one, (2) a friend, (3) a stranger, (4) a disliked other. In
contrast, with the social control function there is much less consistency
between the underlying affect and its behavioral representation. For
example, an employee may strongly dislike his or her boss, but decide
that acting warm and friendly is the best way to insure security and a
good raise. Thus, the employee's close approach, gaze, smiling, and
nodding are managed behaviors designed to portray a positive affect
that is not really felt. This contrast in the affect–behavioral links between
the intimacy and social control functions is one that is apparent in some
of the empirical research discussed in the next section.

RESEARCH EVIDENCE

Intimacy

There is a considerable body of research that focuses on the link between intimacy and nonverbal involvement. Practically, in most of these
studies intimacy may be inferred from the degree of relationship between interacting pairs. That is, it might be assumed that the degree of
intimacy usually decreases as one moves from lovers and family members to friends to acquaintances and finally to strangers. I do not attempt
to review all of that research, but discuss a number of examples in this
section. Representative of the link between relationship level and nonverbal involvement are the following: (1) acquaintance, friend, or related
pairs initiated closer speaking distances than did stranger pairs (Heshka
& Nelson, 1972); (2) pairs of opposite-sex friends were more comfortable
at closer distances (30cm–60cm) and less comfortable at farther distances
(165cm–300cm) than were pairs of strangers (Ashton, Shaw, & Worsham, 1980; Baker, & Shaw, 1980); and (3) the level of tactile involve-

ment in airport greetings was positively correlated with the level of intimacy in a relationship (Heslin & Boss, 1980).

Although there seems to be a clear positive link between relationship intimacy and nonverbal involvement, that link is qualified by the sex composition of the dyad. Specifically, in comparably intimate same-sex relationships, males manifest less nonverbal involvement than do females (Greenbaum & Rosenfeld, 1980; Heshka & Nelson, 1972; Heslin & Boss, 1980). For example, in the Greenbaum and Rosenfeld (1980) study, 79% of all male–male encounters used a handshake, whereas only 7% of the female–male and female–female encounters used a handshake. In place of the handshake, the female–male and female–female pairs used a variety of other greetings of higher tactile involvement such as a hug, embrace, or kiss.

The patterns of nonverbal involvement should be particularly distinct for individuals involved in romantic relationships. The description common in poetry, songs, and literature of extended periods of mutual gaze between lovers has been observed under controlled conditions in the laboratory (Goldstein, Kilroy, & Van de Voort, 1976; Rubin, 1970). Conversely, standardized high levels of mutual gaze within couples has produced attributions of both stronger mutual liking (Kleinke, Meeker, & LaFong, 1974) and higher levels of sexual involvement (Thayer & Schiff, 1977).

Tactile involvement has received considerable attention in the research on romantic relationships. The classic study in this area was Jourard's (1966) investigation of the frequency and location of touch as a function of relationship. Not surprisingly, Jourard found that his college-age subjects reported higher levels of touch from opposite-sex friends than from parents and same-sex friends. That difference was maximized in body areas that could have sexual meaning, such as the hips, thighs, and chest. A replication of that study 10 years later showed noticeably higher levels of apparently sexual touch in opposite-sex pairs (Rosenfeld, Kartus, & Ray, 1976). Such an increase might reflect a real change in the frequency of such touch, or to some degree simply a change in the norms about reporting such behavior.

Two questionnaire studies specifically examined the meaning of touch as a function of its modality (pat, squeeze, stroke, and accidental brush) and location (M. Nguyen, Heslin, & T. Nguyen, 1976; T. Nguyen, Heslin, & M. Nguyen, 1975). In general, the results showed considerable differences in the interpretation of sexual touches as a function of marital status and sex of respondent. In the first study, unmarried men perceived sexual touching (i.e., receiving sexual touching) positively, whereas unmarried women perceived sexual touching negatively (T.

Nguyen *et al.*, 1975). In the second study, both married and unmarried subjects were surveyed. In general, married men perceived sexual touching more negatively, whereas married women perceived it more positively. That is, the pattern evident in the first was apparently reversed for married men and women in the second study.

The various results cited in this section seem generally to be characteristic of an intimacy function. That is, differential intimacy manifested in liking, loving, or commitment to another person seems to be reflected in differential nonverbal involvement toward that person. The tentative judgment that the patterns described here reflect an intimacy function receives more critical attention in the Discussion Section, after the research on the social control function is discussed.

Social Control

Results supportive of the proposed social control function can be found in research dealing with the effects of interpersonal expectancies on interaction patterns. If the influence of expectancies is analyzed from a "self-fulfilling prophecy" (Merton, 1957, Rosenthal, 1966) or a "behavioral confirmation" perspective, the predicted behavioral adjustments would be very clear. In fact, such adjustments should be consistent with an intimacy function. Specifically, if one has a negative expectancy about another person, the first person's behavior should be relatively negative or noninvolving. The opposing pattern of increased involvement should result from a positive expectancy. Presumably, the expectancy determines the initial positive or negative behavior toward the target person. That behavior, in turn, elicits a behavior pattern (positive or negative) from the target that confirms the validity of the expectancy and promotes continued behavior consistent with the expectancy. It should be noted that this explanation is also consistent with the predictions of the intimacy–arousal model. Specifically, if the involvement level initiated by the target person is sufficient to produce arousal, that arousal should be labeled in accordance with the expectancies and then produce the appropriate behavioral adjustments.

However, there appear to be important exceptions to such a pattern—exceptions in various studies that suggest the operation of a social control function. The first study was specifically designed to test the predictions of the intimacy–arousal model in the context of a confederate– subject interaction. In the first stage of the experiment, positive or negative feedback was given to the subject by the confederate. The effect of that feedback was examined both in a baseline interaction and in later interaction in which the confederate's nonverbal involvement was manipulated (Coutts, Schneider, & Montgomery, 1980).

Although increased involvement by the confederate did produce the hypothesized increase in arousal (a heartrate measure), the behavioral adjustment patterns did not clearly support the predictions of the intimacy–arousal model. The subjects who received positive feedback and increased involvement from the confederate made no significant adjustments in their nonverbal involvement. In addition, the subjects who received negative feedback and increased involvement from the confederate *reciprocated* the confederate's increased involvement. That pattern of reciprocation was directly opposite the predicted pattern of compensation derived from the intimacy–arousal model. One suggestion proposed by Coutts *et al.* (1980) for this latter effect was that the increased involvement that followed negative feedback may have been perceived as a *relative* increase in liking. Such a perception of the confederate's increased involvement would constitute a positive label for the confederate's increased involvement and thereby lead to the subject's reciprocation of involvement. This explanation provides an interpretation that is, in fact, consistent with the intimacy–arousal model. Thus, this explanation suggests a liking or intimacy-based function mediating the subject's nonverbal adjustments.

However, one correlational result is inconsistent with this interpretation. Specifically, for subjects in the negative feedback–increased involvement condition, their level of increased involvement was not generally related to increased liking of the confederate. Because the degree of liking did not predict the level of reciprocated involvement, this first interpretation can be questioned. A second interpretation offered by Coutts *et al.* (1980) may be more defensible. This explanation for the subject's reciprocation of the confederate's involvement suggests a motive that clearly seems to reflect a social control function. Specifically, subjects may have viewed the confederate's increased involvement (after the negative feedback) as a return to a more appropriate level of involvement. To encourage the confederate to maintain that appropriate level of involvement, the subjects may have *exaggerated* their own involvement (Coutts *et al.*, 1980). That is, the subjects may have managed their involvement in order to sustain the new and appropriate level of involvement initiated by the confederate. Finally, it should be noted that this social control explanation is consistent with the lack of correlation between the subject's rated liking of the confederate and her subsequent adjustment. That is, if the purpose of the subject's adjustment is to sustain an appropriate level of confederate involvement, then subject's liking of the confederate may be irrelevant.

This lack of relationship between the underlying affect and the behavioral adjustment is characteristic of the operation of a social control function. It can also be seen in the results of some of our own recent research. Two experiments specifically examined the effects of expectancies on later patterns of nonverbal exchange (Ickes *et al.*, 1982). Although the two experiments were substantially different in many aspects of procedure and methodology, very similar effects were found. In Experiment I, subjects were given either friendly, unfriendly, or no expectancy comments prior to meeting another subject. A variety of nonverbal measures were scored from unobtrusive videotape records of the interaction.

The results showed that friendly *and* unfriendly expectancy subjects initiated greater nonverbal involvement than did the no-expectancy subjects. An especially critical result was the presence of increased smiling in the unfriendly condition relative to both the friendly and no-expectancy conditions. Although the overt behavioral patterns of the friendly and unfriendly conditions were otherwise similar, the patterns of rated impressions of the partners were distinctly opposite. Partners were rated more positively in the friendly than in the unfriendly conditions. Furthermore, there was a greater level of distrust of the partner's seemingly friendly behavior in the unfriendly conditions. In Experiment 2, contrasting positive versus negative expectancies were manipulated in terms of the other's similarity or dissimilarity on several personality measures. The contrast between the effects of the similar and dissimilar conditions exactly paralleled the results of Experiment 1. Specifically, subjects in the dissimilar condition smiled more and, at the same time, judged their partners more negatively than did the subjects in the similar condition. There were other nonsignificant trends for greater involvement in the dissimilar than in the similar condition on the measures of gaze, talking duration, and body orientation. Finally, subjects in the dissimilar condition experienced greater arousal (as measured by electrodermal responses) than those in the similar condition immediately after hearing the expectancy manipulation. Such increased arousal is consistent with the functional model's prediction of greater arousal change in anticipating an unusual interaction.

In both experiments of the Ickes *et al.* (1982) study, the results showed increased involvement, especially smiling, in response to unfriendly or negative expectancies. However, rated attraction to the partner was very low even though the high involvement seemed to indicate the opposite. That pattern in the negative expectancy conditions clearly suggested the operation of a social control function. In contrast, the pattern of relatively high involvement, supplemented by high rated attractiveness of the partner in the positive expectancy condition, was consistent with an intimacy-based function.

In another study, Bond (1972) manipulated the "warm" versus "cold" expectancies given to a naive subject about a confederate posing as another subject. Although specific behavioral measures were not recorded, naive judges completed overall ratings of behavioral warmth of the subject and confederate. The results indicated that the cold expectancy subjects acted *more warmly* with their partner than the warm expectancy subjects did with their partner. In addition, the cold expectancy subjects actually induced the naive confederate to act more warmly in return. Apparently, in line with the Coutts *et al.* (1980) and Ickes *et al.* (1982) results, the cold expectancy subjects initiated a contrasting warm behavioral strategy in an attempt to avert or minimize the anticipated difficulty in interacting with their partners.

SOCIAL CONTROL AND SELF-DISCLOSURE

In the latter section on empirical evidence, the results from different studies showed support for the social control management of nonverbal involvement. Up to this point, I have avoided the discussion of verbal "intimacy" or involvement as manifested in the substantial literature on self-disclosure. However, now that social control has been discussed in the research on nonverbal involvement, it is time to examine the potential applicability of social control in understanding those patterns of self-disclosure.

First, both Firestone (1977) and Cappella (1981), in reviews of verbal and nonverbal exchange, stress the contrasting exchange patterns present between verbal and nonverbal behavior. Specifically, compensatory adjustment is characteristic of reactions to increased *nonverbal* involvement, whereas reciprocal adjustment is characteristic of reactions to increased *verbal* involvement (self-disclosure). If both the verbal and nonverbal behaviors simply reflect different components of total involvement with another person, then why is there such an extreme contrast present in their typical adjustment patterns?

The answer may lie in both the relative ease of managing verbal versus nonverbal behavior and the functional utility of doing so. For example, Cappella (1981) suggests that the pressure for topic continuation may be important in verbal disclosure reciprocity. That is, a comfortable exchange probably requires related responses from the interactants. Although some of that verbal reciprocity or matching may occur spontaneously, much of it may be the product of a managed, social control function designed to influence the other person and/or make the interaction more comfortable. There seems little doubt from the discussion in the last section that a subtle behavior like smiling can be used to influence the behavior of others in an interaction. Furthermore, independent evidence from research on deception suggests that increased smiling may also be a component of a deceptive presentation (Ekman & Friesen, 1974; Mehrabian, 1971). If we are able to manage subtle facial displays effectively, it seems very likely that our verbal behavior may be similarly managed. In fact, we have all experienced a variety of situations in which our verbal behavior is managed to conform either to the content of a partner's or to our perception of the partner's expectancies. Consequently, much of the reciprocation found in self-disclosure research may reflect such a relatively deliberate strategy of matching the partner's comments. Thus, a social control strategy may be designed specifically to make the interaction more pleasant, impress the other person, or facilitate a more positive self-image. To the extent that any one or more of these motives is present, the reciprocation of verbal involvement is not representative of a simple intimacy function.

DISCUSSION

General Issues

This chapter has emphasized a functional approach to the analysis of nonverbal involvement in social interactions. That approach has led first to the identification of several different functions of nonverbal behavior and then to the integration of those functions into a broad sequential model of nonverbal exchange. The assumption that intimacy necessarily mediates patterns of nonverbal adjustments—an assumption characteristic of earlier theories (Argyle & Dean, 1965; Patterson, 1976)—was challenged in the context of this functional perspective. In particular, it was proposed that a social control function, manifested in trying either to influence others or create a good impression, may frequently mediate one's nonverbal involvement. Research on the effects of expectancies on nonverbal involvement provides evidence for the operation of the social control function. Specifically, when subjects anticipate meeting unfriendly or dissimilar others, their nonverbal involvement may increase, rather than decrease, as an intimacy function would predict (Bond, 1972;

Coutts *et al.*, 1980; Ickes *et al.*, 1982). Furthermore, that increased involvement may occur in the context of a continued negative evaluation of the other person (Ickes *et al.*, in press). Smiling may be the most important component in this behavioral strategy that is apparently designed to make their interaction more comfortable. Finally, the common pattern of reciprocation of *verbal* involvement or self-disclosure may also reflect a social control function. That is, in order to impress the partner, or simply to make the interaction more comfortable, a respondent may match or reciprocate the partner's level of self-disclosure.

The distinction proposed here between the functions of intimacy and social control provides a starting point for understanding the different motives that affect nonverbal involvement. However, it is also important to try to predict the circumstances that are likely to instigate one or the other function. In general it is expected that more structured and evaluative interactions (e.g., an employment interview, dinner at the boss's house) are more likely to result in the social control management of nonverbal involvement. That is, nonverbal involvement will be guided in the service of a social control function. As interactions are more casual and less evaluative, nonverbal involvement is more likely to be a product of (1) one's own behavioral predispositions for involvement (i.e., acting as a preinteraction mediator) and (2) the affective reaction toward the other person (intimacy). Ickes *et al.* (in press) speculate about the role of specific expectancies in generating managed nonverbal involvement. They suggest that if the actor views other person's anticipated behavior as undesirable, but believes that it is modifiable, then a behavioral strategy that contrasts with the other person's anticipated behavior may be initiated. That proposal is consistent with the results of the Ickes *et al.* and Bond (1972) studies. Although the complementary prediction was not tested in any of these studies, it is worth noting. That is, if the other person's anticipated behavior is undesirable, but judged *not* modifiable, then a contrasting pattern of involvement would not be initiated. In effect there is no payoff possible in trying to manage one's behavior, so no attempt would be made. In that case, the spontaneous avoidance of an unfriendly person (whose behavior is judged as not modifiable) would reflect a negative intimacy function.

Functional Patterns in Close Relationships

The contrast between the intimacy and social control motives has considerable importance for understanding patterns of nonverbal exchange in close relationships. That contrast might be characterized in terms of two dimensions—self- versus other-concern and spontaneous versus managed behavior. Generally, the intimacy motive is reflected in concern about the other as manifested in a relatively spontaneous behavioral pattern. For example, because I like (or dislike) the other person, I would spontaneously stand closer to (farther from) her, smile more (less), and gaze at her more (less). With respect to positive intimacy (liking or love), McAdams and Powers (1981) suggest that the surrender of manipulative control over the other is a critical characteristic. In contrast, the social control motive is more likely to be focused on self-concerns leading to a managed and often manipulative behavioral routine. For example, my job will probably be more secure, and perhaps I will even be promoted, if I try to act friendly toward the boss—even though I dislike the old turkey.

There are obvious exceptions to the contrasts just described. Some unselfish other-focused concerns may lead to distinctly managed strategies for nonverbal involvement. For example, I may manage a high level of involvement toward a distressed friend (even though I don't feel like doing it) because he needs a behavioral expression of support. If the focus were solely on the spontaneous–managed dimension, such high involvement might be described as reflecting a social control motive. If the emphasis were on the underlying concern for the other person that generated the managed levels of high involvement, then that involvement might be described as reflecting the intimacy motive. Practically, the latter classification may reflect the sense of the intimacy motive better than the former classification.

The discussion of these motives has stressed the encoder's or actor's perspective up to this point. However, it is clear that the decoder or recipient's perception of the underlying motive is a major determinant of the continued pattern of exchange. Such a suggestion is one that is at the foundation of attribution theory and is specifically emphasized in the link between nonverbal behavior and person perception (Schneider *et al.*, 1979). The functional perception of another person's behavior may be especially important in initial relationships because of primacy effects and the generation of specific expectancies, but such functional judgments are also very important in close, established relationships. Although the earlier review of intimacy and nonverbal involvement practically operationalized high intimacy in terms of close relationships, specific encounters in close relationships may be guided by various social control motives. For example, the traditional strategy of "buttering-up the old man" may be initiated by the wife or children to obtain some special favor.[1] The close approach, hug, and complimentary words may precede an expensive or time-consuming request. More subtle, yet similar, strategies are used in a variety of encounters among family members, lovers, and friends. I suspect that even very transparent routines are usually viewed positively, or at least benignly, by the recipient as long as the existing relationship is a good one. That does not mean, however, that the strategy would necessarily succeed.

If patterns of high involvement are only initiated when it appears that the actor wants something, the recipient's perception of a social control motive may produce reactance. A good example of such a situation might be the functional attributions surrounding the initiation of a sexual encounter. If the person who initiates a sexual encounter is perceived by the partner as merely seeking pleasure, releasing tension, or exerting control, then there may be greater concern about that encounter. Such a concern might be expressed in terms of whether the partner really loves me (intimacy) or is merely "using me" (social control). Generally, it might be predicted that consistently perceiving the partner's motives in social control terms would lead to greater ambivalence about future sexual encounters and perhaps even about the partner.

In conclusion, it seems fair to say that intimacy and social control motives are both common in most close relationships. Intimacy might be reflected in the habitual manner that we initiate involvement toward friends and loved ones. However, because we frequently relate to those friends and loved ones in many circumstances that can stimulate positive evaluative reactions, intimacy may also be situationally activated. A variety of social control motives may also determine involvement patterns in close relationships. High involvement with another usually implies a high degree of liking or love of that person, and we are more likely to be influenced when that liking or love is manifested. Consequently, a social control strategy or managing nonverbal involvement may be common across relationship levels. Understanding the relationship between intimacy and social control motives, and determining their effect on nonverbal exchange, will be an important pursuit in future research.

---

[1]A comparable strategy may be directed at the wife/mother in more nontraditional families.

REFERENCES

Abelson, R. P. (1981). Psychological status of the script concept. *American Psychologist, 36,* 715–729.

Argyle, M. (1972). Non-verbal communication in human social interaction. In R. A. Hinde (Ed.), *Non-verbal communication.* Cambridge: Cambridge University Press.

Argyle, M., & Dean, J. (1965). Eye-contact, distance and affiliation. *Sociometry, 28,* 289–304.

Argyle, M., & Kendon, A. (1967). The experimental analysis of social performance. In L. Berkowitz (Ed.), *Advances in experimental social psychology.* New York: Academic Press.

Ashton, N. L., Shaw, M. E., & Worsham, A. N. (1980). Affective reactions to interpersonal distances by friends and strangers. *Bulletin of the Psychonomic Society, 15,* 306–308.

Baker, E., & Shaw, M. E. (1980). Reactions to interperson distance and topic intimacy: A comparison of strangers and friends. *Journal of Nonverbal Behavior, 5,* 80–91.

Bond, M. H. (1972). Effect of an impression set on subsequent behavior. *Journal of Personality and Social Psychology, 24,* 301–305.

Breed, G. (1972). The effect of intimacy: Reciprocity or retreat? *British Journal of Social and Clinical Psychology, 11,* 135–142.

Buck, R. (1980). Nonverbal behavior and the theory of emotion: The facial feedback hypothesis. *Journal of Personality and Social Psychology, 38,* 811–824.

Cappella, J. N. (1981). Mutual influence in expressive behavior: Adult–adult and infant–adult dyadic interaction. *Psychological Bulletin, 89,* 101–132.

Chapman, A. J. (1975). Eye contact, physical proximity and laughter: A reexamination of the equilibrium model of social intimacy. *Social Behavior and Personality, 3,* 143–155.

Coutts, L. M., Schneider, F. W., & Montgomery, S. (1980). An investigation of the arousal model of interpersonal intimacy. *Journal of Experimental Social Psychology, 16,* 545–561.

Ekman, P. (1972). Universals and cultural differences in facial expressions of emotion. In J. Cole (Ed.), *Nebraska symposium on motivation, 1971.* Lincoln: University of Nebraska Press.

Ekman, P., & Friesen, W. V. (1969). The repertoire of nonverbal behavior: Categories, origins, usage and codings. *Semiotica, 1,* 49–97.

Ekman, P., & Friesen, W. V. (1974). Detecting deception from the body or face. *Journal of Personality and Social Psychology, 29,* 288–298.

Ekman, P., & Oster, H. (1979). Facial expressions of emotion. *Annual Review of Psychology, 30,* 527–554.

Feldstein, S., & Welkowitz, J. (1978). A chronography of conversation: In defense of an objective approach. In A. W. Siegman & S. Feldstein (Eds.), *Nonverbal behavior and communication.* Hillsdale, NJ: Erlbaum.

Firestone, I. J. (1977). Reconciling verbal and nonverbal models of dyadic communication. *Environmental Psychology and Nonverbal Behavior, 2,* 30–44.

Foot, H. C., Chapman, A. J., & Smith, J. R. (1977). Friendship and social responsiveness in boys and girls. *Journal of Personality and Social Psychology, 35,* 401–411.

Foot, H. C., Smith, J. R., & Chapman, A. J. (1977). Individual differences in children's responsiveness in humour situations. In A. J. Chapman & H. C. Foot (Eds.), *It's a funny thing, humour.* London: Pergamon.

Gale, A., Lucas, B., Nissim, R., & Harpham, B. (1972). Some EEG correlates of face-to-face contact. *British Journal of Social and Clinical Psychology, 11,* 326–332.

Goffman, E. (1967). *Interaction ritual.* Garden City, NY: Anchor.

Goffman, E. (1972). *Relations in public.* New York: Harper Colophon.

Goldstein, M., Kilroy, M., & Van de Voort, D. (1976). Gaze as a function of conversation and degree of love. *Journal of Psychology, 92,* 227–234.

Greenbaum, P. E., & Rosenfeld, H. M. (1980). Varieties of touching in greetings: Sequential structure and sex-related differences. *Journal of Nonverbal Behavior, 5,* 13–25.

Helson, H. (1964). *Adaptation-level theory.* New York: Harper & Row.

Henley, N. M. (1973). Status and sex: Some touching observations. *Bulletin of the Psychonomic Society, 2,* 91–93.

Henley, N. M. (1977). *Body politics: Power, sex, and nonverbal communication.* Englewood Cliffs, NJ: Prentice-Hall.

Heshka, S., & Nelson, Y. (1972). Interpersonal speaking distance as a function of age, sex, relationship. *Sociometry, 35,* 491–498.

Heslin, R. (1974). *Steps toward a taxonomy of touching.* Paper presented at the Annual Meeting of the Midwestern Psychological Association, Chicago.

Heslin, R., & Boss, D. (1980). Nonverbal intimacy in airport arrival and departure. *Personality and Social Psychology Bulletin, 6,* 248–252.

Ickes, W., Patterson, M. L., & Rajecki, D. W., & Tanford, S. (1982). Behavioral and cognitive consequences of reciprocal versus compensatory responses to pre-interaction expectancies. *Social Cognition, 1,* 160–190.

James, W. (1950). *The principles of psychology.* New York: Dover Publications. (Original work published 1890).

Jourard, S. M. (1966). An exploratory study of body-accessibility. *British Journal of Social and Clinical Psychology, 5,* 221–231.

Jourard, S. M., & Friedman, R. (1970). Experimenter–subject "distance" and self-disclosure. *Journal of Personality and Social Psychology, 15,* 278–282.

Kleinke, C. L., Meeker, F. B., & LaFong, C. (1974). Effects of gaze, touch, and use of name on evaluation of "engaged" couples. *Journal of Research in Personality, 7,* 368–373.

Kleinke, C. L., & Pohlen, P. D. (1971). Affective and emotional responses as a function of other person's gaze and cooperativeness in a two-person game. *Journal of Personality and Social Psychology, 17,* 308–313.

Kraut, R. E. (1978). Verbal and nonverbal cues in the perception of lying. *Journal of Personality and Social Psychology, 36,* 380–391.

McAdams, D. P. (1980). A thematic coding system for the intimacy motive. *Journal of Research in Personality, 14,* 413–432.

McAdams, D. P., & Powers, J. (1981). Themes of intimacy in behavior and thought. *Journal of Personality and Social Psychology, 40,* 573–587.

McBride, G., King, M., & James, J. W. (1965). Social proximity effects of galvanic skin responses in adult humans. *Journal of Psychology, 61,* 153–157.

MacKay, D. M. (1972). Formal analysis of communicative processes. In R. A. Hinde (Ed.), *Non-verbal communication.* Cambridge, England: University Press.

Mandler, G. (1975). *Mind and emotion.* New York: Wiley.

Markus, H. (1977). Self-schemata and processing information about the self. *Journal of Personality and Social Psychology, 35,* 63–78.

Mehrabian, A. (1969). Some referents and measures of nonverbal behavior. *Behavior Research Methods and Instrumentation, 1,* 203–207.

Mehrabian, A. (1970). A semantic space for nonverbal behavior. *Journal of Consulting and Clinical Psychology, 35,* 248–257.

Mehrabian, A. (1971). Nonverbal betrayal of feeling. *Journal of Experimental Research in Personality, 5,* 64–73.

Mehrabian, A., & Ksionzky, S. (1972). Categories of social behavior. *Comparative Group Studies, 3,* 425–436.

Merton, R. K. (1957). *Social theory and social structure.* Glencoe, IL: Free Press.

Milgram, S. (1970). The experience of living in cities. *Science, 167,* 1461–1468.

Nguyen, M. L., Heslin, R., & Nguyen, T. (1976). The meaning of touch: Sex and marital status differences. *Representative Research in Social Psychology, 7,* 13–18.

Nguyen, T., Heslin, R., & Nguyen, M. L. (1975). The meanings of touch: Sex differences. *Journal of Communication, 25,* 92–103.

Nichols, K. A., & Champness, B. G. (1971). Eye gaze and the GSR. *Journal of Experimental Social Psychology, 7,* 623–626.

Patterson, M. L. (1973). Compensation in nonverbal immediacy behaviors: A review. *Sociometry, 36,* 237–252.

Patterson, M. L. (1976). An arousal model of interpersonal intimacy. *Psychological Review, 83,* 235–245.

Patterson, M. L. (1982). A sequential functional model of nonverbal exchange. *Psychological Review, 89,* 231–249.

Patterson, M. L., Jordan, A., Hogan, M. B., & Frerker, D. (1981). Effects of nonverbal intimacy on arousal and behavioral adjustment. *Journal of Nonverbal Behavior, 5,* 184–198.

Patterson, M. L., Roth, C. P., & Schenk, C. (1979). Seating arrangement, activity, and sex differences in small group crowding. *Personality and Social Psychology Bulletin, 5,* 100–103.

Rosenfeld, H. M. (1978). Conversational control functions of nonverbal behavior. In A. W. Siegman & S. Feldstein (Eds.), *Nonverbal behavior and communication.* Hillsdale, NJ: Erlbaum.

Rosenfeld, L. B., Kartus, S., & Ray, C. (1976). Body accessibility revisited. *Journal of Communication, 26,* 27–30.

Rosenthal, R. (1966). *Experimenter effects in behavioral research.* New York: Appleton-Century-Crofts.

Rosenthal, R. (Ed.) (1979). *Skill in nonverbal communication: Individual differences.* Cambridge, MA: Oelgeschlager, Gunn, & Hain.

Rubin, Z. (1970). Measurement of romantic love. *Journal of Personality and Social Psychology, 16,* 265–273.

Schachter, S., & Singer, J. E. (1962). Cognitive, social and physiological determinants of emotional state. *Psychological Review, 69,* 379–329.

Schneider, D. J., Hastorf, A. H., & Ellsworth, P. C. (1979). *Person perception* (2nd ed.). Reading, MA: Addison-Wesley.

Storms, M. D., & Thomas, G. C. (1977). Reactions to physical closeness. *Journal of Personality and Social Psychology, 35,* 412–418.

Thayer, S., & Schiff, W. (1977). Gazing patterns and attribution of sexual involvement. *Journal of Social Psychology, 101,* 235–246.

Whitcher, S. J., & Fisher, J. D. (1979). Multidimensional reaction to therapeutic touch in a hospital setting. *Journal of Personality and Social Psychology, 37,* 87–96.

CHAPTER 6

Implications of Social Psychological Concepts for a Theory of Loneliness*

STEPHEN T. MARGULIS

VALERIAN J. DERLEGA

BARBARA A. WINSTEAD

The chapters in this book highlight the issue of the development and maintenance of intimate relationships. In this chapter we have chosen to study individuals who do not have or who have lost particular friends or intimates and are lonely. We believe that understanding loneliness requires paying explicit attention to the real and imagined relationships that are not available to the person. Thus, we need to understand how and why relationships are established and with what kinds of individuals (i.e., social partners). This book represents a unique opportunity to study loneliness in the context of theories and research on social relationships as Weiss (1982) has encouraged us to do: "Insofar as loneliness is only an alarm signaling a system in want, we have first to understand the system" (p. 78).

STUDYING LONELINESS

If people are inherently social, if they desire social relationships, why do surveys indicate that the experience of loneliness, the embodiment of

*The helpful comments of Dan Perlman and George Levinger on an earlier draft of this chapter are gratefully acknowledged. The authors are also indebted to Kathy Ormsbee for her skill and patience in typing the manuscript.

133

a void in a social relationship, is widespread in North America (Peplau & Perlman, 1982a)? One nationwide survey asked: "During the past few weeks, did you feel very lonely or remote from other people?" (Brad-burn, 1969). Twenty-six percent of the people answered "yes." More than half of a sample of widowed men in a telephone survey reported severe feelings of loneliness in the week before they received the call. A smaller, though still substantial, proportion of widowed women, 29%, also reported that they felt lonely and remote from other people during the same time period (Maisel, 1969). Widowers are less likely than wid-ows to have (or find) meaningful alternative relationships after the spouse's death. If the death of a spouse causes social isolation, as it tends to do for elderly widowers, it places a special burden on them. It is even possible that widowers' susceptibility to social isolation and lone-liness contributes to their high suicide rate (Bock & Webber, 1972). In addition, a study of first-year university students at the University of California, Los Angeles, (UCLA) found that 75% of the students sur-veyed had experienced loneliness occasionally since they had arrived on campus. Over 40% indicated they had experienced moderate to severe levels of loneliness (Cutrona, 1982).

We argue that what ties sociality to loneliness is the realization that close relationships, though desired and desirable, are founded on inter-dependency. The loss of such a relationship can leave an individual without important social resources and can create loneliness.

Research on loneliness has expanded rapidly in the last 20 years (see Peplau & Perlman, 1982a, for a thorough review of research and theory). Most research in this area has been stimulated by the publication of Robert Weiss's important book, *Loneliness: The Experience of Emotional and Social Isolation,* and the development of reliable and easily administered questionnaires to measure individual differences in loneliness, particu-larly the UCLA Loneliness Scale (Russell, 1982; Russell, Peplau, & Fer-guson, 1978) and the NYU (New York University) Loneliness Scale (Rubenstein & Shaver, 1980, 1982). As empirical investigations prolifer-ate, conceptual analyses of loneliness are needed in order to organize findings and to understand and predict when this phenomenon occurs (Perlman & Peplau, 1982).

THEORETICAL STATEMENTS ABOUT LONELINESS: A WORD OF CAUTION

The adequacy of a theory of loneliness depends on the adequacy of its theoretical constructs and of its statement of how these constructs fit together. In an earlier analysis of loneliness, Derlega and Margulis (1982) describe three major stages in concept development:

> There are distinct, but, in practice, overlapping stages in concept development (Margulis, 1977). The first stage justifies interest in a concept such as loneliness by presenting studies, observations, and cases that demonstrate the importance and viability of a behavioral concept of loneliness. This stage is now more or less complete. It includes the work of Bell (1956), Abrahams (1972), and Cottle (1974). The second stage accepts the importance of the concept and attempts to explore it further. This stage includes initial attempts at explication (Peplau & Caldwell, 1978; Weiss, 1973) and attempts to demonstrate similarities and differences between loneliness and cognate concepts (Russell, 1982; Zipris, 1979). This stage characterizes most of the current work on loneliness, both conceptual and research. In the third stage, explication becomes systematic, and the whys and hows of loneliness are directly and fully addressed. This stage will build on Stage 2 analyses, and the results will be theories: systematically related sets of statements, some of whose logical implications are empirically testable. That is, in Stage 3, definitions of loneliness will be theoretical; loneliness will be defined in terms of the laws and lawlike statements in which it occurs. This set of interlocking statements will be a theory of loneliness. (Cronbach & Meehl, 1956)

Speculation on loneliness appears to be firmly in Stage 2. It is not yet clear, for example, that loneliness researchers are studying the same construct. Evidence for convergent and discriminant validity of existing loneliness scales (the UCLA and NYU scales) is weak or lacking (Rubenstein & Shaver, 1982; Russell, 1982), and we are not yet at the point where the construct "loneliness" is clearly elucidated by its connections to other constructs within a nomological network. Since the meaning of a construct derives from its position in such a network, the definition of loneliness is incomplete.

We believe that the experience of loneliness derives from a sense of being cut off from meaningful relationships. Inevitably, then, loneliness depends on the relationships, real or imagined, that lonely persons miss; and, in order to understand loneliness, we must study these relationships whose absence is a necessary condition for loneliness to occur.

Our theoretical analysis of loneliness has the following context:

1. Our aim is to explore established social-psychological concepts and their applicability to loneliness in order to make sense of and offer *explanations* for known observations and, ultimately, to develop testable hypotheses about the phenomenon of loneliness.

2. We do not intend a complete account of loneliness. The investigation is exploratory. We recognize the role of dispositional, cultural, and sociological factors, most of which we ignore. This is not because these factors are unimportant; rather, we are looking where the light is brightest for us. We hope that, unlike the drunk who lost his watch in a dark alley but searches for it under a street lamp because "the light is better

there," we are looking for the lost watch in the right place. But we will never know until we have looked and tested our search.

3. We are going to draw on two definitions of loneliness: the "unsatisfactory relationship" view (e.g., Cutrona, 1982; Perlman & Peplau, 1981) and the "unavailability of some needed relationship" view (e.g., Weiss, 1973). The first definition holds that loneliness is a negative response to a discrepancy between a desired and achieved social relationship. The second definition holds that loneliness is having a social need that no current relationship can fulfill.

4. We are going to apply our analysis to a limited number of instances that have been labeled as loneliness. They have been selected because they share an experiential core the authors associate with loneliness.

ON SOCIAL RELATIONSHIPS

There are at least two models used by loneliness researchers and theorists to explain how antecedent social relationships are related to loneliness (see Figure 6.1). Model 1 treats social relationships and loneliness as the result of personal and social factors. Model 2 posits a direct relationship between characteristics of the antecedent social relationship and of the consequent loneliness, when that relationship is lost. Model 2 recognizes that both social relationships and loneliness can be affected by third variables, including personal factors (such as self-esteem) and social factors (such as the availability of and access to other social part-

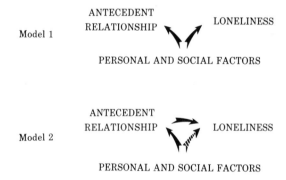

Figure 6.1 Two models used by loneliness researchers to explain how antecedent social relationships are related to loneliness.

ners). Whereas Model 1 identifies the origins of loneliness as personal and social factors, Model 2 treats antecedent social relationships and their vicissitudes as the origins. Model 1 is implicitly accepted by many loneliness researchers. We accept Model 2 and offer it as a workable alternative.

If antecedent relationships are important to understanding loneliness, this calls for an examination of social relationships in terms relevant to loneliness. Our review of the literature on relationship development left us dissatisfied with the classifications of and explanations of relationship development. Thus, to advance our argument, we have settled on (1) a simple scheme for evaluating the quality of relationships and (2) an often-used approach to relationship development, the instrumentalist position.

Mundane and Profound Relationships   Relationships vary in quality from mundane to profound. Mundane relationships involve stereo-typed behavior, role playing, and absence of deep attachment. Profound relationships are deeply moving, caring, loving, and respectful, such as relationships between certain close friends, spouses, and deeply religious people and God.[1] Many relationships cannot be classified as simply mundane or profound. Perhaps our labels represent the ends of a continuum or perhaps there are distinct subcategories of each that would adequately describe most relationships. We reserve judgment on the continuum versus subcategories issue. Evaluating relationships using the mundane–profound distinction requires information about the psychological and emotional quality of a relationship, not just its behavioral manifestations (cf., Chelune, Robison, & Kommor, Chapter 2 of this volume). The relationship between spouses who interact frequently could be closer to mundane than profound if they are playing the parts of spouses, do not share private emotions with one another, and are not deeply attached. On the other hand, persons who rarely see one another can have a profound relationship (e.g., the couple in the popular play–film *Same Time, Next Year*). We argue that the distinction between mundane and profound relationships has implications for an analysis of loneliness. The loss of a profound relationship may be devastating, and the relationship may be difficult to replace; whereas the loss of a mundane relationship may not be particularly upsetting and have

---

[1]This analysis focuses specifically on profound and mundane *relationships*. We recognize that specific experiences, out of which relationships develop, also can be profound or mundane. Moreover, profound *experiences* can be part of mundane relationships (see Derlega & Chaikin, 1977, pp. 108–109). Nevertheless, this chapter focuses on the relationship and not on specific experiences.

little lasting impact. Thus, loneliness is a consequence of an experience of loss and its psychological effects depend on the quality of the lost relationship.

Relationships and Dependency   Consistent with the social exchange approach, we believe that relationships can be described as a series of exchanges that satisfy or frustrate the needs of participants.[2] Moreover, we believe that profound relationships satisfy needs that are inherent rather than learned (cf., Peplau & Perlman, 1982b, pp. 3–5) or, alternatively—here we borrow from Bem's (1970) description of personal beliefs that are central to all others—that such attachments satisfy "zero-order" social needs that are the bedrock of all other social needs.

Profound relationships have several features that are worth noting. Davis (1973), for example, describes intimate relationships among adults in terms of the connectedness of the pair, the establishment of "a common being in order to create a personal relationship of the highest order" (p. 170). This common bond does not preclude individuality, however. In profound mutual relationships, there is a sharpened sense of self and an intensification of individuality. And to give stability and durability to the bond, there is a sense of commitment (Davis, 1973).

Connectedness implies dependency. Dependency, like independence, can be normal and healthy or deviant and unhealthy. Healthy dependency means being sensitive to the needs of those who help us satisfy our own needs, that is, those who are nurturant and supportive. According to Bardwick (1971), "There are always critically important persons whose love and esteem are essential" (p. 116). On the other hand, there are unhealthy forms of dependence. For example, there can be extreme dependence. This could involve hypersensitivity to others' reactions, a hypersensitivity rooted in an egocentric rather than a shared point of view. In addition, dependence could be used aggressively to manipulate and control a partner to meet one's needs, particularly those needs that more independent persons would take responsibility for satisfying on their own. This unhealthy dependence can create, in turn, a greater felt need for support and a consequent increase in dependency (Bardwick, 1971). It is likely that people with healthy dependency have higher self-esteem than those with unhealthy dependency (Conger, 1973).

---

[2]We recognize the limits to instrumentalist (exchange) analyses of social relationships, particularly in the failure to keep clear the distinction between use value and exchange value. According to Csikszentmihalyi (1982), use value refers to an object's intrinsic worth in terms of satisfying human needs. Exchange value refers to an object's extrinsic worth relative to other objects and money. Use value, since it depends on an object's or person's capacity to satisfy human needs, is our focus.

In sum, relationships can be mundane or profound. Relationships that are profound involve being dependent on the other for a wide range of important social needs. Wethington (1982), for example, reports that the "closest" member of a social network (a person you cannot imagine living without) is apt to provide the whole repertoire of social support functions for their partner. We regard this dependency as a healthy one. The impact of pathological dependency on relationships is an important issue, but it will not be discussed further in this chapter. In the remainder of the chapter we argue that a person's (P's) degree of healthy dependency on an other (O) will affect the probability of loneliness, other factors being equal.

NEEDS AND GOALS OF SOCIAL RELATIONSHIPS

Social relationships have goals (i.e., social needs) that they can satisfy. Various classifications have been developed to represent the goals that are obtained from social contact (see Rook & Peplau, 1982). Though these classifications have not been validated empirically, what is critical is the assumption that relationships are associated with the achievement of socially mediated goals. Put differently, we are particularly concerned about those social needs that rest on relationships for their satisfaction and especially those that are associated with the idea of the quality of a relationship.

Sullivan (1953) pointed to a global need for intimacy as *the* goal of relationship development, whereas Weiss (1974) offers six social provisions that individuals seek in relationships. These include

1. attachment, in which a sense of security and commitment is sought, particularly in an intimate relationship with a spouse or a romantic partner;
2. social integration, a feeling of shared activities and concerns that is derived frequently from relationships with friends;
3. opportunity for nurturance, in which one takes responsibility for the well-being of another person, such as a child;
4. reassurance of worth, or the validation of one's sense of competence in a major social role, provided mainly by kin, where one can expect assistance from such persons without having one's past relationship, mutual affection, or one's reciprocation of past help be an issue;

5. sense of reliable alliance, on the expectation of continuing assistance, which is usually provided by kin or family members regardless of past help or mutual affection; and
6. obtaining guidance, particularly when individuals are under stress, where access to a relationship is sought so that someone can provide emotional support and assistance in formulating and evaluating a plan of action to solve a personal problem.

Different relationships may be necessary to satisfy all of these psychological needs, but a single relationship could fulfill more than one of them.

SOCIAL NETWORKS

Humans are inherently social. In our view, relationships with others are a major aspect of human experience. We can easily picture our social relationships with others—family, neighbors, and friends—as networks of social connections. This may explain why network analysis as an approach to describing preferences for others and features of group structure, such as communication patterns and power and status relationships, was in use in the late 1940s and early 1950s (Secord & Backman, 1964), and is in use today in analyses of privacy (Margulis, 1979), support systems (Stokes, 1982), aloneness (Fischer & Phillips, 1982), and relationship development (Milardo, 1982).

As used here, the social relationships that comprise a social network are those that the focal person (P) finds or believes have a high probability of providing rewarding exchanges (Fischer & Phillips, 1982). If we assume that certain rewarding exchanges act to satisfy or achieve particular social objectives, goals, or needs (consistent with an exchange theory approach to relationships), then it is possible that different network members mediate different needs or patterns of needs for P. We shall not explore these differences but wish only to iterate that different social relationships may be required to satisfy P's needs.

Network Elements

Structurally, a network is a set of nodes (e.g., people) connected by a set of ties, for example, relations of some sort (Stokes, 1982). In our analysis the ties are functionally ties of dependency. The nodes are "others," predominantly but not exclusively other people. Psychologically, we treat a variety of objects as "social others," including self as object, imagined others, and mythic others. Romanticized ideal others, such as the "shining knight" or the "waiting princess," can be important elements in an adolescent's social world where imagined encounters and conversations can be more interesting and, perhaps, influential than real ones. Mythic others, by those believing in them, are treated as real and as person-like, in the functional sense. The prototypical example of a mythic other, in the current Western religions, is God.

Suffice it to say, the core of current research on and theory about loneliness focuses on real, actual others. However, we believe a wider view of others could be fruitfully explored (e.g., Paloutzian & Ellison, 1982).

Network Characteristics

For the purposes of this chapter, two characteristics of networks will be introduced: network size and member centrality.[3]

Networks vary in their *size* (how many members there are in each of P's networks) and members of networks vary in their *centrality*, that is, in their association with satisfying P's goals (particularly salient goals). The centrality of a particular network member (O) derives from O's role in mediating (directly, as in supplying, or indirectly, as in helping P to achieve) outcomes desired by P.

Consider the case of P's relationship with O. A number of factors contribute to O's centrality for P, including the number and range of outcomes that O can mediate for P, the importance of the outcomes that O can mediate for P, O's success at producing or helping P to produce the need-satisfying outcomes, and P's satisfaction with O. O's centrality for P is not likely to be salient at all times. It is most likely to be salient when circumstances heighten P's awareness of the relationship or of the needs associated with it. These circumstances could include (1) a change in O that makes him or her less or more capable or willing to mediate desired outcomes, (2) a change in the availability of O under conditions of high need salience for O, or (3) an experience of a particularly satisfy-

---

[3]The present analysis of network characteristics and the applications of an exchange theory approach to networks draws heavily, but loosely, on Stokols and Shumaker's (1981) excellent analysis of place dependence.

ing or unsatisfying outcome mediated by O. It could also include life-cycle changes in P that change the prepotence of his or her needs.

AN EXCHANGE THEORY APPROACH TO RELATIONSHIP CENTRALITY AND NETWORK SIZE

Expectancies, achievements, and desires influence how individuals assess their relationships. We do not define achieved relationships in terms of how many social contacts an individual has (i.e., too few, enough, or too many). Social contacts are evaluated in terms of the quality of the relationship that the individual has with others, unless number of contacts per se is a sought after outcome. Support for our position derives from research by Cutrona and Peplau (1979; also see Cutrona, 1982) who found that individuals' satisfaction with the quality of their relationships was more strongly related to loneliness than was the number of social contacts.

Expectancies influence how individuals assess the effects of exchanges with (actual) others. A useful basis for examining people's expectancies for relationships is Thibaut and Kelley's exchange theory and, in particular, their concepts of comparison level (CL) and comparison level for alternatives (CLalt) (Kelley, Hastorf, Jones, Thibaut, & Usdane, 1960; Thibaut & Kelley, 1959). The comparison level represents a level of outcomes that is experienced as neutral in value. A person with a high CL will expect a great deal from her or his relationships. A person is satisfied with a relationship to the extent that outcomes are above CL. The height of CL may depend on one's past experiences in relationships as well as on comparisons with what kinds of successful relations other people are believed or known to have, especially other people who are seen as similar to oneself.

As stated earlier, a major factor in evaluating O's centrality for P and P's satisfaction with O is O's success in mediating desired outcomes for P. An assessment of satisfaction presumes that P has a certain expectation or standard of comparison for O's role as a mediator of outcomes. It follows that the degree of satisfaction with a relationship is influenced by the difference between P's expectation about O and O's actual performance as a mediator of desired outcomes. The better is O's performance relative to P's expectation, the greater is P's satisfaction. Of course, P's expectation is a response to O's performance as a mediator of goals P seeks in relationships. Thus, over time, the CL (i.e., P's expectation about O) will drop or rise, depending on the performance of O.

Other factors that influence P's CL for O are the number, type, and importance of outcomes that O successfully mediates for P. Important outcomes will have a greater impact on subsequent satisfaction or dissatisfaction than will success or failure with less important outcomes. In relationships that mediate more than one social goal, satisfaction with O is based on the number of mediated outcomes weighted by their importance and averaged over all these outcomes (cf., Stokols & Shumaker, 1981).

In Thibaut and Kelley's theory, comparison level depends largely on previous personal experiences and other sources of expectations. It tends to be a relatively realistic expectation. As applied to social relationships, then, CL represents a person's estimation of probable levels of social exchange. For instance, individuals who move from a large city to a physically isolated community might scale down their expectancies about what they expect to achieve in their relationships.

Another standard for comparison, however, may be desired or ideal social relationships rather than expected ones. The media are potent communicators of what an exciting romantic or a warm familial relationships could be like. Persons who know that they cannot *expect* to achieve such fictional relationships may nevertheless want them. Furthermore, if a "desire," in contrast to an expectancy, for a social relationship refers to a psychologically based need for relationships with others, then this desire should persist unabated or change relatively slowly. The desire might even operate outside of the individuals' awareness of it. As they dream of the unattainable, they may be dissatisfied and disappointed with the attainable (cf., Thibaut & Kelley, 1959, p. 92).

What about the impact of alternative social partners on P's evaluation of her or his social relationships? According to Thibaut and Kelley (1959), comparison level for alternatives (CLalt) refers to the best single alternative, whom we will designate as O_A. In general, dependence of P on O will be less to the extent that O_A is as qualified or able as O to aid P successfully in achieving important outcomes. It is clearly recognized that gaining O_A as an alternative to O rests on a number of preconditions, such as P knows of an O_A, P is able to attract O_A and create a viable relationship with him or her, and O_A is available to P when needed. Availability is particularly important when we are dealing with physical presence as a precondition for successful goal mediation. However, a person needing moral support can draw on anticipated (future) or past interactions with O to succor or sustain them. Also, the God-oriented, religious person can always turn to God, who is omnipresent, for support (Paloutzian & Ellison, 1982).

There is a possible paradox created by having O become central with respect to satisfying important needs. As we become more dependent on O, we may stop searching for or relying on others. In serious relationships that involve the exchange of very intimate information, couples and groups erect barriers to exclude unwanted others, thereby protecting their privacy (Derlega & Chaikin, 1977; Margulis, 1979). The couple or group becomes exclusive—others have limited access to the group and group members are expected to be loyal to the group. For instance, Johnson and Leslie (1982) present data indicating that as dating couples increase their romantic involvement, their friendship networks shrink and those friends who remain in the network are seen as less important and they are disclosed to less intimately. In short—and this states the paradox—as the strength of association (dependency, centrality) increases, the desire to form new relationships to achieve the involved needs should decrease, and the desire to alter the current relationship, particularly if it is a good one, should decrease. However, if the relationship turns sour or O becomes unavailable, P is left alone and potentially without alternative (substitute) relationships.

P can remain dependent on O (O can remain central) without P feeling satisfied with the relationship, such as when a relationship wanes (i.e., P's outcomes fall at or below his or her CL) and alternative social partners (O_A) are not known, accessible, available, or attracted to P or they appear to be no better than O currently is as an outcome mediator for P (i.e., CLalt ≤ CL). Under such conditions, P will remain dependent on O.

Centrality ties directly to the conception of relationships being profound or mundane. By definition, profound relationships are central and mundane relationships less so. We would expect that since profound relationships tend toward exclusivity, then the number of profound relationships will tend to be smaller than the number of mundane relationships in a social network.

Normative research on this aspect of networks is in an early stage of development. Table 6.1 summarizes results of three recent studies. Comparisons of results are clouded by differences in sample characteristics and, as important, in the criterion used to elicit network members. Using a criterion likely to generate profound relationships (Levitt and Antonucci's [1982] inner circle criterion of "you can't imagine living without them"), average numbers of almost three (for men) and four (for women) are reported. Stokes (1982) finds networks with eight confidants. Larger numbers are likely with more "liberal" criteria (see Table 6.1). Equally interesting, Levitt and Antonucci (1982) also report that, in their sample of respondents age 50 and over, less than 1% were isolates (had null networks), and only 4% had no one in their "inner circle" network. In sum, people tend to have profound relationships, usually more than one, and are likely to have additional friends to whom to turn. Table 6.1 does *not* offer strong evidence for or against our hypothesis that the number of profound relationships tends to be smaller than the number of mundane ones within social networks.

Stokes (1982) also reports an interesting relationship between satisfaction with one's social network and network size. He found that satisfac-

TABLE 6.1

Segment Size in Social Networks

Study	N	Characteristics of sample	Network inclusion criteria	Segment size	
Stokes (1982)	82	Undergraduates of mean age 25	"Significant in your life and with whom you have contact at least once a month"	Relatives Friends Total	5.6 9.5 15.1
			"Confides in or turns to for help in an emergency"	Relatives Friends Total	3.7 4.2 7.9
Lowenthal, Thurnher, and Chiriboga (1975)	216	At various stages of life cycle from high school to preretirement	"Friends"	Men Women	5.2 6.3

Levitt and Antonucci (1982)	718	National sample of age 50 and over	Inner Circle: "Can't imagine living without them"	Inner
				  Men
				  Women
					2.8
					4.0

			Middle Circle: Not quite as close but "still very important" to P	Middle
				  Men
				  Women
					1.8
					3.4

			Outer Circle: Not as close but "close enough and important enough" to be in network	Outer
				  Men
				  Women
					3.1
					2.1

				Total
				  Men
				  Women
					7.7
					9.4

tion is optimal with networks of seven confidants. He offers the following explanation for this optimum network size. The opportunities for supportive social interactions increase with group size, but the responsibility and work necessary to maintain relationships also increase. Thus, as the network gets larger, each additional relationship may provide support at a diminishing rate although the cost of maintaining each relationship remains the same or, perhaps, increases (Stokes, 1982).

LONELINESS AND PRIOR SOCIAL RELATIONSHIPS

We suggested that in order to understand loneliness we must first understand the prior relationships of people who become lonely. We have discussed general characteristics of relationships, types of relationships, and ties among relationships. Now we turn to loneliness and address four major topics that research on loneliness raises:

1. the antecedents of loneliness (Why do people become lonely?);
2. the condition of chronic loneliness (Why are some people chronically lonely and others not?);
3. the affect associated with loneliness (Why do people who become lonely feel the way they do?);
4. hypotheses about linkages between social relationships and loneliness (How do social relationships influence conditions that give rise to loneliness or shape the consequences of it?)

These topics are addressed in turn.

The Antecedents of Loneliness

We posit four conditions that are necessary for loneliness to occur. These are

1. the unavailability of any social partner or of a specific social partner (O) who could assist a person (P) in achieving (important) other-contingent goals, objectives, or needs;
2. the belief that the unavailability will endure;
3. the instigation of salient other-mediated needs or the instigation of thoughts of O;
4. a continuing desire for (the availability of) the social partner.

One posited condition for loneliness is the *unavailability of an appropriate other or a specific other*. If O has to be physically present to help P achieve a goal or satisfy a need, then physical separation from O would constitute unavailability. If P can reach his or her goal by speaking to O by telephone in order to share an intimacy, for example, we would not say O was unavailable (Fischer & Phillips, 1982). The nature of O's unavailability is tied functionally to the goal of P that is salient.

We distinguish between the unavailability of others in general and the unavailability of a specific other. In some cases P may find himself or herself without any appropriate social partner either because of situational (e.g., moving to another town) or dispositional (e.g., low self-esteem, socially unskilled) factors. In other cases, even when appropriate social partners are available, the absence of a specific desirable other (e.g., a spouse goes on a business trip) must be considered as a case of unavailability.

If P or O or their relationship changed such that O was no longer willing or able to satisfy a particular need of P, would loneliness arise? Factors that can mediate P's reactions to this condition include the sharpness of the onset of these circumstances and the reasons for them. Let us start with O losing the ability to satisfy P's needs. This can stem from changes in P (e.g., life cycle changes with concomitant changes in P's needs) or changes in O. The change in P should preclude loneliness since the need associated with O has changed, therefore making P less dependent on O. In the case of O becoming unable to satisfy P's need(s), a sudden onset could be traumatic. When the death of a loved one has a gradual onset, one possible reaction is to reduce dependency through an emotional decathexis, a phenomenon observed in families in which a member is slowly dying of a terminal illness (Friedman, Chodoff, Mason, & Hamburg, 1977). In this example, to become less dependent does not mean a withdrawal of love, merely a reduction of one's reliance on the other for satisfaction of specific needs O is unable to address. In the case where O becomes unwilling to help P, then we would expect frustration and anger to result if the unwillingness constituted deliberate goal blocking.

The belief that the *unavailability will endure* simply means that loneliness is temporally bound. It is not necessary that the unavailability be forever. Rather, what is critical is that P finds herself or himself at a juncture between what was (O was available) and what will be (O is not available) (Zipris, 1979). This is a keenly experienced asymmetry. The unavailability must appear at this juncture to have a duration that will be longer than P feels he or she can endure. The foreseeable future stretches ahead as an emptiness with no clear boundary. P must be physically or psychologically committed to this unavailability; if it could be undone, loneliness could be avoided or escaped.

The *instigation of salient, other-mediated goals or the instigation of thoughts of O* is another precondition for loneliness. Weiss (1973) views the inability to achieve a certain social provision (or goal) as *the* critical factor in accounting for loneliness. We agree that the failure of O to help P to achieve a socially mediated goal probably plays a role in loneliness, but not, in every case, in the manner that Weiss (1973) suggests. When unavailability is not an attack by O on the P–O relationship, when it is not a malicious, intentional withholding of help and of self by O, when unavailability is chosen by P, or when it is forced on O by reasonable pressures (e.g., a family crisis takes a spouse out of town), then thoughts of O may be more crucial than thoughts of other-mediated goals as an antecedent of loneliness. When the unavailability represents a deliberate attack on the P–O bond, need salience, as Weiss has argued, may be a precondition for loneliness. In the former case, P is lonely for O or because of O's absence; in the latter, P is lonely for someone to help P satisfy his or her needs.[4]

The *continuing desire for the availability of the unavailable partner* is the fourth condition for loneliness. Why should the unavailable other be on P's mind? It is a consequence of the salience of the need that is contingent on O for its satisfaction and, further, on the degree of dependency on O (profound versus mundane relationship). The greater the dependence on O, then the greater the range of needs mediated by O, and the more the possible reasons to think about O. As long as P continues to experience the relevant social needs, that is, as long as no change in P alters these needs, and as long as no O_A shows up who can satisfy these needs for P the way O used to, longing for O will continue.

It is also possible that unavailability could *increase* the attractiveness of O and make the loneliness even more painful. This is clearly the case when P has chosen some alternative to being with O (e.g., going out of town on a business trip). Research by Festinger and Walster (Festinger & Walster, 1964; Walster, 1964) indicates that in the period immediately after making a decision, persons tend to direct their attention in particular to the good features of the now unavailable alternative. As a result, the unavailable alternative becomes increasingly attractive. This phenomenon is called *regret*. It results in an attempt to reverse or undo the

---

[4]This argument modifies our earlier position (see Derlega and Margulis, 1982, p. 161). We then held that thoughts of the absent other were more important than the failure to achieve a socially mediated goal in contributing to the loneliness experience, but we hadn't considered the circumstances of the loss as an influential variable.

decision, if this is possible (Festinger & Walster, 1964), or to reevaluate the alternatives such that the unavailable alternative becomes less attractive and the available (chosen) alternative becomes more attractive (Walster, 1964). This reevaluation illustrates dissonance reduction.

If the decision cannot be undone and if the dissonance associated with a decision is difficult to reduce, the period of regret could last a long time. The regret about the unavailable partner may be labeled and experienced as loneliness and it may continue as long as postdecisional regret is salient.

The analysis above, derived from cognitive dissonance theory, presumes that the person is responsible for the absence of the unavailable alternative (Wicklund & Brehm, 1976). However, we suggest that commitment to a loss might be sufficient to create regret and the consequent overevaluation of the lost partner (Margulis, 1967). Evidence for this proposition is indirect. One source is research on Brehm's (1966, 1976) theory of psychological reactance. According to Brehm, if an alternative is eliminated by personal or impersonal events, and if the impersonal elimination is unjustified in P's view, then P should experience reactance and, consequently, should regard the eliminated alternative as increasingly attractive. Furthermore, in Brehm's (1966, p. 19) analysis, object attractiveness implies the potential of the object to satisfy needs. This is consistent with our position that social partners associated with need satisfaction will be sources of satisfaction and that their unavailability will be psychologically painful. In our view, the increased attractiveness of the unavailable partner, because of his or her absence, may not only signal loneliness but make the loneliness more painful to bear: the person has lost a partner who is more attractive than had earlier been imagined. Thus, the longing for an absent or lost partner (experienced as loneliness) may have, as preconditions, feeling committed to the loss in addition to cognitive reevaluations that heighten the sense of loss.

Other factors equal, what impact should P's responsibility for the loss of O have on the reevaluation of O following the loss? We would predict that if P was responsible for the loss, then a reduction in regret (i.e., a working through of the affect and an increasingly realistic assessment of O, one that is closer to the pre-loss assessment) is more likely if P has a healthy, strong, positive self-concept than if P has a negative self-concept. We also would predict that the more central O is to P then, following a loss, P would be more likely to devalue the self than O if P had a low rather than a high self-concept. This is predicated on the idea that P's self-concept would be a less resistant element than P's view of O. Last, we would predict that idealization would remain longer if P was not responsible for the loss than if P was responsible. This is based on P's responsibility leading to active attempts to reevaluate O. We are specifically excluding the case in which the loss is seen by P as an intentional act to hurt P by O (e.g., to withhold rewards from P, to punish or to attempt to control or manipulate P).

The Condition of Chronic Loneliness

Chronic loneliness refers to individuals who have experienced this state for a period of years. It seems to be different from the experiences of individuals who are reacting to a sudden or temporary change in their social environment, such as losing a spouse or leaving home for college.[5] There is an interesting implication of our analysis that suggests a partial explanation of chronic loneliness. It rests on two assumptions: First, chronically lonely people lack social skills and, second, a lack of social skills will be associated with low self-esteem. It is likely that these people find it difficult to hold on to socially attractive partners (particularly non-kin). These losses, resulting from inadequate social skills, result in regret. If self-esteem is low, then a loss is consonant with the self-evaluation. It makes this negative self-evaluation stronger and leads, eventually, to the consonant belief that others are beyond their reach. If these people lack the psychological resources to become self-sufficient, then they will dwell on their continuing need for others and their inability to satisfy the need. Observation of persons with successful relationships may further exacerbate their feelings of loneliness.

There is some evidence, consistent with this explanation, that severe, prolonged loneliness can lower a person's self-esteem if it is assessed as a social failure, and this consequence is made worse if the loneliness is attributed, by P, to a personal defect or a personal characteristic. Specifically, many lonely people do blame themselves for their social failure (Anderson, Horowitz, & French, 1983). Furthermore, severe losses are particularly devastating to the self-image and, at least in the short run, can result in lowered self-esteem (Peplau, Miceli, & Morasch, 1982).

This analysis suggests that chronically lonely people will have networks that are impoverished with regard to non-kin, central others (cf., Young, 1982). They are unlikely to have substitutes or buffers at times

---

[5]See Beck and Young (1978), Cutrona (1982), DeJong-Gierveld and Raadschelders (1982), and Young (1982) for other analyses of the chronicity of loneliness.

when they need support. (Substitutes versus buffers is discussed on pp. 153–155.) Nor are they able to fill their impoverished networks.

This discussion also suggests a possible basis for predicting when "absence makes the heart grow fonder" and when to expect "out of sight, out of mind." We would associate the former with profound relationships and the latter with mundane ones. In profound relationships, important needs for P are implicated, and when these needs become salient, it is likely that through their association with O, O becomes "cognitively salient." The regret associated with the loss of O, under these conditions, could make the heart grow fonder—one longs for the source of need satisfaction. In mundane relationships, not only are the needs not strongly tied to particular people, but the needs themselves are not strong (they are less important), and it is probably more likely that another source can be easily found to satisfy them (e.g., you can find another bowling, tennis, golf, skating partner). For this reason, thoughts of O are unlikely to be instigated because of the weak relationship between P's goal and O and because others are associated with the goal as well. Hence, for O, "out of sight, out of mind."

The Affect Associated with Loneliness

We have argued that the affective response to loneliness is associated with the commitment to the loss of a source of outcome mediation. What should that affective response be? We cannot see how a definitive answer can be given.[6] Losses vary in their personal significance and people vary in the capacity to deal with losses. It seems reasonable to assume that the more significant the loss (that is, the greater the dependency), the "greater" the emotional reaction should be, other factors equal. Reaction can range from the trifling regret of individuals who miss a "familiar face" at a local "watering hole" to acute grief at the death of a loved one (cf., Peplau & Perlman, 1982a). Moreover, deciding on appropriate labels for emotional reactions to these losses may be a futile exercise. The individual's choice of labels may be as much a consequence of sociolinguistic factors (how we learned from others to label our internal states) as of the influence of social and other cues on self-labeling (Schachter, 1959).

---

[6]For alternative positions, see the discussions of affective responses to loneliness in Peplau and Perlman's (1982a) book. Check, in their subject index, under "Emotions associated with loneliness" (p. 428).

We must also recognize that emotional reactions to losses can be inappropriate. There are people who profess not to grieve the loss of a loved one (in a culture where grief is expected) and there are people whose overwrought displays of emotions at funerals are inconsistent with the (apparent) centrality of O to them (in a culture in which the most profound expressions of grief are "reserved" for those close to the deceased). The attributional and clinical implications of inappropriate affect, and their relevance for analyses of loneliness, fall beyond the scope of this chapter.

Hypotheses Concerning Social Relationships and Loneliness

We have argued that loneliness is likely to be a problem for P if a satisfying O is inaccessible or unavailable when P has important outcomes or many outcomes to be achieved and if P believes he or she needs O in order to obtain these outcomes. Based on this unavailability notion, predictions can be generated about the effects of P's social network on the occurrence of loneliness.

The probability of loneliness is a direct function of the centrality of the unavailable social partner. The greater the centrality of the absent partner, the greater the likelihood of loneliness occurring. That is, vulnerability to loneliness is based on P's degree of dependency on certain others to assist in satisfying certain needs. If there is less dependency on O, there should be less reason for loneliness under conditions that would otherwise give rise to loneliness. For instance, Lowenthal and Haven (1968) report that "there are some lifelong isolates and near-isolates whose later-life adaptation apparently is not related to social resources" (p. 25). These persons presumably have developed their own inner resources to satisfy their needs.

The probability and duration of loneliness is an inverse function of the number of central others in the network. Assume that central members that serve the same need are substitutable. Then, loneliness is less likely (and should be shorter in duration) if there is more than one central other that can and will help satisfy a need and if substitution of social partners is not otherwise precluded. Is it reasonable to assume that there are alternatives who can substitute for O? Support for this assumption derives from research that finds that elderly widows are more likely than widowers to belong to organizations, maintain social ties, and have intimate contacts outside of the relationship with their spouse. In many cases, the wife was the only central partner for the elderly husband, whereas the husband was just one of multiple social partners available to the elderly wife (Bock & Webber, 1972; Haas-Hawkings, 1978). Thus, the fact that women are more likely to establish and maintain intimate relationships outside of their marriage may account for their success in adjusting to widowhood (Haas-Hawkings, 1978).

Substitutes and Buffers

The notion of substitutability is not as straightforward as we have been suggesting. First, there is a *normative dimension* to substitution. Some substitutes may be socially acceptable and legitimate and others not. A person who "cheats" on a spouse in order to satisfy sexual needs is involved in a morally dubious substitution. It raises questions about the centrality of the spouse. If the spouse is not central and is treated in an "out of sight, out of mind" fashion, then sexual disloyalty might not be a source of guilt or shame. On the other hand, if there is conflict between the psychological commitment to a spouse and the thrill of the sexual escapade, then the infidelity could lead to guilt or shame if sexual activity, through association with the spouse, makes the spouse salient and the act recognizable as a "loss" of the spouse. We suggest that if O is central, then immediately following the loss of O, when regret is maximal, and all need-related activities instigate thoughts of the lost O, the salience of O should be an obstacle to forming new (transitory or permanent) relationships and, if this constraint is ignored, then it might create the preconditions for guilt or shame through P's "desecration" of O.

Second, there are the social complexities of finding, attracting, and correctly evaluating the need-related relevance of potential substitutes as well as determining the costs of alternative support. There could be a significant difference between P's CL for O and her or his CL for O_A (CLalt). Also, if partners are thought to be substitutable, this implies a network of $N > 1$ comparable individuals. Such a network does not necessarily exist for some persons; relationships may be $N = 1$, which occurs frequently for the older, married man whose wife is the only central other (see studies of social isolation by Bock & Webber, 1972, and Fischer & Phillips, 1982).

Third, some central others can serve as sources of moral support for a lonely P, that is, they can serve as *buffers* in contrast to substitutes for O. The concept of buffer is an important aspect of social relationships. Our position rests on the assumption that individuals may at least occasionally engage in selfless acts though our overall analysis assumes that relationships rest mainly on exchange principles.[7] It follows from this assumption that buffer and substitute are different roles. A principal difference is that P's obligations to a buffer are less than the obligations to a substitute. A buffer will give without expectation of taking or getting. Substitutes, because they are involved in an exchange, give but also expect to take. Buffers are less psychologically taxing on P because they do not create social obligations, particularly at a time when P is emotionally wrought. This distinction between buffer and substitute finds a parallel in the religious distinction between anonymous acts of loving-kindness and public acts of charity and in the psychological distinction between use value (the intrinsic value of a thing or act) and its exchange value (the extrinsic value of a thing or act) (cf., Csikszentmihalyi, 1982).[8]

The role of buffers in social support systems is discussed by Depner, Wethington, and Korshavn (1982). There is the buffering hypothesis that argues that people who serve as social supports can *decrease* the unfavorable effects of stress on outcomes of others. This hypothesis is similar to the position we have advanced. There is a complementary hypothesis, however, of negative buffering. It argues that social support can *increase* the unfavorable effects of stress. These two views of buffers, like Stokes' (1982) explanation of optimal network size (see pp. 145–146 of this chapter), underscores that social relationships can generate both costs and rewards. These ideas, though not explored here, deserve consideration in future attempts to link social relationships to loneliness.

What are the consequences of failure to find a successful substitute? Given the likelihood that what it takes to meet the "need profile" of a person is often very specialized (like the song said, "I want a girl just like the girl that married dear old dad"), finding a successful substitute, especially for a central O, could be unsuccessful. Accepting such failures and continuing to search unsuccessfully could reduce self-esteem. Altman (1975) has argued that self-concept could suffer since it is built, in part, on successes and failures of interaction management. As another option, P could make others psychologically less significant in their lives. That is, by relying on our own personal resources, we can main-

---

[7]See Karylowski (1982) for an analysis of different types of helping behavior.

[8]The authors have debated whether attachment is reducible to need satisfaction (exchange value, instrumental value) or whether it is more fundamental and intrinsic. The person unable to create attachments (healthy attachments or attachments at all) with others in our culture is likely to be "crazy" or "criminal". This inability is likely to represent a psychological deficit rather than an actualization of self.

tain our sociality but reduce our dependency (see Zipris, 1979). There are other options. Our conceptual analysis cannot predict, however, which path would be taken or, if a path was taken, what its probable outcome would be.

There is a special case in which P is relatively unlikely to find O unavailable. This is people's personal relationship with their God (at least in the Judeo–Christian view; Paloutzian & Ellison, 1982; Wilson, 1976). Wilson (1976), in a study of Christian conversion, found that "awareness of God's surveillance and encouragement over his omniscience was positively related to optimism about the future" (p. 311). That is, a believer's awareness of God's presence and acceptance is psychologically supporting. This is precisely what networks are for (Stokes, 1982). Paloutzian and Ellison (1982, p. 234) found that Christian respondents reporting their religious commitment as a personal relationship (e.g., "I have a personally meaningful relationship with God," "I believe that God is concerned about my problems") scored lower on measures of loneliness than respondents espousing a nonreligious, ethical approach to Christianity. These data support our view that physical presence (as in a face-to-face relationship) is not necessary for social or moral support (a view that reference group theory would predict; see Merton, 1957).

MUST PEOPLE BE AWARE THAT THEY ARE LONELY TO BE LONELY?

We must be aware of something (if you prefer, be able to discriminate cues) that we can label as "being lonely" or "loneliness." This is our basis for learning to use this word and having it part of a common (shared) code, a prerequisite for social communication. Nevertheless, people might say "He (or she) is lonely" and yet not recognize that state in themselves. People are not always willing or able to recognize certain states in themselves (Peplau, 1955; Rook & Peplau, 1982; Young, 1982).

If people cannot always identify certain psychological states, this raises an interesting question: How many people say they are lonely—and are trying to be truthful—but are not regarded by others as being lonely and how many people believe they are not lonely but would be described by observers as being or acting lonely? If the number is sizable, this raises doubts, on this ground alone, with the use of self-report as the criterion for loneliness. (Peplau, April 1980, personal communication, says it is currently the most widely used criterion.) Why should there be this discrepancy? It could be based on insensitivity to cues (lack of skill or training) or on motivation (a desire to hide from the truth) or it might reflect our difficulty distinguishing essential from associated characteristics of loneliness. This difficulty might reflect poor socialization or it might reflect the ineluctable problems in learning the meanings of linguistically vague and ambiguous terms.

We think that much of the research on *what* loneliness is does not adequately address this question. Moreover, even if it did, we would still have doubts about it unless it was conceptually grounded. Going further, researchers who rely on survey questionnaires, in contrast to interviews, to study loneliness will fail to capture the phenomenon of loneliness as it is lived in daily life. The examination of phenomena as lived is the hallmark of the phenomenological approach. Zipris (1979) is applying just this approach to loneliness.

However, we still remain uncomfortable. The authors' experience with the voluminous literature on privacy makes it abundantly clear that the presence or absence of the word "privacy" in an article was no guide to what one could learn about privacy from the article (Berscheid, 1977; Derlega & Chaikin, 1977; Margulis, 1977). Thus, the implicit theories of respondents should not become the "naive" theories of researchers.

We believe that one must address the *why* of loneliness first on the grounds that concepts guide measurement, direct our understanding, and organize disparate events; moreover, explication forces a consideration of initial and boundary conditions. However, concept building, although it has the built-in capacity for correction through testing, is not without its pitfalls. Just as with privacy (Margulis, 1977), so too with loneliness, the "common core" of experiences about loneliness which theoreticians share as a starting point gives way, under the impetus of divergent theoretical positions, to different statements about the constitutive aspects of loneliness. Zipris (1979), for example, contrasts behaviorist, psychodynamic, humanist, and phenomenological positions, among others, on loneliness. Perlman and Peplau (1982) have identified eight different theoretical positions about loneliness. Admittedly, theoretical and conceptual analyses of loneliness are still at an early stage of development and do not represent fully developed theories at what we call Stage 3 conceptual development. It is hoped that psychological thinking on loneliness in the future will articulate more clearly how loneliness fits into a systematic set of theoretical propositions that define loneliness. The present chapter will have value if it contributes to such a theoretical analysis.

REFERENCES

Abrahams, R. B. (1972). Mutual help for the widowed. *Social Work, 17,* 55–61.

Altman, I. (1975). *The environment and social behavior: Privacy, personal space, territoriality, crowding.* Monterey, CA: Brooks/Cole.

Anderson, C. A., Horowitz, L. M., French, R. de S. (1983). Attributional style in lonely and depressed people. *Journal of Personality and Social Psychology, 45,* 127–136.

Bardwick, J. M. (1971). *Psychology of women: A study of bio-cultural conflicts.*New York: Harper & Row.

Beck, A. T., & Young, J. E. (1978). College blues. *Psychology Today, 12,* 80–81, 85–86, 89, 91–92.

Bell, G. R. (1956). Alcohol and loneliness. *Journal of Social Therapy, 2,* 171–181.

Bem, D. J. (1970). *Beliefs, attitudes, and human behavior.* Belmont, CA: Brooks/Cole.

Berscheid, E. (1977). Privacy: A hidden variable in experimental social psychology. *Journal of Social Issues, 33*(3), 85–101.

Bock, E. W., & Webber, I. L. (1972). Suicide among the elderly: Isolating widowhood and mitigating alternatives. *Journal of Marriage and the Family, 34,* 24–31.

Bradburn, N. (1969). *The structure of psychological well-being.* Chicago: Aldine.

Brehm, J. W. (1966). *A theory of psychological reactance.* New York: Academic Press.

Brehm, J. W. (1976). Responses to loss of freedom: A theory of psychological reactance. In J. W. Thibaut, J. T. Spence, & R. C. Carson (Eds.), *Contemporary topics in social psychology.* Morristown, NJ: General Learning Press.

Conger, J. J. (1973). *Adolescence and youth: Psychological development in a changing world.* New York: Harper & Row.

Cottle, T. (1974). The felt sense of studentry. *Interchange, 5,* 31–41.

Cronbach, J., & Meehl, P. E. (1956). Construct validity in psychological tests. In H. Feigel & M. Scriven (Eds.), *Minnesota studies in the philosophy of science* (Vol. I). Minneapolis: University of Minnesota Press.

Csikszentmihalyi, M. (1982). *The symbolic function of possessions: Toward a psychology of materialism.* Paper presented at the Annual Meeting of the American Psychological Association Convention, Washington, DC.

Cutrona, C. E. (1982). Transition to college: Loneliness and the process of social adjustment. In L. A. Peplau & D. Perlman (Eds.), *Loneliness: A sourcebook of current theory, research and therapy.* New York: Wiley (Interscience).

Cutrona, C. E., & Peplau, L. A. (1979). *A longitudinal study of loneliness.* Paper presented at the Annual Meeting of the Western Psychological Association Convention, San Diego.

Davis, M. S. (1973). *Intimate relations.* New York: Free Press.

DeJong-Gierveld, J., & Raadschelders, J. (1982). Types of loneliness. In L. A. Peplau & D. Perlman (Eds.), *Loneliness: A sourcebook of current theory, research and therapy.* New York: Wiley (Interscience).

Depner, C., Wethington, E., & Korshavn, S. (1982). *How social support works: Issues in testing the theory.* Paper presented at the Annual Meeting of the American Psychological Association Convention, Washington, DC.

Derlega, V. J., & Chaikin, A. L. (1977). Privacy and self-disclosure in social relationships. *Journal of Social Issues, 33*(3), 102–115.

Derlega, V. J., & Margulis, S. T. (1982). Why loneliness occurs: The interrelationship of social psychological and privacy concepts. In L. A. Peplau & D. Perlman (Eds.), *Loneliness: A sourcebook of current theory, research and therapy.* New York: Wiley (Interscience).

Festinger, L., & Walster, E. (1964). Post-decision regret and decision reversal. In L. Festinger (Ed.), *Conflict, decision, and dissonance.* Stanford, CA: Stanford University Press.

Fischer, C. S., & Phillips, S. L. (1982). Who is alone? Social characteristics of people with small networks. In L. A. Peplau & D. Perlman (Eds.), *Loneliness: A sourcebook of current theory, research and therapy.* New York: Wiley (Interscience).

Friedman, S. B., Chodoff, P., Mason, J. W., & Hamburg, D. A. (1977). Behavioral observations on parents anticipating the death of a child. In A. Monat & R. S. Lazarus (Eds.), *Stress and coping.* New York: Columbia University Press.

Haas-Hawkings, G. (1978). Intimacy as a moderating influence on the stress of loneliness in widowhood. *Essence, 2,* 249–258.

Johnson, M. P., & Leslie, L. (1982). Couple involvement and network structure: A test of the dyadic withdrawal hypothesis. *Social Psychology Quarterly, 45,* 34–43.

Karylowski, J. (1982). Two types of altruistic behavior: Doing good to feel good or to make the other feel good. In V. J. Derlega & J. Grzelak (Eds.), *Cooperation and helping behavior: Theories and research.* New York: Academic Press.

Kelley, H. H., Hastorf, A. H., Jones, E. E., Thibaut, J. W., & Usdane, W. M. (1960). Some implications of social psychological theory for research on the handicapped. In L. H. Lofquist (Ed.), *Psychological research and rehabilitation.* Washington, DC: American Psychological Association.

Levitt, M. J., & Antonucci, T. C. (1982). *Social support and well-being: Two samples of the elderly.* Paper presented at the Annual Meeting of the American Psychological Association Convention, Washington, DC.

Lowenthal, M. F., & Haven, C. (1968). Interaction and adaptation: Intimacy as a critical variable. *American Sociological Review, 33,* 20–30.

Lowenthal, M. F., Thurnher, M., & Chiriboga, D. (1975). *Four stages of life: A comparative study of women and men facing transitions.* San Francisco: Jossey-Bass.

Maisel, R. (1969). *Report of the continuing audit of public attitudes and concerns.* Unpublished manuscript, Harvard Medical School.

Margulis, S. T. (1967). *On the loss of a partner: The effects of responsibility on post-decisional re-evaluation processes.* Unpublished doctoral dissertation, University of Minnesota.

Margulis, S. T. (1977). Conceptions of privacy: Current status and next steps. *Journal of Social Issues, 33*(3), 5–21.

Margulis, S. T. (1979). *Privacy as information management: A social psychological and environmental framework* (NBSIR 79–1793). Washington, DC: National Bureau of Standards.

Merton, R. K. (1957). *Social theory and social structure* (rev. ed.). Glencoe, IL: Free Press.

Milardo, R. M. (1982). Friendship networks in developing relationships: Converging and diverging social environments. *Social Psychology Quarterly, 45,* 162–172.

Paloutzian, R. F., & Ellison, C. W. (1982). Loneliness, spiritual well-being and the quality of life. In L. A. Peplau & D. Perlman (Eds.), *Loneliness: A sourcebook of current theory, research and theory.* New York: Wiley (Interscience).

Peplau, H. E. (1955). Loneliness. *American Journal of Nursing, 55,* 1476–1481.

Peplau, L. A., & Caldwell, M. A. (1978). Loneliness: A cognitive analysis. *Essence, 2*(4), 207–220

Peplau, L. A., Miceli, M., & Morasch, B. (1982). Loneliness and self-evaluation. In L. A. Peplau & D. Perlman (Eds.), *Loneliness: A sourcebook of current theory, research and therapy.* New York: Wiley (Interscience).

Peplau, L. A., & Perlman, D. (Eds.) (1982a). *Loneliness: A sourcebook of current theory, research and therapy.* New York: Wiley (Interscience).

Peplau, L. A., & Perlman, D. (1982b). Perspectives on loneliness. In L. A. Peplau & D. Perlman (Eds.), *Loneliness: A sourcebook of current theory, research and therapy.* New York: Wiley (Interscience).

Perlman, D., & Peplau, L. A. (1981). Toward a social psychology of loneliness. In R. Gilmour & S. Duck (Eds.), *Personal relationships: 3. Personal relationships in disorder.* London: Academic Press.

Perlman, D., & Peplau, L. A. (1982). Theoretical approaches to loneliness. In L. A. Peplau & D. Perlman (Eds.), *Loneliness: A sourcebook of current theory, research and therapy.* New York: Wiley (Interscience).

Rook, K. S., & Peplau, L. A. (1982). Perspectives on helping the lonely. In L. A. Peplau & D. Perlman (Eds.), *Loneliness: A sourcebook of current theory, research and therapy.* New York: Wiley (Interscience).

Rubenstein, C., & Shaver, P. (1980). Loneliness in two northeastern cities. In J. Hartog & J. Audy (Eds.), *The anatomy of loneliness.* New York: International Universities Press.

Rubenstein, C., & Shaver, P. (1982). The experience of loneliness. In L. A. Peplau & D. Perlman (Eds.), *Loneliness: A sourcebook of current theory, research and therapy.* New York: Wiley (Interscience).

Russell, D. (1982). The measurement of loneliness. In L. A. Peplau & D. Perlman (Eds.), *Loneliness: A sourcebook of current theory, research and therapy.* New York: Wiley (Interscience).

Russell, D., Peplau, L. A., & Ferguson, M. L. (1978). Developing a measure of loneliness. *Journal of Personality Assessment, 42*, 290–294.

Schachter, S. (1959). *The psychology of affiliation.* Stanford, CA: Stanford University Press.

Secord, P. F., & Backman, C. W. (1964). *Social psychology.* New York: McGraw-Hill.

Stokes, J. P. (1982). *Predicting satisfaction with social support from social network structure.* Paper presented at the Annual Meeting of the American Psychological Association Convention, Washington, DC.

Stokols, D., & Shumaker, S. A. (1981). People in places: A transactional view of settings. In J. H. Harvey (Ed.), *Cognition, social behavior, and the environment.* Hillsdale, NJ: Erlbaum.

Sullivan, H. S. (1953). *The interpersonal theory of psychiatry.* New York: Norton.

Thibaut, J., & Kelley, H. H. (1959). *The social psychology of groups.* New York: Wiley.

Walster, E. (1964). The temporal sequence of post-decision processes. In L. Festinger (Ed.), *Conflict, decision, and dissonance.* Stanford, CA: Stanford University Press.

Weiss, R. S. (1973). *Loneliness: The experience of emotional and social isolation.* Cambridge, MA: MIT Press.

Weiss, R. S. (1974). The provisions of social relationships. In Z. Rubin (Ed.), *Doing unto others.* Englewood Cliffs, NJ: Prentice-Hall.

Weiss, R. S. (1982). Issues in the study of loneliness. In L. A. Peplau & D. Perlman (Eds.), *Loneliness: A sourcebook of current theory, research and therapy.* New York: Wiley (Interscience).

Wethington, E. (1982). *Can social support functions be differentiated: A multivariate model.* Paper presented at the Annual Meeting of the Americal Psychological Association Convention, Washington, DC.

Wicklund, R. A., & Brehm, J. W. (1976). *Perspectives on cognitive dissonance.* New York: Erlbaum.

Wilson, R. W. (1976). *A social-psychological study of religious experience with special emphasis on Christian conversion.* Unpublished doctoral dissertation, University of Florida.

Young, J. E. (1982). Loneliness, depression and cognitive therapy: Theory and application. In L. A. Peplau & D. Perlman (Eds.), *Loneliness: A sourcebook of current theory, research and therapy*. New York: Wiley (Interscience).

Zipris, A. (1979). *Being lonely: An empirical-phenomenological investigation*. Unpublished doctoral dissertation proposal, Duquesne University.

Selectivity and Urgency
in Interpersonal Exchange

LYNN C. MILLER
*JOHN H. BERG*_____

INTRODUCTION

The view that human interactions consist chiefly of a process of social exchange between participants is accepted by almost all contemporary investigators of human behavior. In psychology and sociology, the view that all interactions, not just economic ones, will involve exchange can be traced back to the seminal works of Thibaut and Kelley (1959), Homans (1961), and Blau (1964). Friendship formation, romantic attachment, loneliness, the formation and maintenance of status hierarchies, cooperation and competition between both individuals and groups, and interpersonal communication are only a few of the areas in which social exchange principles have been applied since these original formulations.

Prior investigators of social exchange have tended to focus upon the manner in which people attempt to maximize their outcomes in social exchanges and their reactions to these outcomes (e.g., Thibaut & Kelley, 1959; Walster, Berscheid, & Walster, 1973) and upon the nature of the resources that people exchange with one another (e.g., Foa & Foa, 1974, 1976). Less attention has been paid to the issues of how a person selects a particular resource for exchange with another and the urgency he or

COMMUNICATION, INTIMACY,
AND CLOSE RELATIONSHIPS
161

she feels to make such a selection after having received a resource from the other. It is the intent of this chapter to explore the issues of selectivity and urgency in exchange and to point out how these constructs are relevant to close and intimate relationships. Individuals in close relationships should be particularly concerned about choosing or selecting those benefits that most meet the needs, desires, and wants of the other and less concerned with quickly returning some benefit simply to discharge an obligation. In short, intimate relationships may be governed by different principles of exchange than nonintimate relationships (Mills & Clark, 1982). To a large extent such differences may involve the issues of selectivity and urgency.

While it is not the intent of this chapter to provide a comprehensive description of social exchange theories or their basic principles (for reviews see Burgess & Huston, 1979; Roloff, 1981; Simpson, 1976), we need to discuss some of this literature initially to examine two basic issues: (1) why are people concerned with providing benefits to others? and (2) what types of benefits are available for exchange? We then present a discussion of those factors and individual differences that we see as important in the process of selecting a particular resource to return to another. We conclude with a discussion of the relationships among selectivity and four related concepts or topics: communal and exchange relationships, reciprocity, rules of fairness, and responsiveness. Throughout this chapter exchange is broadly defined and includes social and communicative as well as more "economic" exchanges.

THE DESIRE TO BENEFIT AN INTERACTION PARTNER

The Norm of Reciprocity and Equity Theory

Gouldner (1960) proposed that human interactions are governed by a "norm of reciprocity." He viewed this norm as minimally prescribing that we help those who have helped us and that we refrain from harming those who have helped us. This first requirement provides one reason people will be motivated to return benefits to a person who has benefited them. The norm of reciprocity has formed one of the bases of equity theory (Adams, 1965; Walster *et al.*, 1973) and has frequently been invoked to explain reciprocity in exchanges of self-disclosure (e.g., Chaikin & Derlega, 1974; Derlega, Harris, & Chaikin, 1973). Particularly in the latter case, the norm of reciprocity has been taken to imply that recipients of another's self-disclosure are under an obligation to return disclosure of comparable value (intimacy). While other explanations for disclosure reciprocity have been proposed, the normative approach appears to have the greatest experimental support (Archer, 1979).

Equity theory highlights the fact that in considering what one participant in an exchange "owes" the other, attention must be given to each person's inputs or contributions to the relationship as well as their outcomes. An exchange or a relationship is held to be equitable when the ratio of outcomes to inputs for each participant is equal to the ratio of outcomes to inputs for the other participant(s). The person who has contributed more should receive better outcomes than a person who has contributed less.

Equity researchers have shown that subjects who find themselves in inequitable exchanges will feel distressed and aroused, compared to those for whom the situation is equitable (Austin & Walster, 1974). Moreover, this distress will result regardless of whether the person is being underbenefited or overbenefited in comparison to his or her contributions. In addition, it has been shown that when subjects find themselves in an inequitable situation, they will attempt to restore equity to it. Walster *et al.* (1973) note two general ways in which equity is generally restored. First, a party who is being overbenefited may attempt to compensate the other, exploited party (Berscheid, Walster, & Barclay, 1969). A second type of response involves restoring psychological rather than actual, equity to the situation. A person who has exploited or harmed another may convince him or herself that the situation is still an equitable one through derogating the exploited party (Davis & Jones, 1964; Sykes & Matza, 1957) or by minimizing the person's suffering or their own responsibility for it (Brock & Buss, 1964; Sykes & Matza, 1957). The adequacy of available compensations for complete restoration of equity appears to be a highly important factor in determining which of these two responses will occur. Berscheid and Walster (1967) and Berscheid *et al.* (1969) find that compensation is more likely when the available means of compensation will completely restore equity to the situation than when they are either too small to compensate for the former inequity or so large that they would overcompensate for it.

The internalization of the principle of equity should be one factor leading a person to reciprocate or return benefits he or she has received from an exchange partner. To the extent that the individual subscribes to the principle of equity, he or she feels a greater urgency to repay the other. Also this sense of urgency should increase as the degree to which he or she has been benefited increases. Other factors that will affect the sense of urgency a person feels to benefit another who has previously helped him or her may include the type of benefit received and the attributions made for the benefactor's behavior.

While few persons would question the proposition that equity principles are operative in governing exchanges in relatively casual or business relationships, Hatfield, Utne, and Traupmann (1979) note that there is considerable debate over whether or not such principles are operative in close or love relationships. They note that some theorists (e.g., Fromm, 1956; Rubin 1973) view love as transcending the principles of exchange. The fact that equity considerations are operative within close relationships is illustrated in a study by Walster, Walster, and Traupmann (1978). These researchers found that as compared to persons who felt they were in less equitable relationships, those in more equitable ones reported feeling happier and more content and were more certain that their relationships would continue in the future.

While acknowledging that love relationships and close relationships differ from other relationships in a number of ways including intensity of affect, the depth and breadth of participants' knowledge of one another, and the value and variety of the resources that are exchanged, Walster et al. (1973) and Hatfield et al. (1979) argue that these differences should simply affect the ease with which equity is calculated in close versus casual relationships and the means participants in such relationships are likely to choose to restore or maintain equity. Regarding the first point, it may be that determinations of equity are both more difficult and less frequently made in close relationships than in casual ones. Because close relationships are extended in time, participants will have to draw upon a large number of experiences in determining whether their relationship is fair. The temporal duration of these relationships may also affect the manner in which participants choose to benefit one another or restore equity. For example, if one participant knows the other will be needing a certain benefit in the future he or she may not be concerned with the immediate degree of equity in the relationship, realizing that he or she will benefit the other at this later time. The partner, too, may well understand this and so not be distressed that a benefit is not immediately reciprocated. This is of course, due to the fact that the process of becoming closer has resulted in the development of trust between individuals. One person no longer needs to be concerned with being exploited by or with exploiting the other. To the extent participants trust one another it is unnecessary to examine the fairness of the relationship. In fact, it may even be detrimental. Levinger (1979) notes that one sign that a relationship is in trouble is when participants begin to question whether or not they are receiving as much as they should be.

Outcome Interdependence

It is apparent from the above discussion that we may benefit others in part due to a feeling of obligation or a desire to maintain equity. A theory of outcome interdependence (Kelley, 1979; Kelley & Thibaut, 1978; Thibaut & Kelley, 1959) provides a framework suggesting several additional factors that may lead one individual to provide benefits to an interaction partner.

To provide some background, Thibaut & Kelley (1959) examined how interactions might be understood from the perspective of the outcomes received by participants in the interactions. Outcomes were very broadly defined and represented the net differences between the rewards obtained through interaction and the costs incurred in the course of that interaction. Thibaut and Kelley noted that such outcomes are generally determined by the actions of both the participants in an interaction. By varying their behavior, people will influence not only their own rewards and costs but also the rewards and costs of others. Like all social exchange theorists, Thibaut and Kelley assumed that people were motivated to maximize their rewards while minimizing their costs.

In later reformulations and extentions of the theory (Kelley, 1979; Kelley & Thibaut, 1978) it was emphasized that participants will take the outcomes received by a partner as well as their own outcomes into consideration when deciding how to act and when evaluating an interaction. Considering the other's outcomes in addition to one's own will lead to a reconsideration of environmentally given patterns of rewards and costs and to the transformation of these patterns.

While not representing a true example of interdependence, an example may help clarify some of what is involved in one type of transformation. Consider an individual, Jane, who is attempting to decide between two courses of action. One of these actions, (Act A), provides Jane with a net reward of '3' and her interaction partner with a net reward of '0'. The other course of action, (Act B), would provide both Jane and her partner with outcomes of '2.' Jane would choose Act A if she were motivated to maximize her own outcomes ('3' > '2') or to maximize her gains relative to her partner (a difference of '3' as opposed to '0'). However, when Jane takes her partner's outcomes into account, she would choose Act B if she desired to maintain equality in the relationship (both receive a reward of '2') or if she were attempting to maximize the total amount of benefit received by the pair ('4' > '3') or if she wished to maximize her partner's outcomes ('2' > '0'). In each of the above examples Jane is said to have "transformed" the environmentally given patterns into behaviorally effective patterns and it is the latter that will determine her behavior.

The fact that people do make transformations similar to the ones just described indicates that motives other than merely the desire to maximize one's own outcomes may be operative in interpersonal interactions. Such motives may arise through socialization, because of the situation in which a specific interaction occurs or due to personal characteristics of an individual. The socialization experiences of most people should lead them to view a concern with benefiting another and with maximizing joint rewards as appropriate in close or intimate relationships. In addition, Kelley (1979) notes that the act of expressing personal dispositions may be rewarding in and of itself. Thus a competitive person finds the act of competing rewarding and an altruistic person is rewarded by helping. In close relationships in which people care deeply about one another, one would expect the dispositions a person finds rewarding to involve demonstrating concern with another's outcomes and with the joint outcomes received by the pair.

Thus a person may provide benefits to another because of the transformations they make (due to socialization, the nature of the situation or personal dispositions). They may also provide benefits because they receive rewards themselves through the act of benefiting a partner. These factors provide two reasons in addition to the concern with reciprocity or equity previously considered, that may lead people to benefit an interaction partner.

Because individuals' transformations, and thus their interpersonal dispositions, are reflected in their behavior, Kelley (1979) notes that people will use the choices another makes to infer that person's traits or dispositions. For instance, did Jane in the above example choose Act B because she was attempting to maximize her partner's outcomes (was altruistic) or because she was very concerned with maintaining equality? The view that people will tend to make dispositional attributions is consistent with the idea that they are motivated to identify relatively invariant causes for behavior (Heider, 1958). If the cause of behaviors or transformational tendencies is located in stable dispositions of the other, these may subsequently be drawn upon in order to plan one's own future actions. Kelley (1979) holds that the tendency to make such dispositional attributions will be greatest in close relationships. The repeated interactions that such relationships involve make it most important that participants understand the manner in which their partner is likely to transform given patterns of rewards and costs in order for either the individual or the pair to achieve maximal benefit. Moreover, because any single behavior is likely to be ambiguous in terms of the disposition it reflects, stable attributions may require repeated interactions. Given the importance of such attributions when continued interaction is expected, one might predict that people are more likely to make attributions about a partner's dispositions when future interactions are expected than when they are not.

The types of dispositions that an individual infers an interaction partner to possess may have consequences for (1) the degree to which that person will reciprocate benefits, (2) the form such reciprocation will take, (3) and the speed with which behavior is reciprocated. To return to our earlier example, if I infer that Jane's choice of Act B stems from a concern that I be benefited as much as possible, I may be more concerned with providing her with rewards than if I had attributed her action to a desire to ensure equity. Given the importance that the attributions one makes about a partner's dispositions can have, and the ambiguity that may be involved in making such inferences, it is not surprising that disagreements over whether or not a given behavior reflects an underlying trait or over which trait it reflects are frequent sources of conflict in close relationships (Braiker & Kelley, 1979; Orvis, Kelley, & Butler, 1976).

Several points can be noted in summarizing the preceding section. First, there is a social norm that obligates people to return benefits to those who have benefited them and to maintain equity in their relationships. Second, individuals in close relationships, and some individuals in general, may find it intrinsically rewarding to benefit an interaction partner. Finally, whether individuals provide another with benefits and the nature of the benefits they provide may depend upon the attributions they have made concerning the other's transformational tendencies and dispositions.

RESOURCE THEORY—WHAT IS EXCHANGED?

Once a person has decided to return a resource, he or she must decide what specific resource to give. While we said earlier that this chapter would employ a broad definition of exchange, this does not imply that we view all exchanges of all things as equivalent. The type of resource that is received may have important consequences for the type of resource that is returned and both given and returned resources may impact on the relationship between exchange partners. Thus, before considering the manner in which a recipient selects a particular resource to return, it is important to give some attention to the different types of resources that are exchanged and the likely effects of receiving a particular type of resource.

Work in this area has been relatively sparse, compared to the amount of attention that has been given to factors that motivate a recipient to return benefits or that affect evaluations of exchanges. However, Foa and Foa (1974, 1976, 1980) have proposed and investigated one general system for the classification of resources. They first distinguish six general classes of resources: money, goods, services, love, status and information. They next propose that these six classes may be arrayed along two dimensions. The first of these dimensions is termed particularism and refers to the extent to which a resource derives value because of the particular person giving it. Love is seen as the most particularistic type of resource. It typically matters a great deal who it is that says "I love you" or otherwise expresses affection. Status and services are viewed as somewhat less particularistic in nature. Information and goods derive still less of their value on the basis of the particular person providing them and money will be the least particularistic resource, having the same value regardless of who is providing it. The second dimension Foa and Foa distinguish deals with how concrete or symbolic a resource is. Along this dimension, goods and services are seen as very concrete resources. Information and status, on the other hand, are extremely symbolic since they are typically conveyed only through verbal channels. Love and money are viewed as intermediate between these two extremes along the dimension of concreteness.

Foa and Foa (1974) provided subjects with messages designed to illustrate a benefit in each of the six classes and instructed them to sort the messages into as many categories as they thought appropriate. Results were generally supportive of the proposed structure. Where confusions did occur they involved the confusion of adjacent classes. More recently, Brinberg and Castell (1982) asked subjects to rate the similarity–dissimilarity of 12 behaviors designed to illustrate the different resource classes. The similarity ratings were then subjected to a multidimensional scaling analysis. Again results generally confirmed the structure that Foa and Foa had proposed. One exception in the Brinberg and Castell (1982) study involved the fact that in their college student sample, money was seen as being more similar to love than the model would predict. Brinberg and Castell speculate that this may be due to the fact that within a student sample, money may be a relatively scarce resource. Other research (e.g., Brock, 1968) suggests that the value of a "resource" will increase in proportion to its scarcity. It would seem reasonable to assume that scarce and valued resources would be viewed as being exchanged only between those persons who had a more unique relationship to each other. Thus, these resources would appear similar.

If, as the above line of reasoning suggests, the value of a resource will increase as that resource becomes more particularistic, it is almost certain that particularistic resources will be freely exchanged only among those who have a close relationship. As Altman and Taylor (1973) have noted, as the potential benefits of an exchange or a relationship increase, the potential costs will also increase. Thus before highly valued, particularistic, resources are given, there must exist a feeling of trust that the exchange will be completed and that the other will also provide benefits.

Foa and Foa (1976) also describe several studies bearing on the type of resource that is selected for return after having received a resource. Both subjects who were interacting with a confederate and subjects who were asked to imagine that they had just provided a certain resource to a friend expressed greater satisfaction with returned benefits that were similar to those they had initially given. Two additional findings from subjects imagining exchanges with a friend are noteworthy. First, the preference for receiving a resource from the same class as the resource initially provided became more pronounced as the initial resource became more particularistic. Second, there was a general preference for receiving love as a returned benefit. These latter findings reinforce our belief that exchanges of particularistic resources will be more likely among those who have a close relationship.

Foa and Foa (1974, 1976) also investigated negative exchanges in which a person is initially deprived of a resource. In one study subjects were asked to imagine different interactions in which another first deprived them of a resource from one of the six classes, after which they deprived this person of various resources. Subjects reported greater satisfaction when the resource they denied or took from the other was similar to that which they had been deprived of. In addition, there was also a preference for denying or withdrawing love from the other.

In another study subjects who were initially deprived of a resource from one of the six classes by a confederate were later given the opportunity to retaliate, either by depriving her of money or subjecting her to derogatory statements (taking away love). Results indicated that as the resource available for retaliation (money or love) became more dissimilar to the one subjects were initially deprived of, the intensity of retaliation increased, but that despite this increased intensity, subjects remained more hostile toward the confederate.

It remains to be demonstrated whether similar findings in terms of intensity and satisfaction will occur in positive exchanges. On the basis of Foa and Foa's model, however, it would be predicted that after receiving a benefit in a given class, a subject would repay a greater amount as the resources available for repayment diverged from what he or she received. It would also be predicted that subjects would report less satisfaction with the exchange when they could not return a similar resource.

Foa and Foa's model not only provides us with a means of classifying the types of benefits that are exchanged but also begins to explore how people might selectively choose a certain resource to return to another. It proposes that they will choose one that is similar to the one given them. While Foa and Foa have discussed similarity in terms of the class to which a resource belongs, it is tempting to speculate on whether or not the same reasoning might not apply in terms of the needs met by a resource. If a person provides a resource that satisfies a need of the other, will the exchange be more satisfying if the recipient returns a similar resource or a dissimilar one that reduces a need of the original donor to a similar extent?

The choice of a certain type of resource to return will also be affected by several other factors. The effect that the closeness of a relationship is likely to have was previously noted. Foa and Foa (1976) also point out that the context in which an exchange takes place will influence the type of resource that is returned. They note that the same resource (e.g., a delicious meal) leads to very different types of returned resources depending on whether it is consumed in a restaurant or a friend's home. Different individuals may also have differing preferences for returning certain types of resources. In later sections of this chapter we will address the manner in which individual differences and other situational factors may influence the manner in which a person selects benefits to return.

SELECTIVITY IN SOCIAL EXCHANGE

The process of selecting a benefit for another implies that an individual P has determined that it is appropriate and/or desirable to return a benefit to another O. Having decided to return a benefit, what does P give? Selectivity refers to the process by which P chooses a benefit to bestow upon O. The more that P's chosen benefit to O meets O's desires, needs, and preferences, the more selective the benefit is viewed as being.

Selectivity implies a choice between a number of possible options. In choosing a benefit for another, P must decide what he or she *can* provide as a benefit. Two issues are relevant here: (1) P's perceived time frame (whether there are possible future options and the urgency which P feels to repay a benefit), and (2) the resources P has available within that time frame. Given what P *could* provide, what P decides *to* provide given these constraints is apt to depend upon at least three additional factors: (1) social constraints such as norms, perceptions of socially appropriate behavior, and the physical constraints of the contexts, (2) perceptions of O and the relationship (e.g., knowledge of the other, past interactions, and perceptions of the other's characteristics, intentions and goals) and (3) P's own goals, expectations, motives, and characteristics. Let us consider each of these factors in greater detail.

Benefits Available for Return

Time Frame and Urgency

The time frame is the period of time in which an individual P perceives that he or she ought to reciprocate by giving a benefit or benefits in exchange for a benefit received from another individual. The time frame may be short because the perceived duration of the relationship itself is short (e.g., we don't expect to see this person in the future) or because there is a stimulus or external event which poses a time limit (e.g., a wedding or birthday present usually must be purchased before the event). The shorter the perceived time frame, the less likely we are to choose a selective benefit. As the time frame increases we (1) have more time within which to plan and contemplate giving a selective benefit, and (2) have access to a wider range of resources and options from which to choose a more selective benefit. However, while taking a longer period of time within which to choose a benefit may provide one with more of an *opportunity* to be selective, a longer time span (period of time which elapses before P bestows a benefit upon O) does *not* mean that an individual will choose a more selective benefit. Consider a man who puts off repaying a neighbor for a favor because he can't find that "perfect" benefit to return. Such a man runs the risk of never returning a benefit to his neighbor. In a later section, the implied relationship here between selectivity, time-span, and equity will be discussed further.

The shorter the perceived time frame the more we are likely to feel a sense of urgency to find something to return quickly. At this point the giver of the benefit may be more concerned with meeting social obligations or reciprocity norms than with the needs, desires or wishes of the recipient of the benefit. Even when the time frame is relatively long, some individuals may be especially likely to repay a benefit quickly in order to discharge a perceived obligation as soon as possible. We will discuss such individual difference factors in a later section.

Resources Available

Within a particular time frame, individuals usually have a variety of resources available to them. Several general classes of resources are described here, including the following ones:

1. Personal and affiliative resources. These involve being able to offer such benefits as companionship, support, affection, and praise. Also included here are resources that have a unique personal meaning and are apt to be irreplaceable. Examples might include a ring given to us by a parent, a family heirloom, or a pipe smoked by a now-deceased father. Giving this type of benefit to another is likely to occur only in close relationships and to have special meaning for both the giver and the recipient.

2. Resources drawing on general or specific areas of knowledge that enable one to provide needed or desired information or services to the other. Examples might include offering to cook a gourmet meal or using one's knowledge of plumbing to repair a leaky faucet.

3. Resources stemming from one's social position that involve the ability to provide the other with power, status, wealth or material resources.

4. Time resources that enhance the selection and giving of appropriate benefits.

Having resources such as the ones distinguished above at one's disposal would allow one to provide a host of economic and social rewards (see Buss, 1983; Foa & Foa, 1974). While we have available at our disposal a number of resources, even within a relatively short time-frame, simply because these resources are available does not mean that we will necessarily use them to provide a benefit. We have a limited store of most resources and in considering what benefit to provide to another we need to take into account what other commitments of our resources have been made or will be made. As Foa and Foa (1974) have noted, many of our resources, once given, reduce our own store. This is most clearly the case with concrete goods that are transferred to another, but it also applies to any service or act that requires the expenditure of our time. In short, the set of probable benefits to provide to another will be typically smaller than the total set of resources a person possesses for exchange. Some social norms and rules provide guidelines in assessing to what extent we should use available resources in returning a benefit to another. Several such norms have received empirical attention and we address their influence in the section on related concepts.

Benefits Selected for Return

Knowledge of the Other

One of the most important factors influencing our ability to be selective in returning a benefit is our knowledge (or lack of knowledge) about the other. Presumably, the closer our relationship to the other and the longer we have known the other, the more likely it is that we will have detailed and extensive knowledge of that other's desires, needs and preferences (person-specific information). We may have such knowledge of others because they have explicitly told us verbally what they desire or need or because they have indicated such a need or desire implicitly via nonverbal, verbal or other cues. Another possibility is that we may determine what the other is likely to need from some other source who has access to information about the other's desires or needs (e.g., someone in this other's social network). Finally, we may infer the other's desires or needs from a common knowledge of what individuals need or desire in particular contexts. Thus, for example, suitable benefits to give a woman whose husband has just died include an arrangement of flowers, a letter of condolence, a look of concern, an offer to help out, a casserole, a hug, saying "I'm sorry," and so forth. Suitable benefits to give another whose daughter has just married, (where the mother likes the new son-in-law) include smiling and hugging, complimenting the mother on her dress (or the house, the reception or the food), giving the daughter a gift, and so on. There are clearly classes of appropriate benefits to give depending upon the situation. It would be considered in poor taste, for example, to give a bride (even one who is pregnant) a baby carriage for a wedding present (unless the couple requested the present).

In all, there seem to be four types of knowledge that are likely to affect how selective the benefit is that we are returning to another:

General Knowledge is knowledge of what people in general across a broad number of contexts desire, want, or need. For example, individuals generally want or need such things as food, money, and clothing. This involves awareness of the class of social and economic reinforcers that have been discussed elsewhere (Buss, 1983; Foa & Foa, 1974).

Person-Specific Knowledge is knowledge that involves knowing what a particular individual desires, wants or needs. For example, we know that a best friend generally likes to receive yellow roses or that a parent prefers receiving antiques over receiving a trip as a present.

Context-Specific Knowledge is knowledge that involves knowing what most individuals want or desire in a particular context. For example, speakers who are giving a talk generally would enjoy having a glass of water handy. This is a context in which a glass of water would be highly desired.

Person/Context-Specific Knowledge involves knowledge of what a particular individual would especially desire, need or want in a specific context. One woman we know likes to have her husband rub her stomach when she is anxious and she and her husband are alone in a private place. However, she doesn't like to have her stomach rubbed under any other circumstances.

General knowledge and context-specific knowledge both seem to tap into normative knowledge about what to give another in general or in specific contexts (e.g., most people in this context would prefer, like or need "x"). Person-specific knowledge and person/context-specific knowledge involve knowing specific information about particular individuals' preferences (that diverge from general preferences): information that is more detailed than general knowledge. Because most individuals in a given culture are likely to be aware of that culture's norms, individual differences and degree of relationship with a particular other are apt to be most relevant when what a particular individual desires or wants diverges from or is more detailed than the average "normative" benefit. For example, we might expect that as they spend more time with another, and as the relationship develops, roommates should become better at discovering and meeting each other's needs. Berg (in press) found precisely that in a recent study. Furthermore, as self-disclosure to one's roommate (one index of supplying person-specific knowledge about oneself to another) increased, so too did both the total number of benefits subjects received and the number of times they received those benefits that they most wanted.

Attributions Made For Initial Benefit

Our perceptions of the other's characteristics and motives for providing benefits, as well as the nature of the relationship also affect the benefit we select. Why has the other provided us with a benefit in the first place? In the course of day-to-day interactions with others, people whom we barely know, as well as strangers and close friends, may bestow "benefits" upon us. They may provide us with money, compliments, a seat in a bus, a match, directions downtown or an umbrella in a rainstorm. What do we make of these benefits? Is the salesman giving us a road atlas because he really wants us to buy an auto from his lot? Is this student paying us a compliment because he or she hopes to get a better grade in a course? In short, we need to interpret the giving behavior of the other.

Three classes of giving behavior can be identified. First, *obligatory* •
giving is giving which tends to be normatively based. We tell the hostess the dinner was delicious even though we thought it was horrible. We give a wedding present or birthday present because it is expected that we do so if we attend the affair. *Instrumental giving* is giving through which the giver hopes to accomplish some goal (e.g., the giver wants you to buy something, or do something for him or her). With this type of giving, providing the recipient with a benefit is an ingratiation technique (cf., Jones, 1964) or a means to an end (e.g., the service, good or information the giver desires to receive in return). A third type of giving is more altruistic: It can be called *pleasure-based* giving. Someone gives a benefit because he or she enjoys giving benefits to others or feels bad watching someone else in distress. Perhaps for this individual, giving is consistent with a self-concept of being altruistic and giving makes such a person feel good. Another example of pleasure-based giving is giving so that the other will feel good or not incur a harmful or unpleasant experience. When we decide that the nature of the giving falls into one of these three categories, we are likely to make matching inferences about the giver and his or her motives, as indicated in Table 7.1.

When the giver's behavior falls within boundaries of social norms we would typically assume that the person is simply being polite and thus be unlikely to return a benefit beyond a simple "thank you" or smile. But, once these boundaries are exceeded, then the receiver must decide why he or she is such a recipient. At least one of three inferences are possible: (1) the giver wants something from me in return, (2) the giver is doing this because it makes him or her feel good, or (3) the giver cares about me and my needs.

In the process of making these attributions, individuals must bring to the fore information about the person who provided the benefit (and the category of individuals that this person belongs to), the nature of the relationship that they share with the giver, as well as social information about norms, expectations, and goals. Such information is useful not only in interpreting why others may be bestowing particular benefits,

TABLE 7.1

Relations Among Types of Giving, Perceived Goals, and Attributions

Giving type	Perceived goal of other	Likely attribution concerning the other
Obligatory	to be polite	person is courteous (normative behavior)
Instrumental	other wants you to do something	Person is Machiavellian, manipulative, aggressive. You are only a means to an end for the other
Pleasure-based	providing benefit makes the person feel good or avoid feeling bad or having an unpleasant experience	person is kind, altruistic, giving
	to make you feel good	Person is a good friend, and cares about you personally, or is an empathic person

but also in evaluating such benefits, deciding whether to return a benefit and choosing a specific benefit to return.

Suppose we begin with the characteristics of the individual. If this person is a stranger, we may try to determine first if the motive for giving is likely to be instrumental. We may look to see if they are trying to sell us something. Or, we may consider the individual's occupation (e.g., is the person an insurance agent). Because of our past experiences with members of particular categories and our stereotypes about certain groups of individuals, we may decide that simply knowing that an individual is a member of a certain category (e.g., an insurance agent) makes their giving behavior suspect. That is, even if they don't mention insurance, we may suspect that a new neighbor who is an insurance agent and who provides us with a benefit (e.g., a welcome mat for our new home) is doing so because he or she is going to try to sell us insurance. Even if we can't immediately confirm that the giving is instrumentally based, we may continue to be suspicious of this person's motives, making it difficult to conclude that the giving of the insurance salesman was pleasure-based (e.g., this is a very giving person who likes to help people and make them feel welcome in a community).

What is the result of such attributions? One hypothesis seems reasonable: To the extent that we decide that the benefactor's giving behavior is instrumentally based, we are less likely to be selective if we return a benefit and perhaps even less likely to return a benefit (Brehm & Cole,

1966) than we are when we decide that the giving is more pleasure-based. Given the same benefit, we are probably also more apt to like someone who provides us with a benefit we perceive as pleasure-based than one we perceive as instrumentally based.

What happens when the person who has benefited us is a friend, acquaintance or someone we know something about through a mutual acquaintance or friend? In such cases, we would be expected to use this knowledge in making attributions for his or her giving behavior. It is also likely that with friends we start out with the presumption that they are providing a benefit because of the type of person they are or because of our relationship with them (i.e., an attribution of pleasure-based giving). We feel disappointed and even angered if we discover that the benefit was instrumentally based instead. Consider what happens when a friend or relative invites us to come over for a party. We arrive, expecting that we will receive a benefit (dinner and a relaxing evening) because our friends enjoy our company and they wish to make us feel good, only to discover that this is an Amway party, where we are going to be asked to look at various goods for sale and possibly listen to a lecture to get us to become distributors of this product. Even though our friends have provided a benefit (dinner) we may decide that we do not have to stay around for the "demo" and we may not feel we need to return a benefit. We may feel that our friends have taken advantage of our friendship and that such instrumentally based giving suggests that we may not be the friends we thought we were.

The manner in which the nature of the relationship may affect reactions to receiving a benefit has been described in detail by Clark (1983). We will discuss the manner in which Clark's views relate to the issue of selectivity in more detail later in the section dealing with communal and exchange relationships. Here we would only note that Clark and Mills (1979) provide evidence suggesting that if a benefit received from a friend is perceived as a case of obligatory giving, attraction for the giver may decline.

The attribution made by a recipient may also be affected by the giver's selection of a benefit. Was the resource given something that required a large amount of the donor's time and/or resources? To what degree was the benefit received selective and/or personalistic? Did the recipient specifically request that particular benefit?

If the benefit received is perceived to have required more of the donor's time and/or resources or if the recipient explicitly requested some benefit, a greater feeling of obligation and indebtedness (Greenberg, 1980) is likely to result. The recipient may then feel a greater sense of urgency to return some benefit. This may be especially likely when the relationship between giver and recipient is not a close one. It is also possible, however, that a personalistic benefit (i.e., one perceived by a recipient as specifically intended for him or her), that is given too soon in a relationship might arouse reactance (Brehm & Cole, 1966; Worchel, Andreoli, & Archer, 1976). In this case it would be less likely that a recipient would reciprocate a benefit. The previously mentioned reactions would seem to be less likely when the resource is given by a close friend (Nadler, Fisher, & Streufort, 1974, 1976). In communal relationships, such as those between close friends, there is an obligation to attempt to meet the needs of the other. Giving the resource would be attributed to the relationship between donor and recipient and the recipient should not feel any new obligation unless the donor has incurred a need in the course of providing that benefit (Clark, 1983). A result that is likely to occur is that the recipient should now feel more confident about the relationship with the other and may experience an increased sense of commitment to that relationship.

INDIVIDUAL DIFFERENCES IN SELECTIVITY

Obtaining Knowledge of Others

Presumably, the longer we have known someone, the more selective is our choice of a benefit for them, in general, because we have access to additional categories of knowledge concerning the other (e.g., person-specific and person/context–specific information). In addition, we have more time and therefore more opportunities to give selectively. Even so, among individuals who have known a given other for the same period of time, some people are simply better at choosing benefits that are more desired, needed, or wanted. What individual differences might affect the extent to which individuals are knowledgeable about specific benefits to give particular others under varying contexts?

Although this discussion is speculative, in that there is little data with which to address these issues, it seems reasonable that one factor involves individual differences in attentiveness to what others are saying in conversations: more attentive individuals should acquire more knowledge about others. In fact, some recent research suggests that individuals do vary considerably in how attentive they believe they are when others are conversing (Miller & Mueller, 1983) and these differences are related to what individuals can accurately remember about conversations that they have heard. In one study, undergraduates at

Northern Illinois University first indicated the extent to which they felt that they were attentive listeners, responding to such items as "I listen attentively to the conversations of others". Then these undergraduates watched a videotape of a woman being interviewed. After the interview tape, subjects were asked to indicate how confident they were that the woman being interviewed had said or not said each of 40 statements (20 of which had been said). There was a significant relationship between reported attentiveness to conversations (conversational attentiveness) and ability to remember accurately what was said during the 10-minute videotape. Greater attentiveness during conversations should increase the likelihood that individuals will encode and later be able to remember preferences, desires, and needs that were stated during the conversation. Other research also suggests that other individual differences may affect the ability to remember conversations accurately. One of these characteristics includes vividness of visual imagery (Swann & Miller, 1982). Individuals who score higher on Mark's Visual Imagery Scale (Mark, 1973), were more accurate at remembering what was said during a conversation when they saw the interactant compared to those low in vividness of imagery.

Some individuals may be more knowledgeable about others because they encourage or are able to get others to disclose more about themselves. One relevant individual difference measure involves the Opener Scale (Miller, Berg, & Archer, 1983). Items on this measure include, "I've been told that I'm a good listener" and "I easily get people to 'open up'". Individuals who endorse items on this scale have been found to elicit more disclosure from both strangers in the lab (Miller *et al.*, 1983, Study 2) and acquaintances and friends in the field, (Miller *et al.*, 1983, Study 3). Recent work suggests that high Openers may be more responsive (in the sense that they provide speakers with nonverbal encouragements such as backchannel communications, smiles and eye contact) than low Openers (Purvis, Dabbs, & Hopper, 1981) and it seems likely that this differential responsiveness of Openers partially accounts for their tendency to elicit more intimate disclosure from their partners. In any event, because high Openers elicit more intimate disclosures from their partners, high Openers are apt to know more about their partners than low Openers. A second relevant measure involves individual differences in the tendency to self-disclose. Individuals who are themselves high disclosers may encourage their partners to disclose in turn (Jourard & Resnick, 1970). High disclosers then might have more knowledge of others because others tell them more intimate things. A third personality characteristic that seems relevant here is sociability. More sociable individuals would be expected (by definition) to have a wider circle of friends and acquaintances and thus would be more apt to secure specific knowledge about an individual through their network of friends and associates. Furthermore, one important aspect of sociability is warmth (Buss & Plomin, 1975) which should enhance perceived responsiveness. In a similar vein, the "expressivity scale" (formally the femininity scale) devised by Spence, Helmreich, & Stapp (1974) includes items that ask subjects to judge the extent to which they are "kind," "warm" and "willing to devote themselves to others." Individuals who score high on this dimension may be especially concerned with choosing a benefit that meets the other's needs.

On the other hand, some characteristics of persons may detract from or inhibit learning about others' needs and desires. Shyness and audience anxiety seem likely candidates. Shy individuals may be so worried about what they are saying that they may attend less to what others are saying. Support for this notion comes from a recent study by Stafford and Daly (1983). In that study, individuals who scored high on an audience apprehension measure were less likely to recall information about what was said during a conversation than individuals who scored low on the apprehension measure.

Resources Available

Several personality variables are relevant concerning the resources individuals have available to give to others. Regarding affiliative resources, more sociable individuals may be better at giving companionship than less sociable individuals. Openers may be better at listening to others and seem to be more responsive listeners (Miller, 1982; Purvis et al., 1981). In terms of specific skills, more creative, intelligent, and athletic individuals may have more resources available to them than less creative and talented individuals. Also, some individuals may be especially likely to achieve and receive higher salaries and thus acquire a greater pool of possible resources to provide to others. For example, Helmreich and Spence (1978) found that individuals who have higher levels of two components of achievement motivation (work and mastery) and lower levels of a third component (competitiveness) may be more likely to receive higher salaries (and possibly achieve higher status).

Motivation

Generally speaking then, individuals with greater resources are better able to be selective in their choice of benefits to bestow on others. Suppose we know what someone else needs, we have the resources to meet the need but we lack the motivation to give the resource. Perhaps we feel we can't afford the benefit. Others may be reluctant to provide a benefit that might aid a perceived competitor. For example, suppose two colleagues are working on a similar problem. One has an insight or gains access to a new resource (e.g., a subject pool that the other is unaware of). Does the one colleague provide the other with the new resource? Colleagues who are more cooperative may be more apt to share scarce professional resources. Colleagues who are more competitive may choose alternative benefits that would be unrelated to productivity. They may offer rides or provide dinners but not scarce professional resources.

It also seems likely that we will provide a benefit to another when we especially like him or her. Prior research suggests that some individuals (those high in private self-consciousness) are particularly aware of their feelings (Scheier, 1976). Thus, liking for another should be particularly salient for them. Perhaps, such salient liking for others could increase the likelihood that individuals high in private self-consciousness will provide more benefits (perhaps more selective benefits) to those whom they most like.

Individuals high in public self-consciousness seem particularly concerned about how they appear to others (Fenigstein, Scheier, & Buss, 1975). Such individuals may be more "conservative" in their choice of benefits for another. That is, they may adopt allocation rules that are more absolute, making sure that they return a benefit that is as valuable as the one they received and perhaps being more concerned about how the gift might look to others. For example, suppose a guest at a wedding has to choose between two equally expensive presents. One is a sterling fork and knife in the bride's pattern and the second is a silverplated coffee and tea service. The guest knows that the bride requested the sterling fork and knife, but somehow the coffee service is a more impressive gift. One would expect individuals who are particularly concerned about "how they look" to choose benefits for others that (1) will fit in with social norms, and (2) are apt to be viewed favorably by others.

Some individuals may also find being with others and interacting with them particularly rewarding. For example, those who are especially sociable may be more motivated to give resources to others because they find the presence of others rewarding. Other personality characteristics may predict reduced likelihood of providing benefits to others. For example, because they are afraid of appearing silly, individuals who are high in fear of embarrassment have been found to be less likely to help than those who are low in such fear (McGovern, 1974). It seems likely

that individuals high in various types of social anxiety might be motivated to avoid providing benefits when there is the threat of potential
embarrassment or they might provide benefits that would be more "normative" or conservative and thus probably less selective.

Whether we choose to give or withhold benefits may depend in part
on how we view ourselves. Individuals who view themselves as altruistic may be especially motivated to help because to do so helps to
maintain their self-concept. The notion that individuals attempt to maintain their self-conceptions by engaging in behaviors consistent with that
self-concept has received recent empirical support when applied to such
characteristics as extroversion and assertiveness (Swann & Hill, 1982;
Swann & Read, 1981).

Additional Factors

Individuals may also differ in their reactions to benefits they receive
from another. Some individuals may be pleased, others distressed and
uncomfortable, perhaps even angry. Partially, such reactions may depend upon how individuals interpret the giving behavior of the other. In
general, if the giving behavior is judged to be pleasure-based we would
expect individuals to react positively. If the giving is perceived to be
instrumentally based, however, individuals may react with a variety of
feelings. They may feel manipulated or decide that their freedom of
choice has been curtailed (e.g., I allowed that salesman to give me a car
sweeper, now I have to buy something). Such attributions, therefore
may easily affect individuals' reactions to benefits. This is especially
likely to be the case for individuals high in private self-consciousness
who are particularly aware of their thoughts and feelings. Such individuals have been shown to react especially negatively for example, to
attempts to coerce them (Gibbons, Scheier, Carver & Hormuth, 1979)
and to experience affect more strongly (Scheier, 1976). In addition, it
seems likely that some individuals are more apt than others (especially
in ambiguous situations) to assume that the motives of the other are
instrumental and not pleasure-based. Individuals who are themselves
highly competitive may question why a worker in their office has offered
to share some "inside information" with them or (in the extreme) why
this person is even friendly toward them. Individuals who are themselves competitive (perhaps Machiavellian as well) may assume that
others function in a similar way. In one prisoner's dilemma game, for
example, whether they choose to compete or cooperate, individuals

expected that their partner would behave the way they behaved (Messe & Sivacek, 1979). Other research (Kelley & Stahelski, 1970) has shown that competitive individuals are especially likely to do this.

While the issue of fairness in social exchange is discussed in detail in the section on related concepts, regarding individual differences it appears that some individuals may react negatively to receiving a benefit because they may feel that the relationship is no longer equitable until they have returned a similar benefit. Such individuals may be particularly distressed if, when given the context and other constraints, they cannot reciprocate with an equivalent benefit. A personality dimension that might be related to such a negative reaction is self-esteem. Individuals high in self-esteem seem to react negatively to aid from others (Nadler, Altman, & Fisher, 1979), compared to those who are low in self-esteem. While receiving a benefit is different from receiving aid (aid implies one requires help and can't handle the situation, while a benefit doesn't necessarily imply this), individuals high in self-esteem might react to both situations in a similar way. After all, someone is offering the individual a benefit. If he or she cannot return a benefit of equal value than that might be a blow to the high self-esteem individual (e.g., if I can't return an equal benefit maybe I'm not as good).

This line of reasoning also suggests that an individual high in self-esteem might feel a more urgent need to repay a benefit as soon as possible since such an individual would not want to feel that he or she was "in debt" to someone else. Individuals who feel a greater need or urgency to repay benefits, as suggested earlier, may be less selective in their choice of a benefit to return or give another because they may allow themselves a relatively small time frame. As the time frame for choosing a benefit decreases, options for benefit choice within that time frame are expected to be reduced. This in turn is expected to reduce the selectivity of the benefit chosen.

However, some individuals may choose the opposite extreme course of action with respect to choosing a benefit. They may keep extending the time frame, hoping that they will find an even more selective benefit as time goes by. Such a strategy has a serious drawback—the individual (trying to find that truly "selective" benefit) may wait so long that it would seem inappropriate to return a benefit. For example, it might seem appropriate to send someone a gourmet cheese basket thanking them for a night's lodging a week after having received the benefit, but not 10 years after receiving the benefit. On the other hand, if we provided our hosts with a room in an unexpected emergency 10 years later, that would be a highly selective benefit and would probably be viewed as more selective than giving the cheese a week after receiving the lodging. In short, we have to eventually chose something as a suitable benefit, or else we may risk not being able to provide a suitable benefit at all. The appropriate time frame for providing a less selective benefit (cheese) may pass and it may be unlikely that we will ever be able to provide the more selective benefit (emergency lodging).

RELATED CONCEPTS ABOUT SOCIAL EXCHANGE

Notions of selectivity and urgency can be seen as closely related to and intertwined with previous concepts in the social exchange literature. In the following section, we focus on four such concepts: (1) the distinction between communal and exchange relationships, (2) reciprocity and the stage of relationship development, (3) norms governing fairness in exchange and allocation of resources and (4) the concept of responsiveness. In linking each of these concepts with selectivity and urgency, we also, whenever feasible, attempt to integrate other concepts in the social exchange literature into our discussion.

Communal and Exchange Relationships

As described by Clark and Mills (e.g., Clark & Mills, 1979; Mills & Clark, 1982), communal relationships correspond to those that would generally be considered close (e.g., relationships between family members, romantic partners and good friends). Exchange relationships are more formal and distant (e.g., casual acquaintanceships, student–teacher and proprietor–customer relationships). Clark and Mills (1979) propose that reactions to receiving a resource from another will differ, depending on whether the recipient views the relationship as an exchange relationship or a communal one. In exchange relationships, a benefit is given to another either in order to repay him or her for a benefit that was previously received or with the firm expectation that the recipient will repay the benefit in the near future. In communal relationships, a benefit is given to another because he or she needs or strongly desires that resource and there is no concomitant obligation for repayment in the absence of a need on the part of the original giver.

The giving of resources or benefits is thus seen as operating in accordance with different rules in communal and exchange relationships. If a participant does not act in accordance with the principle appropriate for the type of relationship he or she has with the other, this is expected to result in a decrease in attraction for that person and negative consequences for the relationship. Clark and Mills (1979) tested this idea in two separate experiments. In the first, they found that when "givers" anticipated a communal relationship with the other, they felt less attraction for a recipient who immediately repayed them for their gift than for a recipient who did not repay the original resource. However, if an exchange relationship was anticipated, greater attraction was expressed for a recipient who did make prompt repayment than for one who did not. In a second study, Clark and Mills (1979) investigated the effect of a request for the repayment of previously given aid. Here, subjects either did or did not receive aid from another person with whom they anticipated having either an exchange or a communal relationship. Following this, the other either did or did not ask the subject to provide her with a resource. When subjects expected an exchange relationship, failing to ask for repayment when aid had been given and asking for a resource when aid had not been given resulted in lower attraction for the other. When a communal relationship with the other was expected, the subject liked her less when she did request repayment after providing aid. If subjects had not received aid but expected a communal relationship, attraction was equivalent in the request and the no-request conditions. In both cases, however, attraction was greater than if the other had both aided subjects *and* asked for repayment. This pair of studies indicates that expectations regarding the type of relationship one has with another (exchange or communal) do affect how individuals evaluate the exchange behaviors of others.

It is expected that recipients in exchange relationships are primarily concerned with repaying a benefit as soon as possible while those in a communal relationship are primarily concerned with meeting the needs of the other. In comparing the concepts of selectivity and urgency with the distinction between exchange and communal relationships, an obvious parallel emerges: exchange relationships should be most influenced by feelings of urgency and communal relationships should be most influenced by selectivity (e.g., meeting the needs of the other). Quickly returning a benefit is not, however, necessarily incompatible with communal exchanges. In general, immediate return may be less likely because a quickly returned benefit is apt to be less selective. But, if the returned benefit did meet a need of the other, rapid repayment should be viewed as very appropriate.

Preliminary evidence on the above point is provided by Miller (1983). Miller's data suggest that individuals who immediately return a highly selective benefit are viewed more favorably than individuals who had an opportunity to provide the highly selective and needed benefit (a sharpened pencil for an exam) but who instead returned either the same resource which they had previously received or no resource at all. In comparison, when individuals did not have an opportunity to choose a selective benefit (there was no exam in which a pencil was badly needed), not providing any resource was viewed more positively than providing either a similar or nonsimilar (pencil) resource. The latter condition conceptually replicates a finding of Clark and Mills (1979, Experiment 1) described earlier. Miller's findings strongly suggest that the emphasis in communal relationships is on selectivity (meeting the needs of the other) whenever one has the opportunity to do so regardless of the timing of such return.

It should be pointed out that there is not a complete parallel between the concepts of selectivity and urgency and the distinction between exchange and communal relationships. As Miller's (1983) study indicates, immediate provision of a selective benefit is quite appropriate. One may also be quite selective in other than communal relationships. We might be particularly selective, for example in picking out a gift for a boss not because we have a communal relationship with him or her, but because we wish to ingratiate ourselves.

In relating the distinction between exchange and communal relationships to other social exchange approaches, several points emerge. First, the findings of Clark and Mills (1979) for subjects anticipating an exchange relationship with their partner are in accordance with and replicate past research on equity (e.g., Gergen, Ellsworth, Maslach, & Siegel, 1975). Also Clark (1983) notes that persons involved in communal relationships will be more interdependent than those in exchange relationships. It is also expected that those in communal relationships may receive intrinsic rewards from the relationship itself and from the act of benefiting the other. This expectation is consistent with Kelley's (1979) view that persons in close relationships will often chose to behave in ways that provide maximal benefit to the partner or to the pair and consistent with Foa and Foa's (1974, 1976) proposal that the provision of the most particularistic resource, love, entails giving to oneself as well as giving to the other.

A point of departure from Foa and Foa's theory concerns the effect of giving a similar resource to a previous benefactor. Research conducted in the framework of resource theory (Foa & Foa, 1976; Turner, Foa, & Foa, 1971) suggests that people will prefer to receive the same or a similar resource after having given a resource to another. However, Clark (1981) has provided evidence suggesting that the provision of the same or a similar benefit is viewed as more likely in exchange relationships than in communal ones. She, therefore, speculates that if a person desires a communal relationship, receiving a resource similar to the one he or she initially provided may decrease attraction for the other because it implies that the other neither views the relationship as communal nor wishes it to become communal. The finding of Miller (1983) that more positive impressions were formed of a recipient who returned a dissimilar but needed resource than of one who returned a similar but less-selective resource strongly supports Clark's view.

Some additional attention should be given to the question of why, in communal relationships, returning a resource that does not help satisfy some need results in *less* attraction than if the other returns no benefit at all, (Clark & Mills, 1979). While one possibility is that the expectations of the original giver have been violated, additional possibilities are suggested by considering concurrently related notions of selectivity, equity, and the time available to a recipient. According to Mills and Clark (1982), in order for a communal relationship to exist, partners must anticipate future interaction. Keeping this in mind, consider a donor who has provided his or her partner with a highly selective (needed) resource. When the recipient quickly returns something that is of equal objective value but does not satisfy a need of the original donor, has equity really been maintained in the relationship? On the one hand, you might argue that of course the exchange was equitable because the objective value of the resources exchanged was equal. On the other hand, it would also appear that the original benefit was "special." It was highly selective and addressed an important need of the recipient. The returned benefit, however was not "special." It was not selected to meet a need of the other. Thus the original benefactor may feel inequitably treated, since the relationship has the potential to be long lasting (communal). The recipient certainly could have had the opportunity in the future to provide a more selective and needed resource. The immediate return implied that any obligation has been repaid but in terms of the degree to which each person's needs are likely to be met, the exchange was inequitable. Distinguishing between equity in terms of the "objective" value of the benefits each partner provides the other and equity in terms of the extent to which each attempts to meet the other's needs may help to resolve the controversy between those theorists who feel that equity considerations do not apply to those persons who have a close intimate relationship (e.g., Murstein, MacDonald, & Cerreto; 1977; Rubin, 1973) and those who view equity as an integral component of both close and casual relationships (e.g., Walster *et al.*, 1973; Hatfield *et al.*, 1979).

Reciprocity and the Stage of a Relationship

The norm of reciprocity (Gouldner, 1960) has perhaps been most employed in investigations of disclosure reciprocity. As noted at the start of the chapter, a great deal of research indicates that a recipient of intimate disclosure from another tends to make an intimate self-disclosure in return (e.g., Archer & Berg, 1978; Cozby, 1972; Derlega & Chaikin, 1976; Derlega et al., 1973; Ehrlich & Graeven, 1971; Jourard, 1959; Worthy, Gary, & Kahn, 1969). Also as noted earlier, while several explanations for disclosure reciprocity have been proposed, the explanation that has received the most experimental support involves social exchange and normative considerations (see Archer, 1979). This view assumes that when one person discloses intimate information to another, the recipient incurs an obligation to return self-disclosure of a comparable intimacy level (Chaikin & Derlega, 1974; Derlega et al., 1973).

In comparing the concept of disclosure reciprocity to related approaches, several assumptions are made. First, it is assumed that self-disclosure represents a resource (Foa & Foa, 1974, 1976) and that exchanges of this resource follow rules similar to those involved in exchanges of other resources. Intimate disclosure, like other resources, may be returned after receiving intimate disclosure in order to discharge an obligation. Just as equity and immediate reciprocation of goods are most often found in initial encounters (see Walster et al., 1973) there seems to be a similar pattern for exchanges of self-disclosure in initial encounters. When one partner discloses intimately, the other immediately reciprocates. And just as providing the other with needed goods rather than immediate reciprocation appears to be the goal in long-term or communal relationships, so, too, disclosures in long-term relationships may be more concerned with meeting the other's needs or enhancing the relationship than with reciprocity per se and discharging obligations (Altman, 1973). This analysis would suggest that disclosure reciprocity would be more immediate between those with a short-term as compared to a long-term relationship and is consistent with the available evidence comparing the degree of disclosure reciprocity shown by strangers to that exhibited by friends (Derlega, Wilson, & Chaikin, 1976) and by spouses (Morton, 1978).

Because of a lessened need for immediate reciprocation, and the expanded time-frame of the relationship, participants in established relationships may be more selective in choosing their responses to a partner's disclosure. At times, the other's needs might be best met by following the issue or topic he or she raised through to some conclusion.

At other times needs might best be met by simply being attentive and encouraging, and at other times by expressing support and sympathy, if appropriate. Research by Berg and Archer (1980) suggests that this latter possibility may be preferable to a reciprocal self-disclosure even in initial encounters.

Altman (1973) suggests that the intimacy of a received disclosure will interact with the stage of a relationship to determine the likelihood of disclosure reciprocity. He suggests that reciprocation of nonintimate disclosure will be maximal during the early stages of a relationship and then decline steadily as the relationship develops. For intimate disclosure, reciprocity is expected to be greatest during the middle stages, when people think they may want to become closer but have not as yet developed full trust in one another. Should individuals receive a disclosure that is extremely intimate early in the relationship, they may experience a reactance-like effect with a corresponding decrease in reciprocity (Archer & Berg, 1978; Archer & Burleson, 1980). It would seem likely that in the early stages of a relationship, extremity of any type (e.g., extremely valuable presents) may prove threatening. Furthermore the recipient of such resources may feel that the donor has violated social norms by giving an inappropriate gift. The recipient may then feel less bound him- or herself by these social norms to reciprocate. If the recipient is unable or unwilling to reciprocate, psychological equity might be achieved by derogating the donor (Walster *et al.*, 1973). Alternatively, he or she might refuse to accept such an extreme gift although it is possible to still feel obligated to reciprocate in some way. Barring extremity in received resources, it does, however, appear that feelings of urgency and immediate reciprocation will be more likely in the formative stages of a relationship than in the later ones.

Fairness in Social Exchange

The desire that the balance of exchange and the distribution of joint resources be fair may often be the force behind a feeling of urgency in social exchanges. We wish to pay back our obligations as soon as possible. But how do we determine that our exchanges are fair? At first glance, it might seem that the question of fairness is relatively easy to determine. An application of the norm of reciprocity or the equity principal would seem a rather straightforward way to make any decisions regarding fairness and what a given participant deserves to receive. However, it should be apparent that strict reciprocity or equity is not the only nor necessarily the most appropriate standard to apply in deciding these questions. In communal relationships, for example, there is no obligation to maintain a balance in the number of benefits that participants provide one another. Berg (in press) demonstrated that roommates did not match each other in terms of the total number of benefits they provided their partner as their relationship became extended in time. Berg and Archer (1980) found that expressing concern for another was seen as a more appropriate response than reciprocal disclosure.

Kelley (1979), Foa and Foa (1980) and Clark (1983) have all noted that a benefactor may derive significant rewards from the act of benefiting the other. The fact that the benefit provided may be needed (selective) should add additional subjective value for both recipient and benefactor. In Foa and Foa's framework, the value of a resource may depend on who is providing that resource. When one begins to consider the subjective states of recipients and benefactors, the identity of the benefactor, and the alternative options that were available, the issue of what constitutes fairness becomes much more complex.

It appears likely that a set of rules or norms exists that will govern exchange in social relationships at different times. Scanzoni (1979) notes that these may either have the status of moral norms that exist prior to and are then brought into a particular interaction or they may arise in the course of interaction and later become linked up with other sets of norms that do have the status of moral principles. In either case, Scanzoni notes that the existence of such norms may simplify the exchange process by eliminating the need for continual bargaining and negotiation. They also will set limits on what may be exchanged, how much may be exchanged, and how existing resources should be allocated.

Leventhal (1976, 1980) describes three rules governing the exchange and allocation of benefits and resources that may be applied in social situations. The first of these, which he refers to as a *contributions rule*, is very similar to the principle of equity, prescribing that individuals receive benefits in proportion to the degree they have contributed to a relationship. A second principle, the *equality rule*, would prescribe that all participants in an interaction share equally in the benefits derived from that interaction regardless of their contributions. Finally, Leventhal notes a third principle, the *needs rule*, which would prescribe that people receive those benefits which they need regardless of their contributions.

How do people decide how much weight to give to a particular rule or which rule to apply? When productivity is an issue, a contributions rule will often be viewed as most applicable (Deutsch, 1975). When cohesiveness or cooperation are overriding concerns, the equality rule may be given greater weight. Some evidence suggests that individuals will indeed allocate resources more on the basis of an equality than a contributions rule when they focus attention on the group rather than on themselves (Giuliano & Wegner, 1981). Several psychologists have suggested that as relationships become closer people will come to view themselves as a unit (e.g., Hatfield & Sprecher, 1983; Levinger, 1979; Wegner & Giuliano, 1982) thinking of themselves in terms of "we" and "us" rather than "me" and "you." When people come to view themselves as a single unit, the needs rule may be more frequently used and more appropriate than either an equality or a contributions rule. Some research provides indirect evidence for this view. For example, Clark and Mills (1979) found that in communal relationships, returning a benefit or requesting that a benefit be returned in the absence of any need resulted in a decrease in attraction. Similarly, Clark (1982) found that individuals who had an exchange relationship were more likely than those in communal relationships to keep track of individual contributions to a joint task, presumably expecting rewards to be allocated using a contributions rule.

The above three rules can all be applied reasonably well to situations in which people must allocate resources from a common pool. However when there is no common resource pool, while use of the needs rule can be distinguished, the difference between an equality and a contributions rule begins to blur. Thus if a friend gives you a sweater, are you applying a contributions rule or an equality rule if you also give him or her a sweater? Which would be in effect if you had given a pair of pants? In addition, in exchanges of this type another rule may be distinguished: a *proportions rule*. Using this type of rule, individuals would return a resource to another that, in proportion to their available supply, is as valuable or uses up as much of this supply as the received resource took from the supply of the initial giver. Such a rule would be most applicable when there are major differences in personal resources between two individuals (e.g., between one brother who has a job and one who does not or between a parent and child).

Responsiveness

Broadly defined, responsiveness can be viewed as the extent to which and the way in which one participant's actions address the previous actions, communications, needs, or wishes of another participant in that interaction. Responsiveness then is a dyadic construct. In order to be considered responsive, an action must be both intended by the actor and perceived by the recipient to be based on the past behavior or concerns of that recipient. This requirement helps to distinguish actions that are *responsive* from actions that are *responses*. A behavior that is automatically elicited by another's previous action (e.g., saying "bless you" when someone sneezes) is viewed as a response. A behavior that is not automatically elicited by the other's previous behavior but which addresses that behavior (e.g., offering to share your umbrella when the other sneezes) may be seen as responsive. However, in order to be considered responsive, the action must also be perceived by the recipient as addressing his or her past behavior or concerns. If the other perceives the offer to share an umbrella as stemming from a desire to get close enough to pick his pocket instead of a concern that he stay dry, the offer can hardly be considered responsive. While this is an extreme example to be sure, the same point regarding a recipient's perception was made by Davis and Perkowitz (1979) when they stated that "responsiveness is in the ear of the beholder" (p. 535).

Responsiveness is a concept that was alluded to by Kelley (1979) when he spoke of exchange partners exhibiting responsiveness to one another's outcomes and by Clark and Mills (1979) when they suggested that communal relationships operate according to a norm of mutual responsiveness. The concept of responsiveness has also been employed in understanding exchanges of self-disclosure (e.g., Berg & Archer, 1980, 1982, in press; Davis & Perkowitz, 1978; Miller *et al.*, 1983). In this section, we will address the manner in which the concept of responsiveness may be employed in understanding social exchanges and the manner in which it may aid in understanding a person's selection of a commodity to be returned in an exchange.

In attempting to conceptualize responsiveness, we have considered two classes of responsiveness that have as their focal point either the conversation (conversational responsiveness) or the patterns of exchanges between participants over the course of a relationship (relational responsiveness). In addition to these two classes of responsiveness, we have also considered three ways in which responsiveness can be manifested given either class of responsiveness. These three aspects of responsiveness include (1) style of responsiveness (how individuals respond), (2) timing of responsive behaviors, and (3) what individuals do in the act of being responsive and why individuals are performing the behavior (i.e., the goals of the participants).

Classes of Responsive Behaviors

Two broad classes of responsive behaviors may be distinguished: communicative, or conversational, responsiveness and relational responsiveness (Berg, 1983). Conversational responsiveness refers to behaviors made by the recipient of another's communication through which the recipient indicates interest in and understanding of that communication. Davis (1982) notes three implicit demands of communication situations and defines responsiveness in terms of how well these demands are met. The three demands are (1) that the recipient of another's communication respond in some way, (2) that this response address the content of the other's preceeding communication, and (3) that the response be of an appropriate degree of elaboration. Conversational responsiveness may be indicated and these demands met in a number of ways. Verbal behaviors have perhaps been the most studied of these. Reciprocal self-disclosure may represent a means by which a response of appropriate elaboration (intimacy) is indicated. Disclosure on the same subject matter would address the content of the other's communication. Verbal behaviors, though, are not the only ways in which responsiveness may be indicated. Both nonverbal behaviors such as eye contact and the use of backchannel communicators (e.g., uh-huh) can convey interest in and understanding of another's communication and would seem to fall under the first of the demands Davis distinguishes, that the recipient respond in some way.

The second general class of responsiveness is termed relational responsiveness and refers to behaviors involving the attainment or distribution of rewards through which a person demonstrates that he or she is concerned with and is taking account of another's outcomes and needs. A distinction between the present view and that of Clark and Mills is that we explicitly assume that responsiveness is a characteristic of interactions in general and may occur in what Clark and Mills term exchange relationships as well as in what they would call communal ones. While responsiveness may foster the development of close or communal relationships, the questions of whether it does this—and when—are ones that must be addressed through future research.

Davis (Davis, 1982; Davis & Perkowitz, 1979) has also distinguished a number of consequences expected to follow from responsive actions. Perhaps the most important of these consequences are that responsive actions are expected to result in an increase in attraction for the person performing them and to lead to the maintenance of interactions with that person. It is expected that conversational and relational responsiveness will be affected by the characteristics of the interactants, the nature of the situation, and the prior behaviors of each partner.

Conversational Responsiveness

Davis and Perkowitz (1979) investigated the effect of variations in the extent to which a confederate responded to a subject's communication and the extent to which the confederate's response addressed the content of the subject's communication. In both cases, it was found that as responsiveness increased, attraction for the confederate increased. A study reported by Berg and Archer (1980) also indicates the beneficial effect responsiveness may have on attraction. In this study, subjects read an account of a first encounter between two women. One of the women made either an intimate or nonintimate disclosure to which the second replied with an intimate disclosure, a nonintimate disclosure, or a statement of concern that expressed sympathy and a willingness to pursue the issues the first woman had raised. In terms of Davis' (1982) criteria for responsive interactions, a returned disclosure (of comparable intimacy to the one received) may be viewed as a "response of appropriate elaboration." Consistent with this view and with earlier work on disclosure reciprocity (e.g., Chaikin & Derlega, 1974; Ehrlich & Graeven, 1971; Worthy et al. 1969), subjects reported greater attraction for the nonintimate respondent when the initial disclosure was nonintimate. When the initial disclosure had been intimate, greater attraction was expressed for the intimate than the nonintimate respondent. What was more interesting, however, was that for both intimate and nonintimate initial disclosures the statement of concern resulted in the greatest attraction for the respondent. The concern response may be seen as both an appropriate degree of elaboration and as addressing the content of the first woman's communication. It would thus be considered more responsive.

The results of the Berg and Archer (1980) study suggest that responsiveness may take a number of forms in an interaction and further suggests as a working hypothesis that attraction will be greatest when responsiveness is maximal, regardless of the form such responsiveness takes. Further support for the latter point comes from an additional experiment (Berg & Archer, in press). In this study, subjects first disclosed on moderately intimate topics to an experimental confederate. The confederate's response either was or was not of an appropriate degree of elaboration (intimate) and either did or did not concern itself with the same subject matter as the original communication. As predicted, attraction for the confederate was greatest when her response did both of these.

The following two sections discuss research dealing with responsivenes and interaction goals and characteristics of the respondent. Although these factors are assumed to be relevant to both conversational and relational responsiveness, the research to date has focused only on their effects on conversational responsiveness.

Responsiveness and Interaction Goals

The research reviewed up to this point might seem to indicate that the particular way a person demonstrates responsiveness may vary little from one situation to another and matter even less. Berg and Archer's 1982 study, however, suggests that one's interaction goals may dramatically affect both the nature of the responsive behavior and the extent to which it occurs. Berg and Archer considered three aspects of a reply to another's self-disclosure that could be viewed as responsive: (1) descriptive intimacy (Morton, 1978), which refers to the intimacy of the factual information that is revealed in a communication, (2) evaluative intimacy (Morton, 1978), which refers to the depth of the affect the communication expresses, and (3) topical reciprocity, which refers to the degree to which replies to another's disclosure deal with the same subject matter as the received disclosure. Variations in descriptive and evaluative intimacy represent ways in which responsiveness may be indicated by varying the elaboration of a response while variations in topical reciprocity vary the extent to which the content of preceeding communication is addressed.

Berg and Archer (1982) investigated several variations in the situation to determine their effect on the predominant form responsiveness would take. Under one set of conditions the interaction goal involved the exchange of information. Subjects were asked to describe themselves so that their partner could form an accurate impression of them. This set of instructions, similar to those used in the typical disclosure reciprocity experiment, is likely to place a premium on the revelation of facts per se and create a situation in which the interaction goal of subjects is to exchange information. In such conditions the only way subjects may be able to indicate responsiveness while at the same time satisfying the situational demand to relay information would be through a returned disclosure of comparable descriptive intimacy. As expected, descriptive intimacy was found to be more pronounced in this condition than in any other. Moreover, in line with past research (e.g., Derlega *et al.*, 1973; Ehrlich & Graeven, 1971; Worthy *et al.*, 1969) subjects' replies contained a greater proportion of descriptively intimate statements when the disclosure they had initially received from a confederate had been intimate than when it had been nonintimate. In contrast, the intimacy of the confederate's disclosure exerted very little influence on the degree of either evaluative intimacy or topical reciprocity found in subject's replies in this Information Exchange condition.

When the demand to exchange information was removed by describing the study as an investigation of conversations and suggesting to subjects that they might call to mind past conversations when making their replies, descriptive intimacy decreased and topical reciprocity became pronounced. When the subjects' interaction goal involved having a conversation, over 80% of the statements made in response to both intimate and nonintimate disclosures dealt with the same content as the original communication. Thus as their interaction goal shifted, subjects focused more on addressing the content of the other's communication. In a third set of conditions, when their interaction goal was to make a positive impression, subjects not only showed the same high levels of topical reciprocity but also demonstrated the greatest degree of matching to the confederate's intimacy level in terms of both descriptive and evaluative intimacy. Responsiveness then appeared most pronounced when being liked by another was one's interaction goal. This suggests that subjects are well aware of the beneficial effects responsiveness can have on attraction.

Characteristics of the Respondent

We noted previously that responsiveness is expected to vary according to the personal characteristics of the respondent. Davis (1982) notes several personality variables that are likely to influence the degree to which a person will be responsive to the communications of others. Among these are self-monitoring, self-consciousness, and introversion–extroversion. Because public self-consciousness may reduce the amount of attention one gives to the nonevaluative behaviors of the other, and may increase attention to the other's evaluative responses, Davis feels unable to make a clear-cut prediction. Although, the publicly self-conscious individual may be more responsive in order to enhance attractiveness to others, he or she may not attend sufficiently to the nonevaluative behaviors of the other in order to respond adequately. Davis suggests that predictions for private self-consciousness are more straightforward: Individuals who tend to focus largely on their own inner thoughts and feelings may attend less to the behaviors of others, thereby reducing their ability to address others' behaviors adequately.

Davis applies a similar line of reasoning to understanding the probable effects of self-monitoring on responsiveness. She notes that if the primary effect of a tendency to self-monitor is to increase the amount of attention paid to another's behavior so that appropriate responses can be selected, then self-monitoring should lead to increases in responsiveness. In terms of extroversion–introversion, she notes that extroverts are more likely to attend closely to the others' behaviors. Because they have been more attentive, they are more apt to be responsive.

Recently, individual differences in responsiveness have been addressed more directly (Miller *et al.*, 1983), using the Opener scale described earlier (see pages 27–28). There we reported that persons scoring high on the Opener scale were more likely to be the recipients of another's self-disclosure. One explanation proposed for this finding was that high Openers are more responsive to their partners and that this greater responsiveness seems to elicit more disclosure. Purvis *et al.* (in press) found that subjective judgments by an independent rater of "involvement indicated that high Openers were more involved with and attentive to their partners than were low Openers." Recently, Miller (1982) conceptually replicated this effect. Individuals who were both low Openers and low Disclosers were less responsive than individuals who were high on at least one of these dimensions. If high Openers are more attentive behaviorally to their partners, are they also more attentive to what their partners are actually saying? Are high Openers better at remembering conversations with their partners? In addition, are high Openers more accurate in interpreting the meaning of interpersonal communications? Currently, the authors are involved in addressing these issues in their research.

Relational Responsiveness

Relational responsiveness refers to a second general class of responsive behaviors involving the attainment and distribution of resources through which a person demonstrates that he or she is taking another's outcomes, needs, or wishes into consideration. The expression of relational responsiveness is expected to change during the course of a relationship, as the nature of the relationship itself changes (e.g., moves from an exchange to a communal relationship, Clark & Mills, 1979). For example, in a recent study by Berg (in press), as time progressed in a relationship between previously unacquainted roommates, the rules of exchange shifted. Early in the year, there was a significant positive correlation between the total number of benefits roommates reported receiving from each other. This correlation disappeared when roommates were tested again in the spring. However, what was present in the spring, but absent in the fall was a significant correlation between the number of most helpful or needed resources which roommates reported receiving. Several possible explanations for these results were discussed but the one which appeared most plausible was that the nature of the relationship between roommates shifted from an exchange relationship (based on equity) to a communal relationship (based on meeting the needs of the partner) over the course of the year.

The concept of relational responsiveness is similar to what Kelley (1979)

meant when he suggested that participants in relationships were responsive to the other's outcomes. Kelley postulates a person's behavior will be
determined by both the outcomes he or she would receive and those
received by the partner. Kelley also expects an increase in the tendency to
take another's outcomes into account as participants become more interdependent. The crucial variable here may be the amount of time participants have spent in a relationship and the existence of some form of prior
interaction with the other (rather than the nature of that prior interaction). This view is consistent with the finding of Harrison and McClintock
(1965) that dyads that had experienced either a prior success or a prior
failure were more cooperative in an experimental game than dyads with
no such experience. In addition, McClintock and McNeel (1967) and
McClintock, Nuttin, and McNeel (1970) demonstrated that competition
would be reduced and cooperation facilitated when playing with either a
liked or disliked other as compared to a stranger. Finally, the idea that the
crucial variable is prior experience rather than the nature of that experience is supported by the finding of Berg (in press) that the number of
desired resources subjects received from a roommate increased over time
and that this effect was independent of subjects' plans to continue living
with that roommate for another year.

Facets of Responsiveness

As described earlier, responsiveness can be manifested in at least
three ways. The first of these ways involves *style*; not what individuals
do but how they do it. For example, in terms of conversational responsiveness, style would involve not what one says (i.e., "I love you") but
how one says those words (i.e., with sincerity and depth or as one might
say "this orange looks moldy"). Presumably, the first response would
be more responsive than the second. For relational responsiveness this
would include how individuals provide a benefit to another. Individuals
may decide to provide another with a benefit that meets that other's
needs, desires, and goals but may deliver the benefit begrudgingly
rather than with a great deal of enthusiasm and delight. The recipient is
apt to view this behavior as unresponsive rather than highly responsive.
One's style of expression is an interaction may, of course, be a function
of one's personality (i.e., activity level, general enthusiasm, excitability,
and warmth), the nature of the situation (who one is interacting with
and the context he or she is in) or a combination of these factors.

The *timing* of individuals' responses may also have a dramatic impact
on perceived responsiveness. In conversations, if Sally pauses too long
before saying "uh-hum" the other may think she is daydreaming and

not really paying attention (or being responsive). Or if Sally responds to a topic that the other discussed an hour ago (but is no longer discussing), Sally's "timing" will be off and her response will probably not be considered as responsive as it might have been if it had occurred immediately after her partner's topic-related comment. In relational responsiveness, timing may also be critical to perceptions of responsiveness. For example, if I write to a friend and he or she does not respond for six months, this will negatively affect my perception of my friend's responsiveness. Unfortunately, we are aware of virtually no direct research that assesses either the role of timing or the role of style on perceptions of responsiveness in interpersonal relations.

A third aspect of responsiveness involves what individuals do in their interactions with the other and the goals that those individuals have while engaging in a specific behavior. As such, it involves two components, the *content* of the behavior and the *goal* of the behavior. Let us consider the content of the behavior first. It is this mode of responsiveness that Davis (1982) seems to be referring to when she defines responsiveness as a response that addresses the content of the other's preceeding communication and is of an appropriate degree of elaboration. Most of the research on responsiveness to date has focused on this aspect of responsiveness. As mentioned earlier, this type of responsiveness has been shown to have a positive effect on interactions (Berg & Archer, 1980, in press; Davis & Perkowitz, 1979). In addition to the content, this third mode of responsiveness involves one's interaction goal. Such goals can affect the form of responsiveness that is demonstrated in an exchange (Berg & Archer, 1982). One such goal in interactions involves meeting social norms. In terms of conversational responsiveness this would involve, for example, responding to the disclosure of the other by disclosing in kind about a similar topic. A second goal of conversational responsiveness involves providing benefits that specifically meet the needs of the other. The work by Berg and Archer (1980) suggests that if a friend reveals she's contemplating a divorce, she would probably consider the woman who offers support and listens to her better at meeting her needs (i.e., more responsive) than the woman who tells her the gory details of her own divorce. Regarding relational responsiveness, in providing a benefit for another, one can focus on social norms of exchange or one can provide a benefit the other really needs.

What then is the overlap between the concept of selectivity and the concept of responsiveness? Selectivity can be viewed as a small subset of responsiveness. When we are talking about choosing a benefit to meet the needs of the other we are talking about selectivity or one aspect of responsiveness in which the goal is to meet the needs of the other (more selective behaviors would be considered more responsive). This view of responsiveness suggests that responsive behaviors have multiple components and that researchers have just begun to explore some of these facets to determine which behaviors by what individuals under which circumstances are perceived to be responsive. Future research needs to be done to determine not only the role of each facet in predicting perceived responsiveness (for both actors and observers) but in predicting how various facets of responsiveness affect one another. For example, if we wait too long to say "uh-hum," that will be viewed as less responsive. But, if we wait an unusually long time after someone has spoken and then say something highly selective does that compensate for the long time gap? What if we choose a highly selective gift for someone and in delivering it we show no affective expression (e.g., no enthusiasm) or even seem distressed? How does that effect perceptions of responsiveness?

CONCLUSION

This chapter has discussed the role that selectivity and urgency play in interpersonal exchanges. Selectivity refers to the degree that a benefit is needed or desired by the recipient of that benefit while urgency refers to the desire of an individual to provide another with a benefit and conclude an exchange quickly. In general, selectivity and urgency will be inversely related to one another. The less time a person has in which to provide another with a benefit, the less likely he or she will be to provide a selective benefit.

In addition to being affected by the time frame allowed for the exchange, selectivity in providing benefits will be influenced by one's knowledge of a potential recipient, the attributions made for past benefits that have been received, and social norms such as equity and reciprocity. All of these factors as well as the balance between selectivity and urgency will be affected by the nature and the stage of the relationship between exchange partners. Those in closer and/or more long-term relationships are expected to feel less urgency to return a benefit after having received one and to provide more selective benefits.

The role of several personality factors that may enhance a sense of urgency or a desire to be more selective in choosing benefits for another were discussed. The concepts of selectivity and urgency were also related to other concepts in social exchange. In general, it appears that the ideas of selectivity and urgency have run through a considerable amount of past theorizing and research but have never been addressed explicitly before. We have attempted to provide this type of discussion, while indicating the importance of considering the concepts of selectivity and urgency for a more complete understanding of the exchange process in both close and casual relationships. It is hoped that such a discussion will lead to more explicit future investigations of these issues.

REFERENCES

Adams, J. (1965). Inequity in social exchanges. In L. Berkowitz (Ed.), *Advances in experimental Social Psychology* (Vol. 2). New York: Academic Press.

Altman, I. (1973). Reciprocity of information exchange. *Journal for the Theory of Social Behavior, 3*, 249–261.

Altman, I., & Taylor, D. A. (1973). *Social penetration: The development of interpersonal relationships.* New York, Holt.

Archer, R. L. (1979). The role of personality and the social situation. In G. J. Chelune (Ed.), *Self-disclosure.* San Francisco, Jossey-Bass.

Archer, R. L., & Berg, J. H. (1978). Disclosure reciprocity and its limits: A reactance analysis. *Journal of Experimental Social Psychology, 14*, 527–540.

Archer, R. L., & Burleson, J. A. (1980). The effects of timing of self-disclosure on attraction and reciprocity. *Journal of Personality and Social Psychology, 38*, 120–130.

Austin, W., & Walster, E. (1974). Participants' reactions to "Equity with the world." *Journal of Experimental Social Psychology, 10*, 528–548.

Berg, J. H. (1983, March). Responsiveness in self-disclosure exchanges and close relationships. In V. J. Derlega (Chair), *Social interaction in personal relationships: Theory, research and methodology.* Symposium conducted at the meeting of the Southeastern Psychological Association, Atlanta.

Berg, J. H. (in press). The development of friendship between roommates. *Journal of Personality and Social Psychology.*

Berg, J. H., & Archer, R. L. (1980). Disclosure or concern: A second look at liking for the norm-breaker. *Journal of Personality, 48*, 245–257.

Berg, J. H., & Archer, R. L. (1982). Responses to self-disclosure and interaction goals. *Journal of Experimental Social Psychology, 18*, 501–512.

Berg, J. H., & Archer, R. L. (1983). The disclosure–liking relationship: Effects of self-perception, order of disclosure and topical similarity. *Human Communication Research. 10*, 283–294.

Berscheid, E., & Walster, E. (1967). When does a harm-doer compensate a victim? *Journal of Personality and Social Psychology, 6*, 435–441.

Berscheid, E., Walster, E., & Barclay, A. (1969). Effect of time on tendency to compensate a victim. *Psychology Reports, 25*, 431–436.

Blau, P. (1964). *Exchange and power in social life.* New York, Wiley.

Braiker, H. B., & Kelley, H. H. (1979). Conflict in the development of close relationships.

In R. L. Burgess & T. L. Huston (Eds.), *Social exchange in developing relationships*. New York: Academic Press.

Brehm, J. W., & Cole, A. (1966). Effect of a favor which reduces freedom. *Journal of Personality and Social Psychology, 3,* 420–426.

Brinberg, D., & Castell, P. (1982). A resource exchange theory approach to interpersonal interactions: A test of Foa and Foa's theory. *Journal of Personality and Social Psychology, 43,* 260–269.

Brock, T. C. (1968). Implications of commodity theory for value change. In A. G. Greenwald, T. C. Brock, & T. M. Ostrom, (Eds.) *Psychological foundations of attitudes.* New York: Academic Press.

Brock, T. C., & Buss, A. H. (1964). Effects of justification of aggression in communication with the victim or postaggression difference. *Journal of Abnormal and Social Psychology, 68,* 403–412.

Burgess, R. L., & Huston, T. L., (Eds.) (1979). *Social exchange in developing relationships.* New York: Academic Press.

Buss, A. H. (1983). Social rewards and personality. *Journal of Personality and Social Psychology, 44,* 553–563.

Buss, A., & Plomin, R. (1975). *A temperament theory of personality development.* New York: Wiley (Interscience).

Chaikin, A. L., & Derlega, V. J. (1974). Liking for the norm-breaker in self-disclosure. *Journal of Personality, 42,* 117–129.

Clark, M. S. (1981). Noncomparability of benefits: A cue to the existence of friendship. *Social Psychology Quarterly, 44,* 375–381.

Clark, M. S. (1982, September). Keeping track of inputs into joint tasks in communal and exchange relationships. In J. Berg & V. Derlega (Co-Chair), *Communication and friendship: An attributional and exchange analysis.* Symposium conducted at the 90th Annual Meeting of the American Psychological Association, Washington, DC.

Clark, M. S. (1983). Reactions to aid in communal and exchange relationships. In J. Fisher, A. Nadler, & B. DePaulo (Eds.), *New directions in research on helping.* Vol. 1: *Recipient reactions to aid.* New York, Academic Press.

Clark, M. S., & Mills, J. (1979). Interpersonal attraction in exchange and communal relationships. *Journal of Personality and Social Psychology, 37,* 12–24.

Cozby, P. C. (1972). Self-disclosure, reciprocity and liking. *Sociometry, 35,* 151–160.

Davis, D. (1982). Determinants of responsiveness in dyadic interactions. In W. Ickes & E. G. Knowles (Eds.), *Personality, roles, and social behavior.* New York: Springer-Verlag.

Davis, D., & Perkowitz, W. T. (1979). Consequences of responsiveness in dyadic interactions: Effects of probability of response and proportion of content related responses. *Journal of Personality and Social Psychology, 37,* 534–550.

Davis, K. E., & Jones, E. E. (1964). Changes in interpersonal perception as a means of reducing cognitive dissonance. *Journal of Abnormal and Social Psychology, 61,* 402–410.

Derlega, V. J., & Chaikin, A. L. (1976). Norms affecting self-disclosure in men & women. *Journal of Consulting & Clinical Psychology, 44,* 376–380.

Derlega, V. J., Harris, M. S., & Chaikin, A. L. (1973). Self-disclosure and reciprocity, liking, and the deviant. *Journal of Experimental Social Psychology, 9,* 227–284.

Derlega, V. J., Wilson, M., & Chaikin, A. L. (1976). Friendship and disclosure reciprocity. *Journal of Personality and Social Psychology, 34,* 578–582.

Deutsch, M. (1975). Equity, equality and need: What determines which value will be used as the basis for distribution justice? *Journal of Social Issues, 31*(4), 137–149.

Ehrlich, J. H., & Graeven, D. B. (1971). Reciprocal self-disclosure in a dyad. *Journal of Experimental Social Psychology, 7,* 389–400.

Fenigstein, A., Scheier, M. F., & Buss, A. H. (1975). Public and private self-consciousness: Assessment and theory. *Journal of Consulting and Clinical Psychology, 43,* 522–527.

Foa, E. B., & Foa, U. G. (1976). Resource theory of social exchange. In J. S. Thibaut, J. Spence, & R. Carson (Eds.), *Contemporary topics in social psychology.* Morristown, NJ: General Learning Press.

Foa, E. B., & Foa, U. G. (1980). Resource theory: Interpersonal behavior in exchange. In K. J. Gergen, M. S. Greenberg, & R. H. Willis (Eds.), *Social exchange: Advances in theory and research.* New York: Plenum.

Foa, U. G., & Foa, E. B. (1974). *Societal structures of the mind.* Springfield, IL: Thomas.

Fromm, E. (1956). *The art of loving,* New York, Harper & Row.

Gergen, K. J., Ellsworth, P., Maslach, C., & Siegel, M. (1975). Obligation, donor resources, and reactions to aid in three nations. *Journal of Personality and Social Psychology, 33,* 396–400.

Gibbons, F. X., Scheier, M. F., Carver, C. S., & Hormuth, S. E. (1979). Self-focused attention, suggestibility and the placebo effect. *Journal of Experimental Social Psychology, 15,* 263–274.

Giuliano, T., & Wegner, D. M. (1981, August). Justice and social awareness. *Justice as a pervasive theme in social behavior.* Symposium conducted at the 89th Annual Meeting of the American Psychological Association, Los Angeles.

Gouldner, A. (1960). The norm of reciprocity: A preliminary statement. *American Sociological Review, 25,* 161–178.

Greenberg, M. S. (1980). A theory of indebtedness. In K. J. Gergen, M. S. Greenberg, & R. H. Wells, (Eds.), *Social exchange: Advances in theory and research.* New York: Plenum.

Harrison, A. H., & McClintock, C. G. (1965). Previous experiences within the dyad and cooperative game behavior. *Journal of Personality and Social Psychology, 1,* 671–675.

Hatfield, E., & Sprecher, S. (1983). Equity theory and recipient reactions to aid. In J. Fisher, A. Nadler, & B. DePaulo (Eds.), *New directions in research on helping* (Vol. 1): *Recipient reactions to aid.* New York: Academic Press.

Hatfield, E., Utne, M. K., & Traupmann, J. (1979). Equity theory and intimate relationships. In R. L. Burgess & T. L. Huston (Eds.), *Social exchange in developing relationships.* New York: Academic Press.

Heider, F. (1958). *The psychology of interpersonal relations.* New York: Wiley.

Helmreich, R. L., & Spence, J. T. (1978). The work and family orientation questionnaire: An objective instrument to assess components of achievement motivation and attitudes toward family and career. *JSAS Catalog of Selected Documents in Psychology, 8,* 35 (Ms. No. 1677).

Homans, G. (1961). *Social behavior: Its elementary forms.* New York: Harcourt, Bruce, Jovanovich.

Jones, E. E. (1964). *Ingratiation.* New York, Appleton-Century-Crofts.

Jourard, S. M. (1959). Self-disclosure and other-cathexis. *Journal of Abnormal and Social Psychology, 59,* 428–431.

Jourard, S. M., & Resnick, J. L. (1970). The effect of high revealing subjects on the self-disclosure of low-revealing subjects. *Journal of Humanistic Psychology, 10,* 84–93.

Kelley, H. H. (1979). *Close relationships: Their structures and processes.* Hillsdale, NJ: Erlbaum.

Kelley, H. H., & Stahelski, A. J. (1970). Social interaction basis of cooperators' and competitors' beliefs about others. *Journal of Personality and Social Psychology, 16,* 66–91.

Kelley, H. H., & Thibaut, J. W. (1978). *Interpersonal relations: A theory of interdependence.* New York: Wiley (Interscience).

Leventhal, G. S. (1976). Fairness in social relationships. In J. S. Thibaut, J. Spence, & R.

Carson, (Eds.), *Contemporary topics in social psychology*. Morristown, NJ. General Learning Press.

Leventhal, G. S. (1980). What should be done with equity theory? New approaches to the study of fairness in social relationships. In K. J. Gergen, M. S. Greenberg, & R. H. Willis (Eds.), *Social exchange: Advances in theory and research*. New York: Plenum.

Levinger, G. (1979). A social exchange view on the dissolution of pair relationships. In R. L. Burgess, & J. L. Huston (Eds.), *Social exchange in developing relationships*. New York: Academic Press.

McClintock, C. G., & McNeel, S. P. (1967). Prior dyadic experience and monetary reward as determinants of cooperative and competitive game behavior. *Journal of Personality and Social Psychology, 5*, 282–294.

McClintock, C. G., Nuttin, J. M., & McNeel, S. P. (1970). Sociometric choice, visual presence, and game playing behavior. *Behavioral Science, 15*, 124–131.

McGovern, L. P. (1974). Dispositional social anxiety and helping behavior under three conditions of threat. *Journal of Personality, 44*, 84–97.

Marks, D. F. (1973). Visual imagery differences in the recall of pictures. *British Journal of Psychology, 64*, 17–24.

Messe, L. A., & Sivacek, J. M. (1979). Predictions of others' responses in a mixed-motive game: Self-justification or false consensus? *Journal of Personality and Social Psychology, 37*, 602–607.

Miller, L. C. (1982). *Patterns of two individual differences relevant to recipient and revealer roles in dyadic interactions: Opening and disclosing*. Unpublished doctoral dissertation, University of Texas at Austin.

Miller, L. C. (1983). *Selectivity in social exchange: Impact on observers' perceptions*. Unpublished manuscript.

Miller, L. C., Berg, J. H., & Archer, R. L. (1983). Openers: Individuals who elicit intimate self-disclosure. *Journal of Personality and Social Psychology, 44*, 1234–1244.

Miller, L. C., & Mueller, J. (1983). *Conversational attentiveness and memory for what people actually said*. Unpublished manuscript.

Mills, J., & Clark, M. S. (1982). Exchange and communal relationships. In L. Wheeler (Ed.), *Review of personality and social psychology* (Vol. 3). Beverly Hills, CA: Sage.

Morton, T. L. (1978). Intimacy and reciprocity of exchange: A comparison of spouses and strangers. *Journal of Personality and Social Psychology, 36*, 72–81.

Muir, D. E., & Weinstein, E. A. (1962). The social debt: An investigation of lower-class and middle-class norms of social obligation. *American Sociological Review, 27*, 532–539.

Murstein, B. I., MacDonald, M. G., & Cerreto, M. (1977). A theory of the effect of exchange-orientation on marriage and friendship. *Journal of Marriage and the Family, 39*, 543–548.

Nadler, A., Altman, A., & Fisher, J. D. (1979). Helping is not enough: Recipients' reactions to aid as a function of positive and negative information about the self. *Journal of Personality, 42*, 615–628.

Nadler, A., Fisher, J. D., & Streufort, S. (1974). The donor's dilemma: Recipient's reactions to aid from friend or foe. *Journal of Applied Social Psychology, 4*, 275–285.

Nadler, A., Fisher, J. D., & Streufort, S. (1976). When helping hurts: Effects of donor–recipient similarity and recipient self-esteem on recipient reactions to aid. *Journal of Personality, 44*, 392–409.

Orvis, B. R., Kelley, H. H., & Butler, D. (1976). Attributional conflict in young couples. In J. H. Harvey, W. J. Ickes, & R. E. Kidd (Eds.), *New directions in attribution research* (Vol. 1). Hillsdale, NJ: Erlbaum.

Purvis, J. A., Dabbs, J., & Hopper, C. (in press). The "opener": Skilled user of facial expression and speech pattern. *Personality and Social Psychology Bulletin.*

Roloff, M. E. (1981). *Interpersonal communication: The social exchange approach.* Beverly Hills, CA: Sage.

Rubin, Z. (1973). *Liking and loving: An invitation to social psychology.* New York: Holt.

Scanzoni, J. (1979). Social exchange and behavioral interdependence. In R. L. Burgess, & T. L. Huston (Eds.), *Social exchange in developing relationships.* New York: Academic Press.

Scheier, M. F. (1976). Self-awareness, self-consciousness and angry aggression. *Journal of Personality, 44,* 627–644.

Simpson, R. L. (1976). Theories of social exchange. In J. S. Thibaut, J. Spence, & R. Carson (Eds.), *Contemporary topics in social psychology,* Morristown, NJ: General Learning Press.

Spence, J. T., & Helmreich, R. L. (1978). *Masculinity and femininity: Their psychological dimensions, correlates, and antecedents.* Austin, TX: University of Texas Press.

Spence, J. T., Helmreich, R. L., & Stapp, J. A. (1974). The personal attributes questionnaire: A measure of sex-role stereotypes and masculinity–femininity. *JSAS Catalog of Selected Documents in Psychology, 4,* 43.

Stafford, L., & Daly, J. A. (1983). Conversational memory: The effects of recall mode and instructional set on memory for natural conversations. Unpublished manuscript.

Swann, W. B., & Hill, C. A. (1982). When our identities are mistaken: Reaffirming self-conceptions through social interaction. *Journal of Personality and Social Psychology, 43,* 59–66.

Swann, W. B., & Miller, L. C. (1982). Why never forgetting a face matters: Visual imagery and social memory. *Journal of Personality and Social Psychology, 43,* 475–480.

Swann, W. B., & Read, S. J. (1981). Self-verification processes: How we sustain our self-perceptions. *Journal of Experimental Social Psychology, 17,* 351–372.

Sykes, G. M., & Matza, D. (1957). Techniques of neutralization: A theory of delinquency. *American Sociological Review, 22,* 664–670.

Thibaut, J. W., & Kelley, H. H. (1959). *The social psychology of groups.* New York, Wiley.

Turner, J. L., Foa, E. B., & Foa, V. G. (1971). Interpersonal reinforcers: Classification, interrelationship, and some differential properties. *Journal of Personality and Social Psychology, 19,* 168–180.

Walster, E., Berscheid, E., & Walster, G. W. (1973). New directions in equity research. *Journal of Personality and Social Psychology, 25,* 151–176.

Walster, E., Walster, G. W., Abrahams, D., & Brown, Z. (1966). The effect of liking on underrating or overrating another. *Journal of Experimental Social Psychology, 2,* 70–84.

Walster, E., Walster, G. W., & Traupmann, J. (1978). Equity and premarital sex. *Journal of Personality and Social Psychology, 36,* 82–92.

Wegner, D. M., & Giuliano, T. (1982). The forms of social awareness. In W. J. Ickes & E. S. Knowles (Eds.), *Personality, roles and social behavior.* New York, Springer-Verlag, 1981.

Worchel, S., Andrioli, V., & Archer, R. (1976). When is a favor a threat to freedom: The effects of attribution and importance of freedom on reciprocity. *Journal of Personality, 44,* 294–310.

Worthy, M., Gary, A. L., & Kahn, G. M. (1969). Self-disclosure as an exchange process. *Journal of Personality and Social Psychology, 13,* 59–63.

The Dangers of Intimacy

ELAINE HATFIELD _____

I have two careers—I am chair of the psychology department at the University of Hawaii and a family therapist at the King Kalakaua Center in Honolulu, Hawaii. In both roles, I'm bombarded with questions about love, sex, and intimacy. One of the most common dilemmas people face is "How intimate dare I be with friends and lovers?"

Theorists and therapists take it for granted that people need intimacy. (In Chapter 2 of this volume, Chelune, Robinson, and Kommor review such theorizing.) In intimate encounters we discover our own and other people's innermost natures. Close family relationships spark the deepest of feelings. It is in our early intimate encounters that we learn our basic strategies for dealing with the world.

Yet most people are wary of intimate encounters. My cotherapist Dr. Richard Rapson and I spend most of our time dealing with people's fears of intimacy. Why? Their caution is not without reason.

In the preceding chapters, theorists and researchers have assumed that intimate relationships are critically important; they have reviewed the conditions under which close relationships flower. (see Chapter 1 of this volume by Derlega.) In this Epilogue, I would like to complete the circle. Here I will discuss some of the reasons why people fear intimate encounters.

INTIMACY: WHAT IS IT?

The word intimacy is derived from the Latin *intimus*, meaning "inner" or "inmost." In a wide variety of languages, the word intimate refers to a person's innermost qualities. For example, the French *intime* signifies "secret, deep, fervent, ardent." The Italian *intimo* conveys "internal, close in friendship." In Spanish, *intimo* means "private, close, innermost." To be intimate means to be close to another.

In this Epilogue, we will define *Intimacy* as: A *process* in which we attempt to get close to another; to explore similarities (and differences) in the ways we both think, feel, and behave. (In Chapter 2, Chelune, Robinson, and Kommor review other possible conceptions of intimacy.)

Intimate relationships have a number of characteristics:

Cognitive: Intimates are willing to reveal themselves to one another. They disclose information about themselves and listen to their partners' confidences.

Research supports the contention that men and women are willing to disclose far more about themselves in intimate relationships than in casual ones. In casual encounters, most people reveal only the sketchiest, most stereotyped information about themselves. Yet, as the French essayist Montaigne (1948) observed, everyone is complex, multifaceted:

All contradictions may be found in me . . . bashful, insolent; chaste, lascivious; talkative, taciturn; tough, delicate; clever, stupid; surly, affable; lying, truthful; learned, ignorant; liberal, miserly and prodigal: all this I see in myself to some extent according to how I turn . . . I have nothing to say about myself absolutely, simply and solidly, without confusion and without mixture, or in one word. (p. 242)

In deeply intimate relationships, friends and lovers feel free to reveal far more facets of themselves. They reveal more of their complexities and contradictions. As a result, intimates share profound information about one another's histories, values, strengths, and weaknesses, idiosyncracies, hopes, ad fears (Altman & Taylor, 1973; Huesmann & Levinger, 1976; Jourard, 1964; Worthy, Gary, & Kahn, 1969). In Chapters 2 and 6 of this volume, Chelune *et al.* and Patterson provide a lengthy discussion of this aspect of intimacy.

Emotional: Intimates care deeply about one another. When discussing intimate encounters, most theorists seem to assume that the more intimate a relationship, the more friends and lovers like and love one another. (See Chapters 3 and 6 of this volume by McAdams and Patterson.) In fact, most scales of liking and loving assume love and intimacy are unidimensional concepts—that human feelings range from love (the high point), through liking, through neutrality, through dislike to hatred (the low point) (Berscheid and Walster [Hatfield], 1968).

Yet folk wisdom and our own experiences tell us that there is something wrong with such a unidimensional view of love—often love and hate go hand in hand. The opposite of love is not hate, but indifference. It is in intimate relationships that we feel most *intensely*. True, we generally feel more intense love for intimates than for anyone else. Yet, because intimates care so much about one another, they have the power to elicit intense pain as well; the dark side of love is jealousy, loneliness, depression, and anger. It is this powerful interplay of conflicting emotions that gives vibrancy to the most intimate of relationships. (See Berscheid, 1979, 1983; Hatfield and Walster, 1981).

Basic to all intimate relationships, of course, is trust.

Behavioral: Intimates are comfortable in close physical proximity. They gaze at one another (Argyle, 1967; Exline, 1972; Rubin, 1970), lean on one another (Galton, 1884; Hatfield, Roberts, & Schmidt, 1980; Mehrabian, 1968), stand close to one another (Allgeier & Byrne, 1973; Byrne, Ervin, & Lambreth; 1970; Goldberg, Kiesler, & Collins, 1969; Sheflen, 1965), and perhaps touch. (In Chapter 5 Patterson provides a review of this literature.)

For most people, their intimate relationships are the most important thing in their lives. (See Berscheid & Peplau, 1983; Cook & Wilson, 1979; Duck & Gilmour, 1980, 1981a, 1981b, 1982; Fisher & Stricker, 1982; Pope, 1980). Clients who come to see us at King Kalakaua clinic are usually seeking intimacy—they are eager to find someone to love, to maintain a faltering love affair, or are adjusting to separation or divorce. Everyone needs intimacy. Why then is it so hard to find? Why are people reluctant to risk it? To understand this, theorists must focus not just on the advantages of intimacy, but on its *risks*. In the following section of this epilogue, we focus on the dangers of intimacy. In the section called "Prescription for Intimacy" we review what theorists and scientist–practitioners know about securing the benefits of intimacy while minimizing its risks.

INTIMACY: WHY NOT?

Why are people reluctant to become intimate with others? There are many reasons:

Fear of Exposure

In deeply intimate relationships we disclose far more about ourselves than in casual encounters. As a consequence, intimates share profound information about one another's histories, values, strengths and weaknesses, idiosyncracies, hopes, and fears. (See Altman & Taylor, 1973; Huesmann & Levinger, 1976; Jourard, 1964; Perlmutter & Hatfield, 1980; Worthy *et al.*, 1969.)

One reason, then, that all of us are afraid of intimacy, is that those we care most about are bound to discover all that is wrong with us—to discover that we possess taboo feelings . . . have done things of which we are deeply ashamed.

Such fears are *not* neurotic. The data make it clear that people who reveal too much to others, too soon, *are* judged to be a little peculiar. (See Derlega & Chaikin, 1975, for a review of this literature.)

Fear of Abandonment

A second reason people fear exposure is because they are concerned that if others get to know them too well, they will abandon them. (In Chapter 6 of this volume, Margulis, Derlega, and Winstead discuss such concerns.) Such concerns, too, are sometimes realistic.

We can think of examples:

One of my favorite graduate students was a beautiful Swedish woman. At one time, three sociologists at the University of Wisconsin were in love with her. Her problem? She pretended to be totally self-confident, bright, charming. In intimate affairs, each time she tried to admit how uncertain she was, to be herself, the men lost interest. They wanted to be in love with a *Star*, not a mere mortal like themselves.

A second reason, then, that people are reluctant to risk intimacy, to admit how needy they are, is that they are terrified that their friends and lovers will abandon them. (In Chapter 6 of this volume, Margulis *et al.* discuss people's fears of abandonment.)

Fear of Angry Attacks

Another reason people are reluctant to reveal themselves to others is the fear that "anything they say will be used against them." Most of us worry that if we reveal confidences to our friends, they will reveal the confidences to their friends, who will reveal them to their friends, etc.

One of my clients was Sara, A Mexican–American army wife. Her parents had divorced when she was three. Her father was granted custody, thereafter she was abused both sexually and physically. Sara was justifiably proud of the fact that she learned to be "a perfect lady" in even the most impossible of circumstances. Her voice was always calm, her emotions in control. She took pride in not ever needing anyone for anything. Her only problem was that she didn't have a single friend in which to confide. At long last, she decided to trust one of her sisters. She painfully revealed that her marriage was falling apart and that she was thinking of leaving. Her sister became enraged and denounced her. What kind of a Catholic was she!

Similarly, a powerful businessman I interviewed observed that if he were to reveal that he was worried about getting old, worried that he was not as smart as his computer-age competition, he could expect his competitors to seize on his revelations with glee.

Sometimes it *is* dangerous to trust.

Fear of Loss of Control

Men and women are sometimes afraid to risk becoming intimate for yet another reason—they fear losing control. Some theorists have speculated that *men* may be particularly afraid of intimacy and the loss of control it brings. (See Hatfield, 1982). Traditionally, men are supposed to be in control—of themselves, of other people, and of the situation. The ideal man carefully controls his *thoughts;* is logical, objective, and unemotional. He hides his *feelings,* or if he does express any feelings, he carefully telescopes the complex array of human emotions into a single powerful emotion: anger. A "real man" is even supposed to dominate nature.

In contrast, the ideal woman is supposed to be expressive and warm. She is comfortable expressing a rainbow of "feminine" feelings—love, anxiety, joy, and depression. (She may be less in touch with anger.) She is responsive to other people and the environment.

Broverman and her colleagues (1972) asked people what men and women *should* be like and what they really *are* like. Their answer was clear: men should be/are in control and instrumental. Women should be/are expressive and nurturant.

According to theorists, there are marked gender differences in three areas: (1) desire to be "in control"; (2) desire to dominate their partners versus submit to them, and (3) desire to "achieve" in their love and sexual relations. If such gender differences exist, it is not surprising that women feel more comfortable with intimacy than do men. Unfortunately, although a great deal has been written about these topics, there is almost no research documenting that such gender differences exist. (See Hatfield, 1982).

Fear of One's Own Destructive Impulses

Men and women sometimes fear intimacy for yet another reason.

Many of my clients keep a tight lid on their emotions. They fear that if they ever got in touch with what they are feeling, they would begin to cry . . . or kill.

One of my Korean clients was a traditional macho man. As he sat in my office he often explained that men *had* to be cool. He refused to even allude to the things that were bothering him. As a therapist, it was obvious to me that he was anything but cool. He looked like a seething volcano. He was an enormous, powerful man—a Tai Chi expert. As he explained "analytically" how he felt about things, his eyes blazed, his jaw clenched, he smashed his fist into the palm of his other hand. People were terrified of him. He had to stay cool at all times he insisted . . . otherwise he would kill.

He was undoubtedly wrong. In therapy, I have found that as people learn to be ever more aware of what they're feeling, they find that their emotions are not as powerful, not nearly so overpowering as they had assumed, that somehow they can learn to express their feelings in a controlled way. Yet the fear is real.

Fear of Losing One's Individuality or of Being Engulfed

When I first began reading the intimacy literature, I discovered that theorists believed that one of the most primitive fears of intimacy was the feeling that one would be engulfed by another, the fear that one would literally disappear as he or she lost himself in another. (See Diamond and Shapiro, 1981, for a discussion of this point.) To me, such a concern was inconceivable.

Then I met the Watsons in therapy, and for the first time got some sense of what it meant to fear engulfment. The Watsons were a bright, delightful, and thoroughly crazy family. The father and the mother insisted that they wanted their girls to become independent, to leave home and build families of their own. However, every time the "girls" (who were 50) showed the least independence, their parents got angry.

They complained that the girls weren't doing "it" right. They should be more relaxed about their endeavors. They should be breezy . . . while succeeding spectacularly. The daughters were the first people I ever heard say they were afraid to get close to anyone for fear that they would be "swallowed up." Basically, Patti and Mary were confused about what they wanted versus what everyone else in the family wanted. Each time they were tempted to express themselves, they would be overtaken by guilt. They began a tortured internal dialogue. Why were they so ungrateful? Demanding? Their parents would be hurt terribly. Was it fair to do that to them? "No." They inevitably decided to remain mute.

Nor were Patti and Mary capable of really listening. If they listened, if they permitted themselves to see what their parents needed, they would be responsible for sacrificing themselves completely to provide it. They would lose their freedom. Even then what could they do? They were too weak.

So everyone stayed in their own shell. No one could ever be really independent: no one could ever be really intimate with others for fear that they would be engulfed.

A PRESCRIPTION FOR INTIMACY

Everyone needs a warm intimate relationship. At the same time, one must recognize that in every social encounter there are some risks. What, then, is the solution? Social psychological research and clinical experience gives us some hints: (See Sprecher & Hatfield, in press)

A basic theoretical assumption provides the framework we use in teaching people how to be intimate with others. People must be capable of independence in order to be intimate with others; capable of intimacy, if they are to be independent. Independence and intimacy are not *opposite* personality traits, but *interlocking* skills. People who lack the ability to be independent *and* intimate can never really be either. They are never really with one another, never really without them.

What we set out to do, then, is to make people comfortable with the notion that they and the intimate are separate people, with separate ideas and feelings, who can sometimes come profoundly close to others.

According to theorists, one of the most primitive tasks people face is to learn how to maintain their own identity and integrity while yet engaging in deeply intimate relationships with others. (For a fuller discussion of this point, see Chapters 3 and 4 in this volume by McAdams and Schlenker, respectively, as well as Erikson, 1968; Fisher & Stricker, 1982; Freud, 1922; Hatfield and Walster, 1981; Kantor & Lehr, 1975; Kaplan, 1978; Maslow, 1954; Pope, 1979.)

Once individuals have the skills to be independent/intimate, they must find an appropriate lover or chum on which to practice their art.

In a few situations, the only thing one can do is to play out a stereo-typed role. In most situations, one has to be at least tactful; in a few, downright manipulative, in order to survive. But on those occasions when real intimacy is possible, men and women can recognize its prom-ise, seize their opportunities, and take a chance. (In Chapters 3 and 5 of this volume) McAdams and Patterson discuss the factors that people use in calculating how intimate it is safe to be.)

Are There Gender Differences in Intimacy?

It may be that men have the easiest time achieving an independent identity; women have the easiest time achieving closeness with others. Napier (1977) describes two types of people who seem, with uncanny accuracy, to attract one another. Type I (usually a woman) is only mini-mally concerned with maintaining her independence. What she cares about is achieving emotional closeness. (She seeks "fusion with the partner," "oneness" or "we-ness" in the marriage. She puts much ener-gy into planning "togetherness" activities.) Type I fears rejection and abandonment.

Type I's partner, Type II (usually a man), is most concerned with maintaining his sense of self and personal freedom and autonomy. He feels a strong need to establish his territory within the common house-hold: to have "my study," "my workshop," "my car." Similarly, he fears being "suffocated," "stifled," or "engulfed," or in some manner intruded on by his wife.

Napier observes that men and women's efforts to get close, but not "too close" for each of them, makes matters worse. Women (seeking more closeness) clasp their mates tightly, thereby contributing to the men's anxiety. The men (seeking more distance) retreat further, which increases their wives' panic, inducing further "clasping."

There is some evidence that men are less comfortable with intimacy than are women. Researchers find:

1. *In casual encounters*, women disclose far more to others than do men (Crozby, 1973; Jourard, 1971). Rubin and his colleagues (1980, p. 306)

point out that the basis for such differences appears to be in socialization practices. In our culture, women have traditionally been encouraged to show feelings; men have been taught to hide their feelings and to avoid displays of weakness. (See also Pleck & Sawyer, 1974). Kate Millett (1975) observes "Women express, men repress."

2. *In their deeply intimate relationships*, however, men and women differ little, if at all, in how much they are willing to reveal to one another. For example, Rubin and his colleagues (1980) asked dating couples via the Jourard Self-Disclosure questionnaire how much they had revealed to their partners. Did they talk about their current relationships? Previous opposite-sex affairs? Their feelings about their parents and friends? Their self-concepts and life views? Their attitudes and interests? Their day-to-day activities? The authors found that, overall, men and women did *not* differ in how much they were willing to confide in their partners.

There was a difference, however, in the *kind* of things men and women were willing to share with those they love. Men were more willing to share their views on politics and their pride in their strengths. Women were more likely to disclose their feelings about other people and their fears. Interestingly enough, Rubin and his colleagues found that that the stereotyped form of communication is most common in traditional men and women.

Some authors have observed than *neither* men or women may be getting exactly the amount of intimacy they would like. Women may want more intimacy than they are getting; men may want far less. There is evidence that couples tend to negotiate a level of self-disclosure that is bearable to both. In the words of the movie *My Fair Lady*, this ensures that *"neither* really gets what either really wants at all" (Chaikin & Derlega, 1975).

3. Women receive more disclosures than do men. This is not surprising in view of the fact that the amount of information people reveal to others has an enormous impact on the amount of information they receive in return (see Altman, 1973; Davis & Skinner, 1978; Jourard, 1964; Jourard & Friedman, 1970; Marlatt, 1971; Rubin, 1970; Worthy, Gary, & Kahn, 1969).

There does seem to be some evidence, then, that women feel slightly more comfortable with intense intimacy in their love relationships than do men, and are far more comfortable revealing themselves in more casual relationships than are men. Tradition dictates that women should be the "intimacy experts." And today, women *are* more comfortable sharing their ideas, feelings, and behavior than are men. But what happens if this situation changes? Rubin and his colleagues (1980) suggest that such changes have already begun.

The prognosis is mixed. Young women usually say that they would be delighted if the men they love could be intimate. I'm a bit skeptical that it will be this easy. Change is always difficult. More than one man has complained that when he finally dared to reveal his weaker aspects to a woman, he soon discovered that she was shocked by his lack of "manliness." Family therapists such as Napier (1977) have warned us that the struggle to find individuality *and* closeness is a problem for everyone. As long as men were fleeing from intimacy, women could safely pursue them. Now that men are turning around to face them, women may well find themselves taking flight. In any case, the confrontation is likely to be exciting.

People need intimacy; yet they have every reason to fear it. What advice can social psychologists give men and women as to how to secure the benefits of deep encounters while not being engulfed by their dangers?

The advice we would give follows directly from the theoretical paradigm we offered earlier—one must be independent before one can be intimate; intimate before one can be independent. How do we teach the impossible? It's easy.

Developing Intimacy Skills

Encouraging People to Accept Themselves as They Are

It is a great temptation to dwell in the realm of absolutes. One is either a saint or a sinner. Many people are determined to be perfect (at least); they can't settle for less.

Yet Saintliness/Evil are the least interesting of human conditions. Real life is lived in the middle zone. Real people inevitably have some real strengths; yet everybody possesses small quirks that makes them what they are. The real trick to enjoying life is not just to accept diversity, but to learn to take pleasure in it.

The first step in learning to be independent/intimate, then, is to come to accept the fact that you are entitled to be what you are—to have the ideas you have, the feelings you feel, to do the best that you can do. And that is good enough.

In therapy, we try to move people from the notion that one should come into the world perfect and continue that way to a realization that one can only gain wisdom in small steps. People must pick one small goal and work to accomplish that. When that's accomplished, they can move on to another. That way change is manageable, possible (Watson & Tharp, 1981). You can never attain perfection, only work toward it.

Encouraging People to Recognize Their Intimates for What They Are

People may be hard on themselves, but they are generally even harder on their partners. Most people have the idea that everyone is entitled to a perfect partner, or at least one a little bit better than the one available. (See Hatfield, Traupmann, Sprecher, Utne, & Hay, in press). If people are going to have an intimate relationship, they have to learn to enjoy others as they are, without hoping to fix them up.

It is extraordinarily difficult for people to accept that their friends are entitled to be the people they are. From our own point of view, it seems so clear that things would be far better if our mates were only the people we wanted them to be. It would take so little for them to change their whole character structure. Why are they so stubborn?

If we can come to the realization that our lover or friend is the person who exists right now—not the person we wish he was, not the person he could be, but what he is—once that realization occurs, intimacy becomes possible.

Encouraging People to Express Themselves

Next, intimates have to learn to be more comfortable about expressing their ideas and feelings. This is harder than one might think.

People's intimate relations are usually their most important relationships. When passions are so intense, consequences so momentous, people are often hesitant to speak the truth. From moment to moment, they are tempted to present a consistent picture. If they're in love, they are hesitant to admit to their niggling doubts. (What if the person they love is hurt? What if their revelations destroy the relationship?) When they are angry, they don't want to speak about their love or their self-doubts, they want to lash out.

To be intimate, people have to push toward a more honest, graceful, complete, and patient communication; to understand that a person's ideas and feelings are necessarily complex, with many nuances, shadings, and inconsistencies. In love, there is time to clear things up.

One interesting thing that people often discover is that their affection increases when they begin to admit their irritations. People are often surprised to discover that sometimes, when they think that they have fallen out of love—they are "bored" with their affair—that as they begin to express their anger and ambivalence, they feel their love come back in a rush.

In *The Family Crucible,* Napier and Whitaker (1978) describe just such a confrontation.

> 1) What followed was a classic confrontation. If John's affair was a kind of reawakening, so now was this marital encounter, though of a very different sort. Eleanor was enraged, hurt, confused, and racked with a sense of failure. John was guilty, also confused, but not apologetic. The two partners fought and cried, talked and searched for an entire night. The next evening, more exhausting encounters. Feelings that had been hidden for years emerged; doubts and accusations that they had never expected to admit articulated.
>
> Eleanor had to find out everything, and the more she discovered, the more insatiable her curiosity became. The more she heard, the guiltier her husband became and the angrier she grew, until he finally cried for a halt. It was his cry for mercy that finally led to a temporary reconciliation of the couple. They cried together for the first time either of them could remember.
>
> For a while they were elated; they had achieved a breakthrough in their silent and dreary marriage. They felt alive together for the first time in years. Somewhat myste-riously, they found themselves going to bed together in the midst of a great tangle of emotions—continuing anger, and hurt, and guilt, and this new quality: abandon. The lovemaking was, they were to admit to each other, "the best it had ever been." How could they have moved through hatred into caring so quickly? (p. 153)

Love and hate tend to flow together. (Hatfield & Walster, 1981; Kaplan, 1979)

Teaching People to Deal with Their Intimate's Reactions

To say that you *should* communicate your ideas and feelings, *must* communicate if you are to have an intimate affair, does not mean your partner is going to like it. You can expect that when you try to express your deepest feeling, it will hurt. Your lovers and friends may tell you frankly how deeply you have hurt them and that will make you feel extremely guilty. Or they may react with intense anger.

Intimates have to learn to stop responding in automatic fashion to such emotional outbursts—to quit backing up, apologizing for what they have said, measuring their words. They have to learn to stay calm, remind themselves that they are entitled to say what they think, feel what they feel, listen to what their partners think and feel and keep on trying.

Only then is there a chance of an intimate encounter.

REFERENCES

Allgeier, A. R., & Byrne, D. (1973). Attraction toward the opposite sex as a determinant of physical proximity. *Journal of Social Psychology, 90,* 213–219.

Altman, I. (1973). Reciprocity of interpersonal exchange. *Journal for the Theory of Social Behavior, 3,* 249–261.

Altman, I., & Taylor, D. A. (1973). *Social penetration: The development of interpersonal relationships.* New York: Holt.

Argyle, M. (1967). *The psychology of interpersonal behavior.* Baltimore, MD: Penguin Books.

Berscheid, E. (1979). *Affect in close relationships.* Unpublished manuscript.

Berscheid, E. (1983). Emotion. In H. H. Kelley *et al.* (Eds.), *Close relationships* (pp. 110–168). NY: Freeman.

Berscheid, E., & Peplau, L. A. (1983). The emerging science of relationships. In Harold H. Kelley *et al.* (Eds.), *Close relationships* (pp. 1–19). NY: Freeman.

Berscheid, E., & Walster (Hatfield), E. (1968). *Interpersonal attraction.* Reading, MA: Addison Wesley.

Broverman, I., Vogel, S., Broverman, D., Clarkson, F., & Rosenkrantz, P. (1972). Sex role stereotypes: A current appraisal. *Journal of Social Issues, 28*(2), 59–78.

Byrne, D., Ervin, C. R., & Lamberth, J. (1970). Continuity between the experimental study of attraction and "real life" computer dating. *Journal of Personality and Social Psychology, 16,* 157–165.

Cook, M., & Wilson, G. (Eds.) (1979). *Love and attraction.* NY: Pergamon.

Cozby, P. C. (1973). Self-disclosure: A literature review. *Psychological Bulletin, 79,* 73–91.

Davis, J. B., & Skinner, A. E. (1978). Reciprocity of self-disclosure in interviews: Modeling of social exchange. *Journal of Personality and Social Psychology, 29,* 779–784.

Derlega, V. J., & Chaikin, A. L. (1975). *Sharing intimacy: What we reveal to others and why.* Englewood Cliffs, NJ: Prentice-Hall.

Diamond, M. J., & Shapiro, J. L. (1981). *The paradoxes of intimate relating.* (Available from Dr. J. L. Shapiro, King Kalakaua Center for Humanistic Psychology, Honolulu, HI 96821.)

Duck, S., & Gilmour, R. (Eds.) (1980). *Personal relationships.* Vol. 1. *Studying personal relationships.* London: Academic Press.

Duck, S., & Gilmour, R. (Eds.) (1981a). *Personal relationships.* Vol. 2. *Developing personal relationships.* London: Academic Press.

Duck, S., & Gilmour, R. (Eds.) (1981b). *Personal relationships.* Vol. 3. *Personal relationships in disorder.* London: Academic Press.

Duck, S., & Gilmour, R. (1982). *Personal relationships.* Vol. 4. New York: Academic Press.

Erikson, E. H. (1968). *Childhood and society* (rev. ed.). New York: Norton.

Exline, R. (1972). Visual interaction: The glances of power and preference. In J. Cole (Ed.), *Nebraska Symposium on Motivation 1971.* Lincoln: University of Nebraska Press.

Fisher, M., & Stricker, G. (Eds.), (1982). *Intimacy.* NY: Plenum.

Freud, S. (1922). *Group psychology and the analysis of the ego.* London: Hogarth.

Galton, F. (1884). Measurement of character. *Fortnightly Review, 36,* 179–185.

Goldberg, G. N., Kiesler, C. A., & Collins, B. E. (1969). Visual behavior and face-to-face distance during interaction. *Sociometry, 32,* 43–53.

Hatfield, E. (1982). What do women and men want from love and sex? In E. R. Allgeier & N. B. McCormick (Eds.), *Gender roles and sexual behavior: The changing boundaries.* Palo Alto, CA: Mayfield.

Hatfield, E., Roberts, D., & Schmidt, L. (1980). The impact of sex and physical attractiveness on an initial social encounter. *Recherches de psychologie sociale, 2,* 27–40.

Hatfield, E., Traupmann, J., Sprecher, S., Utne, M., & Hay, J. (in press). Equity and intimate relations: Recent research. In W. Ickes (Ed.), *Compatible and incompatible relationships.* NY: Springer-Verlag.

Hatfield, E., & Walster, G. W. (1981). *A new look at love.* Reading, MA: Addison-Wesley.

Huesmann, L. R., & Levinger, G. (1976). Incremental exchange theory: A formal model for progression in dyadic social interaction. In L. Berkowitz and E. Hatfield-Walster (Eds.), *Equity theory: Toward a general theory of social interaction*. New York: Academic Press, 9, 192–230.

Jourard, S. M. (1964). *The transparent self*. Princeton, NJ: Van Nostrand.

Jourard, S. (1971). *Self-disclosure: An experimental analysis of the transparent self*. New York: Wiley.

Jourard, S., & Friedman, R. (1970). Experimenter–subject distance in self-disclosure. *Journal of Personality and Social Psychology, 15*, 278–282.

Kantor, D., & Lehr, W. (1975). *Inside the family*. San Francisco: Jossey-Bass.

Kaplan, H. S. (1979). *Disorders of sexual desire*. New York: Simon & Schuster.

Kaplan, L. J. (1978). *Oneness and separateness: From infant to individual*. NY: Simon & Schuster.

Marlatt, G. A. (1971). Exposure to a model and task ambiguity as determinants of verbal behavior in an interview. *Journal of Consulting and Clinical Psychology, 36*, 268–276.

Maslow, A. H. (1954). *Motivation and personality*. NY: Harper.

Mehrabian, A. (1968). Relationship of attitude to seated posture, orientation, and distance. *Journal of Personality and Social Psychology, 10*, 26–30.

Montaigne, M. de. (1948). Of the inconsistency of our actions. In D. M. Frame (Trans.), *Complete essays of Montaigne* (p. 242). Stanford, CA: Stanford University Press.

Napier, A. Y. (1977). *The rejection–intrusion pattern: A central family dynamic*. Unpublished manuscript, School of Family Resources, University of Wisconsin–Madison.

Napier, A. Y., & Whitaker, C. (1978). *The family crucible*. New York: Harper & Rowe.

Perlmutter, M., & Hatfield, E. (1980). Intimacy, intentional metacommunication and second-order change. *American Journal of Family Therapy, 8*, 17–23.

Pleck, J. H., & Sawyer, J. (Eds.) (1974). *Men and masculinity*. Englewood Cliffs, NJ: Prentice-Hall.

Pope, K. S. (1980). Defining and studying romantic love. In K. S. Pope and Associates (Eds.), *On love and loving*. San Francisco, CA: Jossey-Bass.

Rubin, A. (1970). Measurement of romantic love. *Journal of Personality and Social Psychology, 16*, 265–273.

Rubin, A., Hill, C. T., Peplau, L. A., & Dunke-Schetter, C. (1980). Self-disclosure in dating couples: Sex roles and the ethic of openness. *Journal of Marriage and the Family, 42*, 305–317.

Scheflen, A. E. (1965). Quasi-courtship behavior in psychotherapy. *Psychiatry, 28*, 245–257.

Sprecher, S., & Hatfield, E. (in press). Interpersonal attraction. In G. Stricker & R. Keisner (Eds.), *The implications of non-clinical research for clinical practice*. New York: Plenum.

Watson, D. L., & Tharp, R. G. (1981). *Self-directed behavior* (3rd ed.). Monterey, CA: Brooks-Cole.

Worthy, M. A., Gary, L., & Kahn, G. M. (1969). Self-disclosure as an exchange process. *Journal of Personality and Social Psychology, 13*, 63–69.

Author Index

The numerals in italics indicate pages on which the complete references appear.

A

Abelson, R. P., 118, *130*
Abrahams, R. B., 135, *157*
Adler, A., 44, *67*
Alexander, J. F., 30, *39*
Allegeier, A. R., 209, *218*
Allen, A., 19, *36*
Altman, I., 2, 3, 4, *8*, 14, 17, 20, 29, 30, 32, *36, 39*, 62, *67*, 154, *157*, 208, 210, 215, *219*
Anchor, K. N., 62, *69*
Anderson, C. A., 150, *157*
Andreyeva, G. M., 22, *36*
Angyal, A., 44, *67*
Antill, J. K., 13, 34, *37*
Antonucci, T. C., 144, 145, *158*
Archer, R. L., 2, 3, 4, *8*, 22, 23, *36, 39*, 62, *67*
Argyle, M., 22, 23, 24, *36*, 107, 111, 112, 113, 126, *130*, 209, *219*
Aronfreed, J., 18, *36*
Ashton, N. L., 120, *130*
Atkinson, J. W., 43, 46, *67, 69*
Audy, J. R., 66, *68*
Azjen, I., 30, *36*

B

Backman, C. W., 71, 72, 74, 91, 92, 96, 97, 99, *101, 103*

Bakan, D., 41, 44, 45, 50, 53, 57, 58, 60, 64, 65, 66, *67*
Baker, E., 120, *130*
Balint, M., 59, *67*
Bandler, R., 16, 19, *36, 39*
Bandura, A., 83, *101*
Bardwick, J. M., 138, *157*
Bateson, G., 16, *36*
Baumeister, R. F., 97, *101*
Beck, A. T., 150, *157*
Bell, G. R., 135, *157*
Bell, R. R., 55, 62, 63, *67*
Bem, D. J., 19, 24, *36, 37*, 138, *157*
Berg, J. H., 23, *39*
Berger, P. L., 33, *37*
Berscheid, E., 2, *8, 9*, 28, 34, *40*, 72, 84, 85, *101*, 156, *157*, 208, 209, *219*
Blau, P. M., 72, 84, 85, 96, *101*
Bock, E. W., 134, 153, *157*
Bond, M. H., 125, 126, 127, *130*
Booth, L., 50, *68*
Boss, D., 121, *131*
Bouffard, D. L., 22, *39*
Bradburn, N., 134, *157*
Breed, G., 108, *130*
Brehm, J. W., 90, *101*, 149, *157*
Brophy, J. E., 54, 61, *68*
Broverman, D., 211, *219*
Broverman, I., 211, *219*
Brown, B. R., 85
Buber, M., 18, *37*, 59, 60, *67*

Subject Index